3-Tier
Client/Server
At Work

Other books by Jeri Edwards

The Essential Client/Server Survival Guide, Second Edition

The Essential Distributed Objects Survival Guide

Instant CORBA

3-Tier Client/Server At Work

Jeri Edwards

with Deborah DeVoe

WILEY COMPUTER PUBLISHING

JOHN WILEY & SONS, INC.

New York   Chichester   Weinheim   Brisbane   Singapore   Toronto

Publisher: Katherine Schowalter
Editor: Theresa Hudson
Managing Editor: Frank Grazioli
Text Design & Composition: Jeri Edwards
Graphic Art: David Pacheco

Library of Congress Cataloging-in-Publication Data:

ISBN 0 471-18443-8

Printed in the United States of America
10 9 8 7 6 5 4

Foreword

by Robert Orfali

We are living in perpetually changing times. It was only a few short years ago that 2-tier client/server revolutionized the software industry. Today, 3-tier is the rage. In less than two short years, the Web has made 3-tier the de facto client/server model. And this is only the beginning. The Gartner Group estimates that more than 90% of new business-critical applications will be built using ORB-based distributed objects by 1999—ORB-based applications are N-tiered by definition (where N is greater than two).

Because we're in a state of perpetual revolution, no one has taken the time to document how these systems come to life or how they really work. Readers of our books should be familiar by now with the 3-tier foundation technologies—including ORBs, TP Monitors, components, and the Object Web. But you won't find real case studies on how these technologies are used. Why? Because most customers we come in contact with make us sign these infamous legal muzzles called Non-Disclosure Agreements (NDAs). The organizations who break their teeth getting 3-tier applications to work use these NDAs to protect their competitive advantage. Yes, a good, working 3-tier application is handled like a trade secret.

The bottom line is that it's not easy to find people who will let you write about their successful 3-tier applications. So when our co-author, Jeri Edwards, approached me with this 3-tier client/server case study project, I warned her it was going to be mission impossible and wished her the best of luck. I also told Jeri that I'd gladly write this foreword if she could pull off this stunt. She succeeded. So, here I am writing these words.

In reality, getting this book out proved to be even harder than I had predicted. There were lawyers, NDAs, marketing people, and other barriers that make most authors cringe. Jeri and Deborah were successful because: 1) they are extremely persevering people, 2) they had the support of an entire field organization, and 3) this book became a passion for them—they were learning a lot from the designers they interviewed. So hats off to Jeri and Deborah for a job well done.

To the best of my knowledge, this is the first set of documented case studies on client/server. As an added bonus, these case studies are about mission-critical client/server systems that use TP Monitors and—in one case—an ORB. This book shows—in detail—how real applications are conceived, architected, developed, and deployed. Some of the case studies are almost too vivid. Most practitioners will immediately relate to the hurdles these people faced—you get all the gore. There are design patterns and lessons in this extraordinary book that we can all learn from.

Now I can now tell my students to read this book before they build their own client/server systems. They will have examples of successful projects that they can emulate. Most importantly, I can wave this book at people who say "I'm from Missouri—show me." Happy reading.

> — *Robert Orfali*
> *San Jose, California*
> *August, 1997*

Preface

In the heart of Silicon Valley where I live, you'll find the Winchester Mystery House. In the late 19th century, Mrs. Winchester—the widow of a rifle magnate—decided that if she kept building her house, she could keep the grim reaper at bay and live forever. So she employed a bevy of carpenters to work around the clock building staircases to nowhere, installing windows that face walls, and adding doors that open in mid-air. Mrs. Winchester died anyway. But her house is still there. Visitors marvel at its extravagant wastefulness.

The software world is littered with Winchester Mystery House applications. They have lots of nice features, but it's hard to see where they're headed. The original design is long lost, but application development seems to go on forever. It's always "add a door here and a window there." The best thing you can say about these projects is that they provide life-time employment for their development teams. That is, until someone finally notices and pulls the plug.

This book is *not* about Mystery House projects.[1] It's about development teams that have delivered working solutions. I like happy endings. In our case studies, the architects understand the requirements, pick the right technology and tools, create and implement workable designs, and bring their systems into production. We're talking about massive client/server systems that could have failed in many different ways. These stories are about how they got it right.

Why You Should Read This Book

3-tier client/server is taking over the computing universe. What started out as an application discipline for the high-end of the enterprise client/server market is now becoming mainstream. The Internet is making 3-tier client/server ubiquitous. So whether you're a programmer, systems architect, operator, or MIS manager, you will soon be dealing with 3-tier. This book is about the pioneers in this field who have already been there and done that. The applications they created are being used every day by thousands of users. They are bet-your-business applications that process hundreds of thousands (sometimes millions) of business transactions a day. So, you will be learning from the 3-tier client/server masters.

---

[1] A book about why projects fail (or worse, limp along forever) would be extremely enlightening, but—as you can imagine—it is impossible to find anyone willing to talk about them.

Why case studies? Other disciplines use case studies to record and teach best practices. Case studies provide simulations of real-world situations that you can use for target practice before spending your own money. According to Standish Group, businesses in the United States alone spent $275 billion on applications in 1996. This amounts to roughly 200,000 software projects. Now here's the bad news: 53% of these projects failed. These Mystery House projects cost U.S. businesses $145 billion in a single year. Given these statistics, learning from successful projects can only help. Taking a day or two to read the next 230 pages—perhaps, at the beach—could generate a very nice return on your investment (at least, for your company).

What This Book Covers

3-Tier Client/Server At Work documents working mission-critical client/server applications. To get you ready for the tour—and to make this book self-contained—we start with the big picture: what 3-tier client/server is, how it compares with other technologies, and how it is changing to support the intergalactic Internet. We also describe the middleware that supports 3-tier applications.

Next, we visit eight production 3-tier applications—the case studies. We explain why each application was chartered and how it is architected. Then we relive the projects: you get an insight into what went into their design, development, and deployment phases. Sometimes the book feels like an E-ride at Disneyland. Finally, we summarize the key lessons we learned from the architects of these systems.

You should resist the temptation to go straight to the last chapter to get the bottom line. There are tons of application design patterns, project methodologies, and architectural insights throughout the book. We organized this book into three parts:

- **Part 1** is a fast-moving introduction to 3-tier client/server. First, we look at what is driving this new movement from both a business and technical perspective. Then we describe the technology that you will need to run these 3-tier client/server applications—including TP Monitors and Object Request Brokers. The next-generation TP Monitors, called *Object Transaction Monitors*, will incorporate these two technologies. We'll tell you what this will mean to future client/server applications.

  We also include a chapter on Tuxedo because it is the TP Monitor that seven out of eight case studies in this book use.[2] Why Tuxedo? Because most production 3-tier applications are built on TP Monitors today; Tuxedo is the most popular TP Monitor on the market. And, because I work for BEA—the company that

---

[2] The other case study is of a leading bank that uses CORBA-based distributed objects as the foundation for its 3-tier applications.

makes Tuxedo. BEA gave me access to its customer base and the support of the field force to get these applications documented. Without their help, I could never have assembled these case studies. There are undoubtedly great 3-tier applications that use other products, but someone else will have to write that book. In any case, the lessons we learned from these case studies are universally applicable.

■ **Part 2** gives you a rare glimpse of how real mission-critical applications are conceived, designed, built, and deployed. Until now, this was a secret: you had to be a member of the guild to get this type of tour. We chose the applications in this book based on the following criteria:

✔ ***They are large***—as measured by either the number of clients or by transaction volume.

✔ ***They are critical to the business***—in all cases, these applications are at the heart of the business.

✔ ***They are in production now***—we wanted to show you the entire application life cycle. This meant that the applications we selected had to be deployed. We had to skip over many interesting applications that were not quite in production.

We also looked for variety. The projects we chose represent different industries and organizations. Some are large stand-alone applications; others are suites. We worked on making this book global—so there are European, American, and multinational case studies.

■ **Part 3** summarizes the advice the architects gave us most frequently. You will get the ten golden rules that lead to client/server nirvana. But, a word of caution: don't expect instant enlightenment. It turns out that the *real* secret to successful 3-tier applications is to employ good engineering practices—most projects fail because they overlook one of these basic rules.

As you can see, this book starts with the 50,000-foot view of 3-tier technology and where it is going, then dives in to get "up close and personal" with the projects. When you finish this book, we hope you will feel like you've vicariously lived through some interesting experiences.

How to Read This Book

The nice thing about this book is that you can consume it in nibbles if you want. If you are unfamiliar with 3-tier, you should read Part 1 first. From there, you can read any of the case studies that grab your attention in any order: think of them as a collection of short stories. Be sure to read them all: each one has a unique lesson to teach.

What the Boxes Are For

We use shaded boxes as a way to introduce concurrent threads in the presentation material. It's the book's version of multitasking. The *Soapboxes* introduce strong opinions or biases on some of the more controversial topics of client/server computing. The *Briefing* boxes give you background or tutorial type information. The *Detail* boxes cover some esoteric area of technology that may not be of interest to the general readership. Finally, we use *Warning* boxes to let you know where danger lies.

A Sneak Preview of the Eight Case Studies

To whet your appetite, here is a quick peak at our eight case studies:

■ **U.K. Employment Service's Labour Management System** is one of the largest client/server applications in the world. More than 20,000 employment workers throughout England, Wales, and Scotland use it to generate 6.8 million transactions each day. But the most amazing thing about this case is that they delivered the entire project—from design through deployment—in only 12 months.

■ **PeopleSoft** is moving its famous application suite from 2-tier to 3-tier. It has designed a migration strategy that makes this move transparent to the majority of its developers, as well as to its customer base. Who said, "No pain, no gain?"

■ **Wells Fargo Bank** uses a CORBA Object Request Broker to provide a suite of applications that let customers and bank employees access accounts more easily. This suite of integrated applications includes Internet home banking, the customer relationship system, automated call response, and ATM access. To the best of our knowledge, it is the largest CORBA application in production; it handles over 900,000 end-user transactions each day.

■ **AppleOrder Global** is Apple Computer's new electronic ordering application. Thousands of resellers and service providers around the world use it to order Macs and Apple parts. This application front-ends Apple's new SAP corporate information system; it also replaces the five regional ordering systems that Apple previously maintained.

■ **The Customer Transaction Monitoring System at MCI** is used by MCI's largest customers to monitor the quality of service they are getting. While the

system doesn't support a large number of clients, it tracks more than 324,000 transactions each hour.

- **3M Healthcare Enterprise Management System** is a suite of software products that provide an integrated view of a patient's status and treatment—the data comes from a variety of systems spread throughout a healthcare establishment. The application uses artificial intelligence to alert clinicians to issues and contradictions in treatment programs.

- **EUCARIS** is a pan-European message broker; it verifies vehicle registrations and prevents fraud and auto thefts across borders. The system links pre-existing, independent vehicle registration systems throughout much of Europe.

- **The Zenith Project at AT&T** re-engineered the inbound sales application of AT&T's largest business unit, the Consumer and Small Business division. To do this, it built an object-oriented 3-tier application that front-ends a number of legacy systems. Zenith brought on-line customer information to AT&T's nearly 2,000 telemarketing representatives; it significantly reduces the fulfillment time for ordering telephone services.

As you can see, this is quite an interesting collection of case studies. I hope you will find them as fascinating as we did. Enjoy.

Acknowledgments

It takes a village to create a book like this. I'd like to say thanks to each of these people who played an essential role in helping us create *3-Tier Client/Server At Work*:

■ First, to all the architects and developers of the case studies we cover in this book. Without them, there would have been nothing to write about. They shared their projects and architectures with us, and endlessly reviewed our work:

  ✔ *UK Employment Services:* Phil Mullis

  ✔ *PeopleSoft:* Rick Bergquist and Peter Gassner

  ✔ *Wells Fargo and The Cushing Group:* Eric Castain, Erik Townsend, and Michael Ronayne

  ✔ *Apple:* Dean Rally, Michelle Pope, Tom Wilson, and Oisin Clarke

  ✔ *MCI:* Victor Koliczew, Drue Baker, Bodo Krueger, Rob Chung, and Craig Sandin

  ✔ *3M:* Robert Dupont, Mark Scarton, Kent Stevenson, Shane Beeny, Mike Tutor, Kathleen Kingston, and Carolyn Rose

  ✔ *RDW and Unisys (EUCARIS):* Hans van der Bruggen, Erik van Nus, Fred Bosch, and Ruud de Ridder

  ✔ *AT&T:* Mikola Owdij and Andy Schenke

■ And special thanks go to the BEA folks who helped us arrange for the case studies: Glenna Baker, Michelle Cheng, Bob Creegan, Bill Dana, Ed Durney, Amy Friedman, Dave George, Neal Grande, Matt Green, Dennis Lyftogt, Arthur Raguette, Barbara Reed, Stewart Reid, Fiona Robertson, Frank Szczepanski, and Susan Teague.

■ To the BEA customers, developers, and field organization who daily show us how 3-tier is being used in mission-critical environments. Special thanks to the following people for helping us get it right: Sam Cece, Alfred Chuang, Terry Dwyer, Birdie Fenzel, Jay Fry, Joe Glynn, Pete Homan, Jay Krackeler, Dianne Langeland, Hallie Lyons, Cynthia Merlynn, Linda Parker, Norm Robbins, and Eric Warner. Bill Coleman, BEA's CEO, provided insight into what was driving the 3-tier revolution. My boss, Ed Scott, encouraged this effort and put up with my absences from my normal duties while I completed this book.

■ To Robert Orfali and Dan Harkey. They may not be co-authoring this book with me as usual, but I could never have completed it without their help and encouragement.

■ To Dave Pacheco for creating the wonderful technical illustrations in this book. In fact, Dave got to draw them twice when—half way through—I changed their format.

■ To our tireless copy editor, Larry Mackin.

■ To the people at Wiley—especially Terri Hudson, Frank Grazioli, Bob Ipsen, Ellen Reavis, and Katherine Schowalter.

Contents

Chapter 5. PeopleSoft Moves Applications to 3-Tier 89

Chapter 10. 3-Tier Brings Car Registration Protection to Europe 179

Chapter 11. AT&T Takes on Order Turnaround 197

Part 1
3-Tier
Client/Server
Fundamentals

Transactions per Second

An Introduction to Part 1

Welcome to a world of *working* mission-critical client/server applications. That's right—mission-critical client/server is far more than a theory. Every day, millions of electronic business transactions begin on client programs running on PCs and execute on distributed server systems.[1] With client/server, you mix local and remote processing in a single application to get the best of both worlds; it makes mission-critical applications friendly and easier to use. You can use personal and shared applications together without culture shock. And it is also the foundation for the Internet, intranets, and extranets.

However, client/server is far from a sure recipe for success. Like the rest of life, there are choices you can make to improve the odds of having successful client/server projects. The architecture of your application is one of the most critical choices you will make. The architects of the demanding applications in Part 2 made the right choices—their large, production 3-tier client/server applications are the proof.

In Part 1, we explain the importance of 3-tier, and describe the software infrastructures that you can use to build your 3-tier applications. We cover, in detail, the following topics:

■ *Client/server tiers and what all the fuss is about*. What are tiers? Why have we moved from monolithic, single-tier applications to multi-tier intergalactic client/server? What is the driving force behind the fast adoption of 3-tier client/server? Is 3-tier really an N-tier component architecture? (Yes, just when you get comfortable with 3-tier client/server, we explain why it isn't really 3-tier but N-tier.)

■ *The middle-tier infrastructure*. What are the requirements for the middle tier? What capabilities do today's middle-tier platforms—including TP Monitors, ORBs, MOM, and RPCs—provide and when do you use them? How do TP Monitors compare with stored procedures?

■ *The architecture and features of Tuxedo*. Tuxedo is the middle-tier software used by most of the 3-tier applications described in this book. How does it work?

Part 1 gives you the background you will need to understand—and appreciate—the real-world applications we will describe in Part 2. So, without further ado, let's explore the world of 3-tier client/server.

---

[1] Standish Group estimates that 56 million electronic transactions were executed each second in 1995 in the U.S. alone. This is expected to grow to 100 million by the year 2000.

Chapter 1

Why 3-Tier Client/Server Is Hot

Ten years after its introduction, client/server has become the application architecture of choice. Figure 1-1 shows its rising popularity. Client/server applied a giant chainsaw to monolithic mainframe applications to split the processing load between clients and servers. As a result, client/server has revolutionized the way we design and build our applications. And it raised end-user expectations about the "look and feel" of multiuser software.

In its wake, client/server created a huge software industry dominated by adolescent giants like Baan, Informix, Lotus, Microsoft, Novell, Oracle, PeopleSoft, SAP, Sun, and Sybase. These companies are the superstars of the first client/server era. They are now the new computer establishment.

This may come as a big surprise, but there is a silent revolution going on within the client/server revolution. Figure 1-1 also shows that client/server computing is rapidly transforming itself from its 2-tier origins to a 3-tier architecture. The impact of this change will even be more dramatic than the original move from monolithic applications to client/server. The 3-tier movement was initially driven by the need to make client/server work for demanding enterprise-class applications. However, the Internet, intranets, distributed objects, and components are now rocket-boosting 3-tier into the client/server mainstream.

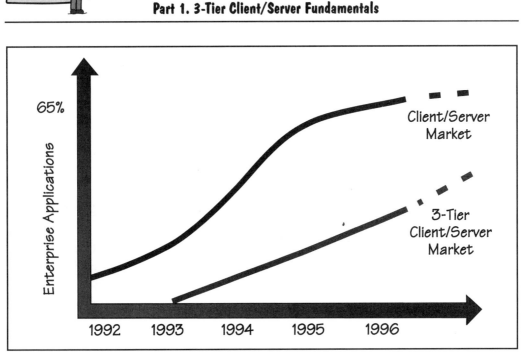

Figure 1-1. 2-Tier Versus 3-Tier Client/Server Growth. (Source: Standish Group, 1996 COMPASS Survey.)

So the news is that client/server has become the dominant form of computing. The other news is that 3-tier is becoming the dominant form of client/server. What is 3-tier? Why is it so important?

WHAT ARE THESE TIERS, ANYWAY?

In the early 1980s, minicomputer vendors introduced the term *3-tier* (as in "3-tier architecture") to describe the physical partitioning of an application across terminals (tier 1), minicomputers (tier 2), and mainframes (tier 3). This gave them an opportunity to sell their mid-range computers as front-ends to mainframes.

Today, we use *tiers* to describe the logical partitioning of an application across clients and servers. Splitting the processing load is a central client/server concept. But it also introduces the previously unnecessary—but now persistent—design issue of where to put these loads. Tiers let us describe the basic architectural choices:

■ *2-tier* splits the processing load in two. The majority of the application logic runs on the client, which typically sends SQL requests to a server-resident database. We call this architecture *fat client* because a big chunk of the application runs on the client side of the equation (see Figure 1-2).

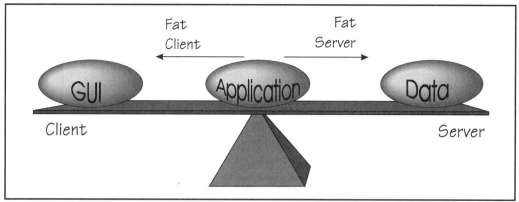

Figure 1-2. Fat Client Versus Fat Server.

- **3-tier** splits the processing load between 1) clients running the graphical user interface (GUI) logic, 2) the application server running the business logic, and 3) the database and/or legacy application. Because 3-tier moves the application logic to the server, it is also referred to as a *fat server*—or more recently, a *thin client*—architecture.

By definition, all client/server applications must have at least two tiers: the user interface resides on the client and the shared data is stored on the server. As you've just seen, an application is 2-tier or 3-tier based on the separation of the application logic from the GUI and the database (see Figure 1-3).

This partitioning is a central design issue that makes a big difference in determining the success of mission-critical applications. Today, application designers and developers are making architectural mistakes that cost millions of dollars. Applications most often fail because of these errors—not because of coding problems. While you can readily fix bugs, a project can almost never recover from a fundamental architectural flaw. The good news is that you can easily avoid these errors with just a basic understanding of the trade-offs between various client/server architectures. We cover these trade-offs in the rest of this chapter—and throughout this book.

The Benefits and Limitations of 2-Tier Architectures

In 2-tier client/server systems, the application logic is either buried inside the user interface on the client or within the database on the server (or both). You run a GUI on the client. It sends SQL, file system calls, or HTTP commands over a network to the server. The server processes your request and returns the results. To access data, clients must know how it is organized and stored on the server side. A variation of the 2-tier approach uses *stored procedures* to off-load some of the processing

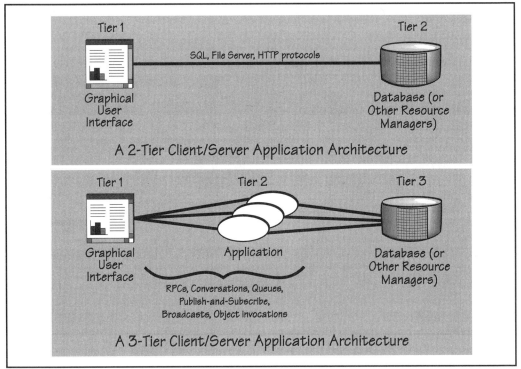

Figure 1-3. 2-Tier Versus 3-Tier Architectures.

to the server side. Instead of sending SQL requests across the network, stored procedures let you invoke a function that runs within a database—you can think of this as 2.5-tier partitioning. (We cover stored procedures in Chapter 2.)

Simplicity is the biggest factor driving the popularity of 2-tier client/server. 2-tier is great for creating applications quickly using visual builder tools. Typically, these are departmental applications, such as decision support and small-scale groupware, or simple Web-based applications.

But as successful departmental applications started to roll out, architects began to depend on 2-tier for mission-critical applications. They soon discovered, though, that the architectures and tools they used so successfully for 2-tier didn't scale. Applications that worked perfectly well in prototypes and small installations fell apart when put into large-scale production. The 2-tier model is not mission-critical. Consequently, application rollouts were delayed. Projects went over budget to create workarounds. Independent software vendors' products reached architectural barriers to growth. Naturally, pundits started to declare that client/server had failed.

What really happened was that client/server was undergoing a transition. We are now deploying enterprise-wide client/server applications and Internet-based electronic commerce. Consequently, we have moved past the traditional 2-tier client/server world that we cut our teeth on. We now face a complex world where applications are split into components and distributed across multiple processors— a world of 3-tier (and N-tier) applications.

Why 3-Tier Client/Server?

In no way does Internet computing replace client/server computing. That's because it already is client/server computing.

> — *Herb Edelstein, Principal*
> *Euclid Associates*

Client/server has outgrown its departmental origins. As you will see in this book, we are now deploying client/server applications that serve thousands of enterprise clients. These applications often run on many servers and consist of hundreds of software components. They run the core functions within an enterprise. And these client/server applications are going intergalactic. With the Internet, servers can get requests from any of the world's millions of connected PCs.

In this new world, transactions can come from consumers (via Internet applications), from suppliers or distributors (via inter-company *extranets*), or from your own far-flung employees. Intergalactic client/server will allow enterprises to thrive in a quickly changing business climate—where they are driven by new demands that must be fulfilled in "Internet years." Here are some examples:

- Businesses will increasingly compete by being the first to market with new electronic goods and services. Their success will be determined by their applications.

- Companies will create *virtual corporations* through alliances with a shifting set of partners. This will allow them to react quickly to new opportunities—and maintain a tight focus on their "core competencies."

- Roles and relationships between enterprises will shift frequently as industries realign. Successful companies will use these dislocations to increase market share and to acquire a dominant industry position. The current corporate trend toward mergers and acquisitions will escalate.

Intergalactic client/server will both enable and drive these massive changes. It will change the way many industries operate. But it would not be fully enabled without several technology breakthroughs—including low-cost, high-speed bandwidth on wide area networks, a new generation of network-enabled desktop operating systems, and a component-oriented distributed infrastructure. Clients and servers do not have to be co-located on the same campus any longer—they can be a world away. We call this "the irrelevance of proximity."

Table 1-1 contrasts the departmental and intergalactic eras of client/server computing. As you can see, the requirements of intergalactic client/server are many orders of magnitude greater than those of departmental client/server. 2-tier client/server did not fail—au contraire, it succeeded beautifully for departmental applications. However, the world has changed. Our applications have outgrown their old departmental boundaries and spilled over into an interconnected world. Intergalactic applications introduce new and more stringent requirements. 3-tier was designed to meet this new challenge.

Table 1-1. Intergalactic Client/Server Versus Departmental Client/Server.

Application Characteristic	Departmental Client/Server	Intergalactic Era Client/Server
Number of clients per application	Less than 100	Millions
Number of servers per application	1 or 2 homogeneous servers	100,000+ "Server mania" with many heterogeneous servers performing different roles
Geography	Campus	Global
Server-to-server interactions	No	Yes
Middleware	SQL and stored procedures	Components on the Internet and intranets
Client/server architecture	2-tier	3-tier (or N-tier)
Transactional updates	Very infrequent	Pervasive
Multimedia content	Low	High
Mobile agents	No	Yes
Client front-ends	Fat clients	On-demand clients, Webtops, compound documents, and shippable places
Timeframe	1985 to present	1997–2000 and beyond

In 3-tier, the client provides the GUI and interacts with the server through remote service or method invocations. The application logic lives in the middle tier—a domain of its own. In 3-tier, processes become first-class citizens. You manage and deploy them separately from the user interface and database. The application logic now has its own separate tier and runs on one or more servers.

3-tier is the new growth area for client/server computing because it meets the requirements of large-scale Internet and intranet client/server applications. 3-tier applications are easier to manage and deploy on the network—most of the code runs on the servers, especially with zero-footprint technologies like Java applets. In addition, 3-tier applications minimize network interchanges by creating abstract levels of service. Instead of interacting with the database directly, the client calls business logic on the server. The business logic then accesses the database on the client's behalf. 3-tier substitutes a few server calls for many SQL queries and updates, so it performs much better than 2-tier. It also provides better security by not exposing the database schema to the client and by enabling more fine-grained authorization on the server.

How Does 2-Tier Compare With 3-Tier?

Table 1-2 compares the 2-tier and 3-tier approaches. When client/server was a departmental or campus-based phenomenon, the shortcomings of 2-tier weren't very important. They certainly didn't outweigh the advantages provided by 2-tier's ease of development. But as client/server grew up to run mission-critical applications—especially those of intergalactic proportions—3-tier became essential.

Table 1-2. 2-Tier Versus 3-Tier Client/Server.

	2-Tier	3-Tier
System administration	Complex (more logic on the client to manage)	Less complex (the application can be centrally managed on the server—application programs are made visible to standard system management tools)
Security	Low (data-level security)	High (fine-tuned at the service or method level)
Encapsulation of data	Low (data tables are exposed)	High (the client invokes services or methods)
Performance	Poor (many SQL statements are sent over the network; selected data must be downloaded for analysis on the client)	Good (only service requests and responses are sent between the client and server)

Table 1-2. 2-Tier Versus 3-Tier Client/Server. (Continued)

	2-Tier	3-Tier
Scale	Poor (limited management of client communications links)	Excellent (concentrates incoming sessions; can distribute loads across multiple servers)
Application reuse	Poor (monolithic application on client)	Excellent (can reuse services and objects)
Ease of development	High	Getting better (standard tools can be used to create the clients, and tools are emerging that you can use to develop both the client and server sides of the application)
Server-to-server infrastructure	No	Yes (via server-side middleware)
Legacy application integration	No	Yes (via gateways encapsulated by services or objects)
Internet support	Poor (Internet bandwidth limitations make it harder to download fat clients and exacerbate the already noted limitations)	Excellent (thin clients are easier to download as applets or beans; remote service invocations distribute the application load to the server)
Heterogeneous database support	No	Yes (3-tier applications can use multiple databases within the same business transaction)
Rich communication choices	No (only synchronous, connection-oriented RPC-like calls)	Yes (supports RPC-like calls, but can also support connectionless messaging, queued delivery, publish-and-subscribe, and broadcast)
Hardware architecture flexibility	Limited (you have a client and a server)	Excellent (all three tiers may reside on different computers, or the second and third tiers may both reside on the same computer; with component-based environments, you can distribute the second tier across multiple servers as well)
Availability	Poor (can't fail over to a backup server)	Excellent (can restart the middle tier components on other servers)

COMPONENTS: WHEN 3-TIER IS N-TIER

The middle tier in most 3-tier applications is not implemented as a monolithic program. Instead, it is implemented as a collection of components that are used in a variety of client-initiated business transactions (see Figure 1-4).

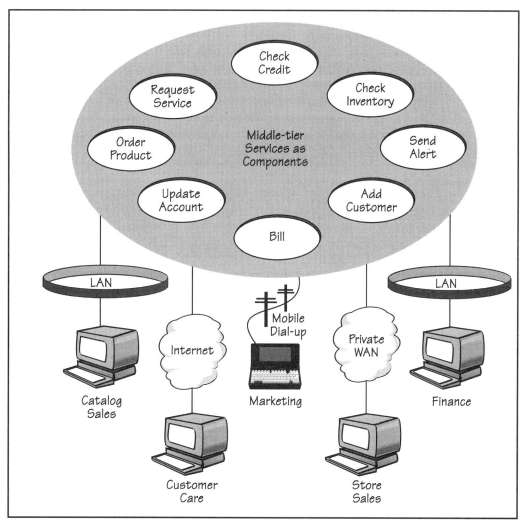

Figure 1-4. Components in an N-tier Architecture.

Each component automates a relatively small business function. Clients frequently combine several middle-tier components within a single business transaction. A component can call other components to help it implement a request. In addition, some components may act as gateways that encapsulate legacy applications running on mainframes. So, most of the time 3-tier is really N-tier.

Benefits of Component-based Architectures

Component-based applications offer significant advantages over monolithic applications. When you design the middle tier as a component-based application, you obtain the following benefits:

- *You can develop big applications in small steps.* Component-based architectures allow you to develop large mission-critical applications as small projects. When you use this step-wise development method, you can put initial versions of applications into production faster. It also reduces your risk. Standish Group reports that the larger a project grows, the more it is likely to fail. They found that 53% of IT projects fail. Small projects that are developed by just four people over four months have the best chance for success. Components lend themselves well to this small-team, incremental development approach.

- *Applications can reuse components.* Unlike object-oriented languages that focus on source code reuse, you reuse components as binary "black boxes." You can recombine them in different ways, depending on the application.

- *Clients can access data and functions easily and safely.* Clients send requests to components to execute a function on their behalf. The server components encapsulate the details of the application logic and thus raise the level of abstraction. Clients do not need to know which database is being accessed to execute the request. And they do not need to know if the request was sent to another component or application for execution. Encapsulation provides consistent, secure, auditable access to data and eliminates random, uncontrolled updates coming from many applications at once.

- *Custom applications can incorporate off-the-shelf components.* Enterprises gain tremendous benefits by buying ready-made components that are packaged as applications. They can also mix and match suites from different software vendors. However, this mix-and-match capability requires some semantic glue (see the next Warning box).

- *Component environments don't get older—they only get better.* Component-based systems grow beyond a single application to become the basis for suites of applications. You can assemble applications very quickly by building new clients, adding a few new middle-tier components, and reusing a number of existing components. You can update components without changing your clients. And you can add new capabilities as your business needs them.

Component Glue Not Necessarily Included

Warning

Mixing and matching components sounds wonderful—and is wonderful. Standard middleware allows seamless communications between clients and server components, as well as between server components. But buying component suites that use the same middleware—even loosely coupled, dynamic messaging mechanisms such as queues and publish-and-subscribe—does not guarantee plug-and-play capability. Components must know how to access each other semantically. One frequently used mechanism for combining component suites is to develop a new client application that bolts them together. Or a component suite offered by a major software vendor can be used as a framework to which smaller vendors add function. In all cases, someone must provide the glue. ❏

Server Component Types

There are two types of middle-tier components:

- **Services** implement a business function—for example, *Update_Checking_Account*. Services are stateless procedures: when a request is received—for example, to update Joe's bank account—the application logic must access and update the data. In this case, the data is Joe's bank account. Most of today's transactional middleware products support procedural services.

- **Objects** expose a set of related procedures or "methods," not just a single procedure. The infrastructure manages all the related methods for bank accounts—such as update, delete, and audit methods—as a unit. Today, *Object Request Brokers* (*ORBs*) provide a distributed object infrastructure. They typically allow objects to communicate across languages, operating systems, and networks. Depending on their implementations, ORBs can support either stateless or stateful object-oriented components.

  - ✔ **Stateless Objects** do not have a unique state—for example, a *bank_account* object would be stateless, whereas *joe's_bank_account* is stateful. When a stateless object is called, it must determine what instance data it needs and then retrieve it from a database. When it's done, it must update the database. Microsoft's *Distributed Component Object Model*

(*DCOM*) is an example of a stateless object environment.[1] And while the *Common Object Request Broker Architecture* (*CORBA*) ORB standard supports both stateless and stateful objects, most ORBs are stateless today.

✔ *Stateful Objects* enable clients to request services of a specific object using a unique object identifier. The middle-tier software must deliver the request to that specific object. If it is not already in memory, the infrastructure must find and load the object's state and methods. After the request completes, the infrastructure must store (or *commit*) the state and delete (or *garbage-collect*) the object from memory. Some ORBs work with an Object Database Management System to store state. In the future, *Object Transaction Managers* (*OTMs*) will manage stateful objects, ensuring that the object is safely put away after transactions complete (we discuss ORBs and OTMs in the next chapter).

How Components Talk to Each Other

Clients send requests to components using logical names instead of physical addresses. The middle-tier infrastructure maps these logical names to physical locations and ensures the delivery of the messages. This mapping provides location transparency for server components. Obviously, this makes life easier for clients that are looking for components to invoke. It lets the middle-tier infrastructure manage component replicas to safeguard the application from system failures. The infrastructure also uses replicas to handle increased loads and balance variable loads. The middle-tier infrastructure routes the request to the physical location where the component is currently running.

Naturally, the programming model of the middle-tier infrastructure determines whether it will call services or objects. Today, transactional middleware (a.k.a. Transaction Processing Monitors, or TP Monitors) are service-oriented, while ORBs are object-oriented. However, ORBs are starting to morph with TP Monitors (more on this later).

The middle-tier infrastructure can provide any (or all) of the following messaging alternatives:

■ *Conversations* support an ongoing dialog involving many interactions between clients and server components. Examples include TCP/IP sockets and IBM's CPI-C.

---

[1] DCOM partially overcomes this limitation by providing a level of indirection using *Monikers*.

- **Request-response** supports a single interaction between client and server components. Examples include remote procedure calls (RPCs) and ORB remote method invocations.

- **Queues** decouple the client and server interactions. Messages are queued for servers. Servers access them when they are ready. Queues can support messages of different priorities. They also support time-triggered dequeuing. Queues are a great—and often necessary—addition to a 3-tier environment. When you are connecting existing applications together, they may be the only communications model you need (see the next Soapbox). When you build new 3-tier applications, they are normally used to supplement synchronous communications. Message-Oriented Middleware (MOM) and TP Monitors currently implement queues. The CORBA 3.0 standard will also include support for queues.

- **Publish-and-subscribe** enables clients (or server components) to register their interest in certain messages with an event manager. Server components (or clients) then "publish" messages to the event manager. The event manager acts as a matchmaker, sending published messages to subscribers that have declared an interest in particular types of messages. Advanced publish-and-subscribe environments support scripted filters that can finely tune the conditions under which a message is forwarded. They can also specify alternate actions, such as queuing the message to a different component. Examples of publish-and-subscribe systems include CORBA's event service and specialized event services that come with MOMs and TP Monitors.

- **Broadcasts and datagrams** allow one-way communication to one or more components or clients. Examples include CORBA's one-way invocation and (again) the specialized services of TP Monitors.

Message Brokers: Fast and Loose Isn't Always Enough

Soapbox

Message Brokers are an exciting and important new trend. They use a coordinated, many-to-many approach to attack the challenge of integrating disparate application systems.

— Roy Schulte
Gartner Group

Message-Oriented Middleware (MOM) is queue-based middleware that allows an application to notify other applications of an event. The application that is the source of the message hands it to the MOM. The MOM then queues it for delivery. It can deliver it when the recipient is available or on a timed trigger. Message Brokers go beyond these functions—they also translate the message from one format to another.

Message Brokers have been touted as the answer to IT's application integration problems. However, they are not a substitute for synchronizing important updates within or between applications. Message Brokers are like chocolate sundaes. They are great when used in moderation—overuse, however, leads to serious side effects. Here's why. Let's assume you want to notify several applications that Joe just opened a checking account. Queued messages will work well in this environment if the other applications can't veto Joe opening the account. But if one of these applications can veto the action—for example, if it checks Joe's credit rating—you can have a messy situation. The application that opened the account must now implement a *compensating transaction* to close the account. It must then send a message to all the applications that received the original notice informing them that Joe's account is no longer open. Each of the recipients must also perform a compensating transaction.

In general, you will find that synchronized transactions are better for applications that depend on each other for their actions. You are assured that everything is OK before the transaction is committed. You do not need to write compensating transactions to undo updates in case of failures. Standards for synchronizing transactions include CICS' 2-Phase Commit protocol, X/Open's OSI/TP, and OMG's Object Transaction Service. These standards allow heterogeneous components to play together in distributed transactions. ❑

WHEN SHOULD YOU USE 3-TIER?

3-tier is rapidly growing in popularity, but 2-tier is far from dead. There are still a number of applications that are ideal for 2-tier architectures. So, how do you know which model to use? We like Gartner Group's answer to this question (see Figure 1-5). The figure shows that—for smaller projects—2-tier applications are easier to develop than 3-tier. However, as applications become more complex, 2-tier applications become exponentially harder to develop.

So, where is the crossover point? According to Gartner Group, you should use 3-tier if your application has any of the following characteristics:

■ Many application services or classes—more than 50

■ Applications programmed in different languages or written by different organizations

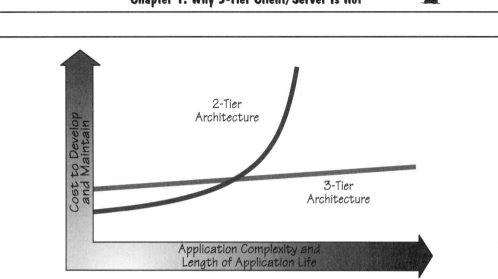

Figure 1-5. 2-Tier and 3-Tier Compared. (Source: Gartner Group.)

■ Two or more heterogeneous data sources—such as two different DBMSs or a DBMS and a file system

■ An application life that is longer than three years—especially if you expect many modifications or additions

■ A high-volume workload—more than 50,000 transactions per day or more than 300 concurrent users on the same system accessing the same database

■ Significant inter-application communication—including inter-enterprise communication such as *electronic data interchange* (*EDI*)

■ The expectation that the application will grow over time so that one of the previous conditions will apply

CONCLUSION

Generally speaking, it has become a safe bet to implement your applications using a 3-tier client/server architecture—especially if you pick a solid infrastructure. In today's world of intranet and Internet applications, 3-tier is the odds-on favorite. It lets you start small—both in scale and function—and then grow your application to intergalactic proportions. It also lets you create a catalog of custom and purchased components that you quickly assemble to produce new applications. You can publish the interfaces to these components, and use GUI tools to access them. Consequently, departmental programmers can include them in their applications. You can even encapsulate and "reuse" legacy applications.

So the message is that client/server has grown up—and proven itself. As you will read in this book, enterprises are now entrusting this technology with their key mission-critical applications. When the going gets tough, smart architects choose 3-tier.

Chapter 2

TP Monitors: The 3-Tier Workhorse

Transaction Processing Monitors (TP Monitors) are being rediscovered by a new generation of software architects. According to Standish Group, TP Monitors became one of the hottest IT technologies in 1996—57% of mission-critical applications were built on TP Monitors. So why this sudden craze for a technology that has its roots in the mainframe world? The answer is that today's generation of open TP Monitors play a key role in 3-tier client/server systems—the fastest growing segment of the client/server market. They provide frameworks that run middle-tier processes as first-class citizens.[1]

TP Monitors have solid credentials—they've been used for many years to keep the biggest of "big iron" applications running. In the mainframe world, a TP Monitor is sold with every mission-critical database. The mainframe folks realized many moons ago that you can't create mission-critical applications without managing the programs (or processes) that operate on the data (see the next Warning box). TP Monitors were born to manage processes and to orchestrate programs. They do this by breaking complex applications into pieces of code called *services*. Using *transactions*, a TP Monitor can get these pieces of software that know nothing about each other to act in total unison. This is obviously a very desirable function

---

[1] This chapter is adapted from **The Essential Client/Server Survival Guide, Second Edition**, by Orfali, Harkey, and Edwards (Wiley, 1996).

in intergalactic client/server environments like the Internet. These environments must eventually be able to deal with billions of daily transactions running anywhere on a network of thousands of servers.

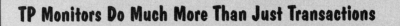

TP Monitors Do Much More Than Just Transactions

Warning

TP Monitors have become associated with the two-phase commit protocol they use to ensure application integrity—so much so that some people believe that it is all they do! In reality, only between five and ten percent of the code in TP Monitors is about synchronizing transactions. Many vendors of TP Monitors find this misunderstanding so pervasive that they have begun using other labels for their software, such as *transactional middleware*. Everyone admits that this falls short of being a satisfying name. However, it is the vendor's attempt to indicate that TP Monitors do much more than just transactions. We've chosen to use the term *TP Monitor* in this book, and describe the broader scope of their capabilities in this chapter. ❏

WHAT TP MONITORS DO

TP Monitors were introduced to run classes of applications that could service thousands of clients. They do this by providing an environment that interjects itself between the remote clients and the server resources (see Figure 2-1). By interjecting themselves between clients and servers, TP Monitors can manage transactions, route them across systems, load-balance their execution, and restart them after failures. They improve overall system performance. TP Monitors manage transactions from their point of origin—typically on the client—across one or more servers, and then back to the originating client. And, of course, TP Monitors ensure that the transactions are completed accurately.

TP Monitors control all the traffic that links hundreds (or thousands) of clients with application programs and the back-end resources. These processes now have a separate existence outside the database or GUI. This means that you can distribute them across machines and networks to wherever it makes the most sense.

One of the great appeals of a TP Monitor is that it is the overseer of all aspects of a distributed application, regardless of the systems or resource managers used. It can manage resources on a single server or multiple servers, and it can cooperate with other TP Monitors in federated arrangements. Future TP Monitors may reside on every client machine to bring desktop resources—such as the user interface, local data warehouses, or personal agents—within a distributed transaction's reach.

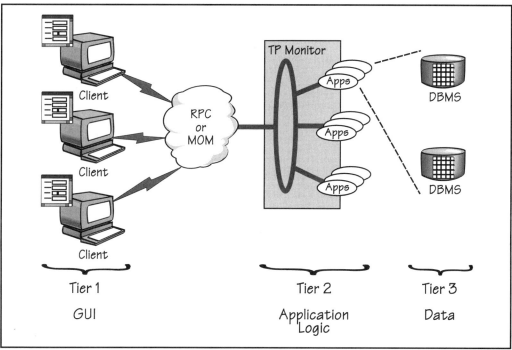

Figure 2-1. 3-Tier Client/Server, TP Monitor Style.

TP Monitors can save you money. According to Standish Group, TP Monitors may result in total system cost savings of greater than 30%—depending on system scale—over a more database-centric approach. In addition, Standish Group research shows that companies can achieve significant "development time" savings—up to 40% or 50%.[2] TP Monitors, with their load balancing, also provide better performance using the same system resources; this means that you can run your application on less expensive hardware. Finally, TP Monitors don't lock you into a vendor-specific database solution—which makes the acquisition process more competitive and adds to cost savings. And if you use a standard transaction interface, you can even avoid getting locked into the TP Monitor.

How TP Monitor-Based Applications Work

You can think of a TP Monitor as providing a pre-built *framework* that helps you build, run, and administer a client/server application so that you don't have to start from ground zero. TP Monitors provide an excellent platform for quickly developing robust, high-performance client/server applications.

---

[2] One of our cases—MCI—actually achieved a 75% reduction in project cost over a previously-developed 2-tier version of the application.

TP Monitors provide a framework for client/server application development. Increasingly, visual tool vendors are directly supporting RPCs and making the TP Monitor transparent to the developers. On the server side, TP Monitors encourage you to create modular, reusable procedures—called *services*—that encapsulate resource managers. A resource manager is any piece of software that manages shared resources—such as a database manager, a persistent queue, or a transactional file system. TP Monitors provide general-purpose server shells (called *server classes*) that run your middle-tier services.

The TP Monitor introduces an event-driven programming style on the server side by letting you associate services—which act as event handlers—with server events. You export the function call and not the data itself. This means that you can keep adding new function calls and let the TP Monitor distribute that function over multiple servers. TP Monitors allow you to create highly complex applications by just adding more services.

The TP Monitor guarantees that unrelated services work together in *ACID* unison. ACID stands for atomicity, consistency, isolation, and durability—principles transaction processing applications live by (see the next Briefing box). The TP Monitor runtime enforces the ACID discipline without requiring any specialized application code other than *begin/end transaction*.

The TP Monitor also lets you mix resource managers, so you can start with one resource manager and then move to another one while preserving your investment in your existing function calls. All services—even legacy ones—join the TP Monitor-managed pool of reusable procedures. In other words, TP Monitors let you add heterogeneous server resources anywhere without altering the existing application architecture.

 Transactions and the ACID Properties

Briefing

From a business point of view, a transaction is an action that changes the state of an enterprise—for example, a customer depositing money in a checking account constitutes a banking transaction. Technically speaking, a transaction is a collection of actions that are governed by "ACID properties." TP Monitors and ORBs with Object Transaction Services provide these properties to applications. ACID—a term coined by Andreas Reuter in 1983—stands for Atomicity, Consistency, Isolation, and Durability. Here's what it means:

■ ***Atomicity*** means a transaction is an indivisible unit of work: all of its actions succeed or they all fail. It's an all-or-nothing proposition. The actions under the transaction's umbrella may include the message queues, updates to a database, and the display of results on the client's screen. Atomicity is defined from the perspective of the instigator of the transaction, usually the client.

■ ***Consistency*** means that after a transaction executes, it must leave the system in a correct state or it must abort. If the transaction cannot achieve a stable end state, it must return the system to its initial state.

■ ***Isolation*** means that a transaction's behavior is not affected by other transactions that execute concurrently. The transaction must serialize all access to shared resources and guarantee that concurrent programs will not corrupt each other's operations. A multiuser program running under transactional protection must behave exactly as it would in a single-user environment. The changes that a transaction makes to shared resources must not become visible outside the transaction until it commits.

■ ***Durability*** means that a transaction's effects are permanent after it commits. Its changes should survive system failures. The term *persistent* is a synonym for *durable*.

A transaction becomes the fundamental unit of recovery, consistency, and concurrency in a client/server system. Why is that important? Take a simple debit-credit banking operation. You'd like to see all credits made to *your* account succeed. Any losses would be unacceptable (of course, any unexpected credits are always welcome). This means you're relying on the application to provide the integrity expected in a real-life business transaction. The application, in turn, relies on the underlying system—usually the TP Monitor—to help achieve this level of transactional integrity. The programmer should not have to develop tons of code that reinvents the transaction wheel.

A more subtle point is that all the participating programs must adhere to the transactional discipline because a single faulty program can corrupt an entire system. A transaction that unknowingly uses corrupted initial data—produced by a non-transactional program—builds on top of a corrupt foundation.

In an ideal world, *all* client/server programs are written as transactions. ACID is the motherhood and apple pie of client/server applications, even—or maybe, especially—for those of intergalactic proportions. ❑

So What Exactly Is a TP Monitor?

TP Monitors first appeared on mainframes to provide robust run-time environments that could support large-scale on-line transaction processing (OLTP) applications—applications that require immediate responses, such as airline and hotel reservations, banking, credit authorization, and stock brokerage systems. Since then, OLTP has spread to almost every type of business application—including hospitals, manufacturing, point-of-sales retail systems, and automated gas pumps. TP Monitors provide the services that keep these OLTP applications running in the style they're accustomed to: highly reactive, available, and well-managed. With OLTP moving to client/server architectures and open platforms, a new breed of TP Monitors has emerged to help make these new environments hospitable to mission-critical applications.

It should come as no surprise that our industry has no commonly accepted definition of a TP Monitor. We like to think of a TP Monitor as an operating system for transaction processing applications. It is also a framework for running middle-tier server applications. In a nutshell, a TP Monitor does three things extremely well:

■ *Process management* includes starting server processes, funneling work to them, monitoring their execution, and balancing their workloads.

■ *Transaction management* means that the TP Monitor guarantees the ACID properties to all programs that run under its protection.

■ *Client/server communications management* allows clients (and services) to invoke an application component in a variety of ways—including request-response, conversations, queuing, publish-and-subscribe, or broadcast.

TP Monitors and OSs: The Great Funneling Act

TP Monitors were originally introduced to run classes of applications that could service hundreds and sometimes thousands of clients (think of an airline reservation application). If each of these thousands of clients were given all the resources it needed on a server—typically a communication connection, half a megabyte of memory, one or two processes, and a dozen open file handles—even the largest mainframe server would fall on its knees (see Figure 2-2). Luckily, not all the clients require service at the same time. However, when they do require it, they want their service *immediately*. Humans on the other end have a "tolerance for waiting" of two seconds or less. TP Monitors provide an operating system—on top of existing operating systems—that connects, in real time, these thousands of impatient humans with a pool of shared server processes. The TP Monitor balances the use of resources among the clients on a demand basis—this is called *funneling*.

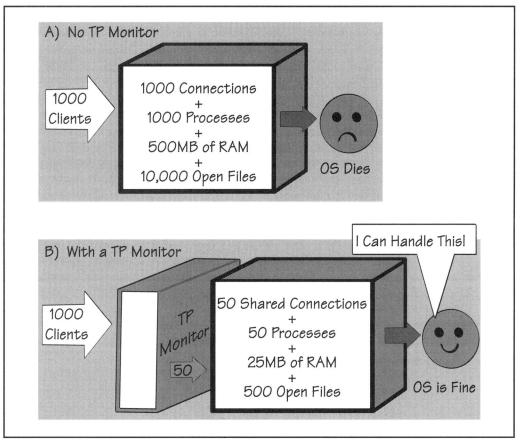

Figure 2-2. Why a Server Operating System Needs a TP Monitor.

The "funneling act" is part of what a TP Monitor must do to efficiently manage the server side of an OLTP application. The server side of the OLTP application is typically packaged as a set of services that contains a number of related functions. The TP Monitor assigns the execution of each service to *server classes*, which are pools of prestarted application processes or threads waiting for work.[3] Each process or thread in a server class is capable of doing the work. The TP Monitor balances the workload between them. Each application can have one or more server classes.[4]

---

[3] As we will explain in the next chapter, Tuxedo calls server classes *Tuxedo servers*. We have decided to call them *server classes* in this book. We don't want you to confuse them with server machines. Now if you meet a Tuxedo developer walking down the street and she starts talking about her 70 servers, you'll understand what she's talking about.

[4] Well, now we need to clarify something more. TP Monitor server classes are not classes in the object-oriented sense of the word. Imagine how much fun it's going to be when OTMs have server classes that manage object classes.

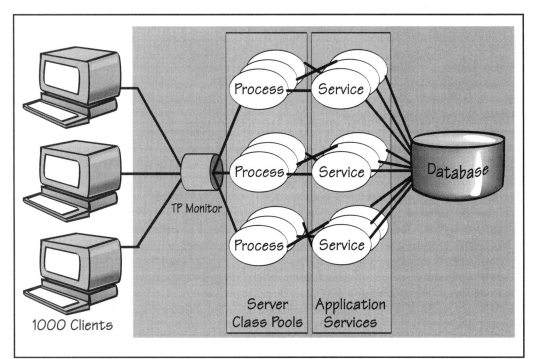

Figure 2-3. How the TP Monitor Performs its Funneling Act.

When a client sends a service request, the TP Monitor hands it to an available process in the server class pool (see Figure 2-3). The server process dynamically links to the service function called by the client, invokes it, oversees its execution, and returns the results to the client. After that completes, another client can reuse the server process. The operating system keeps the already loaded services in memory, where they can be shared across processes. It doesn't get better!

In essence, the TP Monitor removes the process-per-client requirement by funneling incoming client requests to shared server processes. If the number of incoming client requests exceeds the number of processes in a server class, the TP Monitor may dynamically start new ones—this is called *load balancing*. The more sophisticated TP Monitors can distribute the process load across multiple CPUs in SMP or MPP environments. Part of the load-balancing act involves managing the priorities of the incoming requests. The TP Monitor does that by running some high-priority server classes and dynamically assigning them to the VIP clients.

Important, short-running functions are often packaged in high-priority server classes. Batch and low-priority functions are assigned to low-priority server classes. You can also partition server classes by application type, desired response time, the resources they manage, fault-tolerance requirements, and client/server interaction modes—including queued, conversational, or RPC. In addition to providing dynamic load balancing, most TP Monitors let you manually control how many processes or threads are available to each process class.

In their load-balancing capacity, TP Monitors play the role of a client/server *traffic cop*. They route client requests to pools of application processes spread across multiple servers—some of which consist of multiple processors in SMP or MPP configurations.

TP Monitors and Transaction Management

The transaction discipline was introduced in the early TP Monitors to ensure the robustness of multiuser applications that ran on the servers. These applications had to be bulletproof and highly reliable if they were going to serve thousands of users in "bet-your-business" situations. TP Monitors were developed from the ground up as operating systems for business transactions. The unit of management, execution, and recovery is the transaction and the programs that invoked them. The job of a TP Monitor is to guarantee the ACID properties while maintaining high transaction throughput. To do that, it must manage the execution, distribution, and synchronization of transaction *workloads*.

As component-based middleware becomes dominant, transaction coordination becomes even more important. Clients mix-and-match several components to implement a single business transaction. Each of these components may make an update to a database. They become "mini-programs." As a result, their updates need to be coordinated. TP Monitors play this role by providing the ACID properties to the application. For example, components may update the same database or different databases—maybe even different types of databases. What happens if the business transaction is stopped or fails in the middle of all these updates? The TP Monitor ensures that all the updates associated with an aborted transaction are removed or "rolled back." It can even perform this trick when the components are on different servers and are updating different databases from different vendors. When the resource managers are across networks, the TP Monitor synchronizes all the transaction's updates using a two-phase commit protocol (see the next Details box).

With TP Monitors, the application programmers don't have to concern themselves with issues like concurrency, failures, broken connections, load balancing, and the synchronization of resources across multiple nodes. All this is made transparent to them—very much like an operating system makes the hardware transparent to ordinary programs. Simply put, TP Monitors provide the run-time engines for running business transactions—they do that on top of ordinary hardware and operating systems. They also provide a framework for running your server applications.

What's a Two-Phase Commit Protocol?

Details

The *two-phase commit* protocol synchronizes updates so they either all fail or all succeed. This is done by centralizing the decision to commit but giving each participant the right of veto. It's like a Christian marriage: you're given one last chance to back out of the transaction when you're at the altar. If none of the parties present object, the marriage takes place.

Each commercial implementation of the two-phase commit protocol introduces its own variation—and they don't interoperate. But of course, there are standards bodies that are trying to make it all work together. In December 1992—after a five-year development cycle—ISO published its OSI-TP standard that defines very *rigidly* how a two-phase commit is to be implemented (see Figure 2-4). So, OSI-TP allows different TP Monitors to work together to synchronize transactions. Let's go over the mechanics of this protocol:

1. ***In the first phase of a commit***, the *commit manager* node—also known as the *root node* or the *transaction coordinator*—sends *prepare-to-commit* commands to all the *subordinate* nodes that were directly asked to participate in the transaction. The subordinates may have spawned pieces of the transaction on other nodes (or resource managers) to which they must

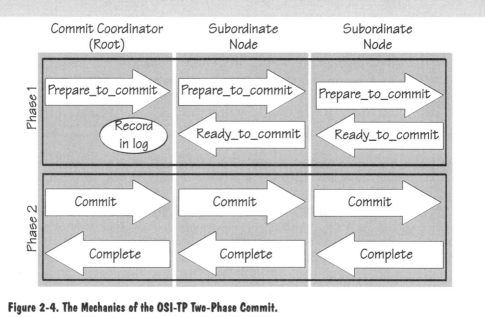

Figure 2-4. The Mechanics of the OSI-TP Two-Phase Commit.

propagate the prepare-to-commit command. It becomes a transaction tree, with the coordinator at the root.

2. ***The first phase of the commit terminates*** when the root node receives *ready-to-commit* signals from all its direct subordinate nodes that participate in the transaction. This means the transaction has executed successfully so far on all the nodes, and they're now ready to do a final commit. The root node logs that fact in a safe place used to recover from a root-node failure.

3. ***The second phase of the commit starts*** after the root node makes the decision to *commit* the transaction—based on the unanimous yes vote. It tells its subordinates to commit. They, in turn, tell their subordinates to do the same, and the order ripples down the tree.

4. ***The second phase of the commit terminates*** when all the nodes involved have safely committed their part of the transaction and made it durable. The root receives all the confirmations and can tell its client that the transaction completed. It can then relax until the next transaction.

5. ***The two-phase commit aborts*** if any of the participants return a *refuse* indication, meaning that their part of the transaction failed. In that case, the root node tells all its subordinates to perform a rollback. And they, in turn, do the same for their subordinates.

The X/Open XA specification defines a set of APIs that work with the underlying OSI-TP protocol. To participate in an XA-defined two-phase commit, TP Monitors and resource managers (such as databases and message queues) must map their private two-phase commit protocols to the XA commands. They must also be willing to let somebody else drive the transaction—something they're not accustomed to doing. The XA specification allows participants to withdraw from further participation in the global transaction during Phase 1 if they do not have to update resources. In XA, a TP Monitor can also use a one-phase commit if it is dealing with a single resource manager.

In early 1996, most TP Monitors could easily handle transactions that spanned across 100 two-phase commit engines. However, the two-phase commit protocol is by no means perfect. Here are some of its limitations:

■ ***Performance overhead*** is introduced by all the message exchanges. The protocol has no way of discerning valuable transactions that need this kind of protection from the more tolerant transactions that don't need protection. It generates messages for all transactions, even read-only ones. So, architects tend to use application designs that keep their database reads outside the transaction's boundaries.

■ ***Hazard windows***, where certain failures can be a problem. For example, if the root node crashes after the first phase of the commit, the subordinates may be left in disarray. Who cleans up this mess? There are always workarounds, but it's a tricky business. It helps if you use some fault-tolerant hardware in your system to coordinate the transaction.

Many TP Monitor vendors have also implemented support for *delegated commit* as a practical necessity in a client/server environment. Delegated commit means a transaction originating from an unreliable platform—such as a personal computer—can delegate the commit coordination to an alternate node. ❑

XA, OSI-TP, and Other Transaction Standards

The X/Open standards body has defined a set of specifications that allows applications, resource managers (such as databases), and transaction managers to synchronize distributed transactions. This is called the X/Open Distributed Transaction Processing (DTP) standard (see Figure 2-5). Because there are multiple players involved in a transaction, multiple interfaces need to be defined. Here are the most important of these interfaces:

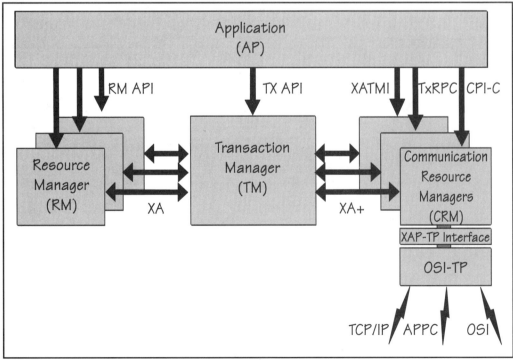

Figure 2-5. X/Open 1994 Distributed Transaction Processing Reference Model.

- **RM API** is used by an application to query and update resources that are owned by a Resource Manager (RM).

- **TX API** is used by an application to signal the transaction manager that it is beginning a transaction, ready to commit it, or wants to abort it.

- **XA API** is used by the transaction manager to coordinate transaction updates across resource managers. Through this interface, the transaction manager tells the resource managers when to "prepare to commit," "commit," "end," or "roll back" transactions.

- **OSI-TP** protocols allow heterogeneous transaction managers to work together to coordinate transactions.

- **XATMI, TxRPC, and CPI-C** are transactional communication programming interfaces. You have your choice of standards. XATMI is based on BEA Tuxedo's Application-to-Transaction Monitor Interface (ATMI), a message-oriented interface; TxRPC is based on the Distributed Computing Environment (DCE) remote procedure call interface; and CPI-C is a peer-to-peer conversational interface based on IBM's CPI-C. There is a standard here to please every camp! Note that some transaction managers support more than one interface. For example, Tuxedo supports both XATMI and TxRPC.

The good news is that you, the programmer, only have to use TX and one of the remote communications interfaces. The rest are under-the-cover interfaces that each of your transaction managers and resource managers should support. The other good news is that CORBA ORBs have built-in transaction support. The CORBA *Object Transaction Service (OTS)* is patterned after XA. In addition, support for transactions is built directly into the ORB's communication service, which makes their propagation transparent to ordinary objects.

Transactional Communications

Ordinary operating systems must understand the nature of the jobs and resources they manage. This is also true for TP Monitors—they must provide an optimized environment for the execution of the transactions that run under their control. This means they must load the server programs, dynamically assign incoming client requests to server processes, recover from failures, return the replies to the clients, and make sure high-priority traffic gets through first.

One of the jobs TP Monitors have is to provide communications between clients and servers—and between the servers. They need to do this while maintaining the ACID properties. So what kind of transactional communications do TP Monitors provide? They typically support one or all of these facilities: conversational, RPC, queued, publish-and-subscribe, and batch (see Figure 2-6). Conversational and RPC transactions usually involve a human user that requires immediate attention; they run in high-priority mode. Publish-and-subscribe transactions usually run as high-priority messages too. Batch transactions typically run in low-priority mode. MOM-based queued transactions can be of either type.

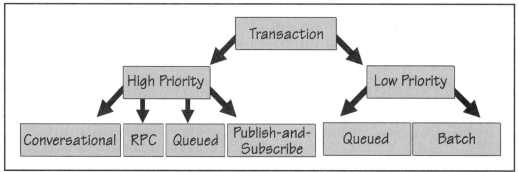

Figure 2-6. Client/Server Transaction Profiles.

TP Monitors complement Message Brokers (or MOMs) very well. Together they can support long-lived transactions and workflow applications. TP Monitors can act as the transaction coordinator for work exchanged through transactional queues. The queued events can trigger server processes managed by the TP Monitor.

What Makes Transactional Communications Different?

On the surface, transactional client/server exchanges appear to use traditional communication models: RPCs, queues, ORB invocations, publish-and-subscribe, and conversational peer-to-peer. This is not so. They're using highly augmented versions of these traditional communication mechanisms. However, most of the value-added elements are made transparent to the programmer—they look like ordinary exchanges bracketed by start and end transaction calls. The transactional versions augment the familiar communications exchanges with the following value-added extensions:

■ They piggyback *transactional delimiters* that allow a client to specify the begin-transaction and end-transaction boundaries. The actual commit mechanics are usually *delegated* to one of the server TP Monitors—otherwise each client would need to manage ACID properties and maintain transactional logs, which would be an unmanageable and unreliable situation.

■ They introduce—under-the-cover—a three-way exchange between a client, server, and TP Monitor (the transaction manager). A new transaction is assigned a unique ID by the coordinating TP Monitor. All subsequent message exchanges between the participants are tagged with that transaction ID. The message exchanges allow the TP Monitor to keep track of what Microsoft's Jim Gray calls the "dynamically expanding web" of resource managers participating in a distributed transaction. TP Monitors need that information to coordinate the two-phase commit with all the participants in a transaction.

■ They embed transactional state information within each of the messages exchanged. This information helps the TP Monitor identify the state of the distributed transaction and figure out what to do next.

■ They allow a TP Monitor to enforce *exactly-once* semantics—this means that the message only gets executed once.

■ They guarantee that a server process is at the receiving end of the message. Traditional RPCs and MOMs don't worry about this kind of stuff—they assume that a program will "automagically" appear on the receiving end.

■ They provide server routing based on server classes, server loads, automatic failover, and other factors.

As you can see, there's a lot more going on here than a simple RPC, MOM, or ORB exchange. The literature calls these enhanced services *Transactional RPC (TRPC), Transactional Queues, Transactional Publish-and-Subscribe, Transactional Conversations, and Transactional ORB Invocations*. The distinguishing factor is that all resource managers and processes invoked through these calls become part of the transaction. The TP Monitor is informed of any service calls; it uses that information to orchestrate the actions of all the participants, enforce their ACID behavior, and make them act as part of a transaction. In contrast, traditional RPCs, messages, and queue invocations are between separate programs that are not bound by a transaction discipline. Table 2-1 summarizes the differences between transactional communication mechanisms and their non-transactional equivalents.

Examples of commercial implementations of transactional RPCs include Transarc/IBM's Encina Transactional RPC, BEA's Tuxedo TxRPC, and IBM's CICS External Call Interface (ECI). Examples of conversational transactional interfaces are found in Tuxedo ATMI, Tandem's RSC, and IBM's APPC. IBM's MQSeries and BEA's MessageQ are examples of a transactional implementation of an "open" MOM queue. Some TP Monitors also include their own bundled versions of recoverable queues—in Encina's case, it is RQS; in Tuxedo, it is /Q; and CICS uses transient queues. In addition, Tuxedo has a transactional publish-and-subscribe subsystem called the EventBroker. Finally, commercial implementations of CORBA OTS are beginning to appear in ORBs such as Iona's Orbix, BEA's Iceberg, and IBM's Component Broker.

Table 2-1. Transactional Versus Non-Transactional Communications.

Feature	Ordinary Queues, RPCs, ORBs, Publish-and-Subscribe, and Conversational Communications	Transactional Queues, RPCs, ORBs, Publish-and-Subscribe, and Conversational Communications
Participants	Loosely-coupled client/server programs.	Transactionally bound client/server and server/server programs. The message invocation causes the recipient program to join the transaction.
Commit synchronization	No	Yes
Only-once semantics	No	Yes
Server management on the recipient node	No. It's just a delivery mechanism. (ORBs provide minimal server management.)	Yes. The process that receives the message is started, load-balanced, monitored, and tracked as part of the transaction.
Load balancing	Using the directory services. The first server to register becomes a hotspot. No dynamic load balancing is provided.	Uses the TP Monitor's sophisticated load-balancing algorithms. Can spread work across multiple SMP machines and dynamically add more processes to cover hotspots of activity. Several servers can read from the same queue.
Supervised exchanges	No. Exchanges are simply between the client and the server. The exchanges are transient. No crash recovery or error management is provided. You're on your own.	The TP Monitor supervises the entire exchange, restarts communication links, redirects messages to an alternate server process if the first one gets hung, performs retries, and provides persistent queues and crash recovery.

TP-LITE VERSUS TP-HEAVY

TP-Lite systems may not solve all the world's problems, but they solve many simple ones. According to Ziph's law, most problems are simple.

> — Jim Gray,
> Microsoft

If I had to do an application that had a lot of processing, I'd use a distributed TP Monitor.

> — Ed Wood, VP of Interoperability
> Sybase

Stored procedures may be the most intense competition TP Monitors face. Database vendors introduced the concept of stored procedures to increase the performance of 2-tier architectures. Stored procedures consist of SQL statements and business logic—typically implemented in the database vendor's 4GL. Industry pundits call this approach *TP-Lite*. The database model does not treat processes as independent first-class citizens—the procedures are stored and executed inside the database. So even though stored procedures have a 3-tier veneer, their packaging is the epitome of 2-tier.

In some ways, TP-Lite integrates some of the functions of a TP Monitor directly into the database engine. But only a few of the functions are currently integrated—including some level of client communications concentration, single-function transaction management, and RPC-like calls. As a result, TP-Lite fixes some of the problems inherent to 2-tier—but it also introduces some new problems. There is a long list of functions that are not implemented; the TP Monitor people have a ten-year head start. This is why TP Monitor-based architectures are known as *TP-Heavy*.

A feature-by-feature comparison between TP-Lite and TP-Heavy is painfully unequal. It's like comparing a Harley-Davidson motorcycle with a bicycle. TP-Lite can best be defined by what it lacks, which is a long list of functions. In a nutshell, TP-Lite functions don't execute under global transaction control, there is no global supervisor, and the process management environment is very primitive. TP-Lite server functions only work with a single resource manager (the local database), and they don't support any form of ACID nesting. Here are the biggest differences between these two technologies.

Scope of the Commit

A TP-Lite stored procedure is written in a database-vendor proprietary procedural language—PL/SQL, Transact SQL, and so on—and it is stored in the database. A stored procedure is a transactional unit, but it can't participate with other transactional units in a global transaction. It can't call another transaction and have it execute within the same transaction boundary. As shown in Figure 2-7, if stored procedure A dies after invoking stored procedure B, A's work will automatically be rolled back while B's work is committed for posterity. This is a violation of the ACID all-or-nothing proposition. This limitation causes you to write large stored procedures that put everything within the scope of the commit. It doesn't help the cause of modularization or writing reusable functions.

In contrast, TP-Heavy procedures are written using standard procedural languages. They can easily provide all-or-nothing protection in situations like the one shown in the right-hand side of Figure 2-7. For TP-Heavy, dealing with global transactions is second nature.

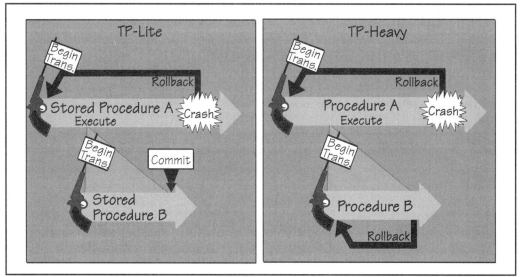

Figure 2-7. Scope of the Commit.

Managing Heterogeneous Resources

RDBMSs do not support the notion of a global transaction that encompasses more than one program.

— *Richard Finkelstein, President*
Performance Computing

A TP-Lite stored procedure can only commit transaction resources that are on the vendor's database or resource manager (see Figure 2-8). It cannot synchronize or commit work that is on a foreign database or resource manager—whether local or remote. In contrast, TP-Heavy procedures can easily handle ACID updates on multiple heterogeneous resource managers within the scope of the single transaction.

Note that some database vendors can extend two-phase commit to multiple databases—usually their own. Oracle7's Open Gateway even lets you manage the two-phase commit across heterogeneous XA-compliant databases. However, the catch is that gateways are built on the assumption that a stored procedure within a single database is the entire application (and also the point of origin of the transaction). Gateways do not allow multiple applications (or stored procedures) to participate in a transaction. Gateways also lock you into a database vendor's proprietary stored procedure environment. On the other hand, TP-Heavy really makes your applications resource-neutral.

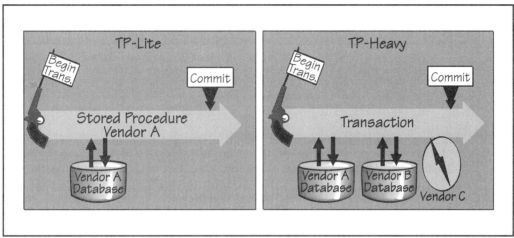

Figure 2-8. Synchronizing Heterogeneous Resource Managers.

Process Management

A TP-Lite stored procedure is invoked, executed under ACID protection (within a single-phase commit), and *may* then be cached in memory for future reuse. That's about it.

In contrast, TP-Heavy processes are prestarted and managed as server classes (see Figure 2-9). Server classes run copies of the application's business logic—so they are ready to act on incoming requests from clients. Loads are balanced across the server classes. If the load on a server class gets too heavy, more processes are automatically started. Server classes support priorities and other class-of-service attributes. Server processes have firewalls around them so that the programs running within them don't interfere with each other. If a server class process dies,

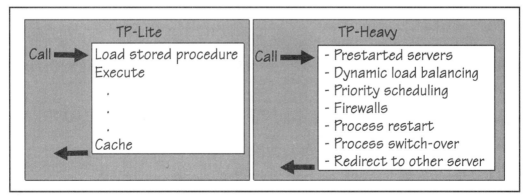

Figure 2-9. TP-Lite Versus TP-Heavy Process Management.

it is restarted or the transaction can be reassigned to another process in that server class. The TP Monitor constantly supervises the entire environment. The server class concept helps the TP Monitor understand what class of service is required by the user for a particular group of functions. It's an intelligently managed environment. These features mean that TP-Heavy applications can scale—the same application, without code changes, can serve a few clients to many thousands.

Client/Server Invocations

The TP-Lite stored procedure invocation is extremely non-standard. Vendors provide their own proprietary RPC invocation mechanism. The RPCs are not defined using an Interface Definition Language (IDL). And they're not integrated with global directory, security, and authentication services. These omissions make them especially unsuitable for Internet transactions. The communications links are not automatically restarted, they aren't load-balanced for efficiency, and they're not under transactional protection. In addition, TP-Lite does not support communications alternatives like conversations, queues, or publish-and-subscribe.

In contrast, the TP-Heavy environment is very open to different communications styles (see Figure 2-10). Client sessions are authenticated. Clients access components through logical names. Clients also define transaction boundaries, can call multiple components, and include legacy systems in the business transaction.

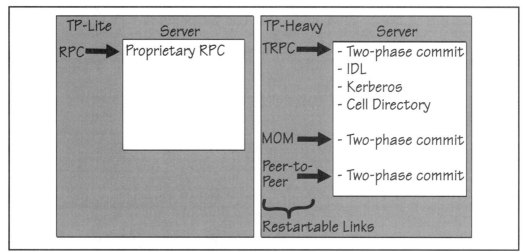

Figure 2-10. TP-Lite Versus TP-Heavy Client/Server Invocation.

Performance

Because they cut down on network traffic, TP-Lite stored procedures are much faster than either networked static or dynamic SQL. However, they don't perform as well as TP-Heavy managed procedures, especially under heavy loads. Most stored procedures dynamically interpret each SQL statement for each transaction and then recreate the access plan. In addition, most stored procedures are written using interpreted 4GLs, which are slow. In mid-1997, *all* of the top 25 TPC-C database benchmark scores were achieved using a TP Monitor (see Table 2-2).[5]

Table 2-2. The Top 25 TPC-C Benchmark Results.

Submitting Company	Throughput (tpmC)	Database	Operating System	TP Monitor	Qty/Processors/MHz
Sun	31,147	Oracle8	Solaris 2.6	Tuxedo	24/UltraSPARC/250MHz
Digital	30,390	Oracle7	Digital UNIX V4.0A	Tuxedo	32/DECchip 21164/350MHz
SGI	25,309	Informix	IRIX 6.4 S2MP	Tuxedo	28/R10000/195MHz
Sun	23,144	Oracle7	Solaris 2.6	Tuxedo	16/UltraSPARC/250MHz
Sun	18,439	Sybase	Solaris 2.5.1	Tuxedo	20/UltraSPARC/250MHz
HP	17,827	Oracle7	HP-UX 10.20	Tuxedo	48/PA-RISC 7150/120MHz
Sun	15,462	Informix	Solaris 2.6	Tuxedo	14/UltraSPARC/250MHz
HP	14,739	Sybase	HP-UX 10.30	Tuxedo	4/PA-RISC 8000/180MHz
Bull	14,286	Oracle7	System AIX 4.1.5	Tuxedo	8/PowerPC 604/112MHz
IBM	14,286	Oracle7	AIX 4.1.5	Tuxedo	8/PowerPC 604/112MHz
Digital	14,227	Oracle7	Open VMS 7.1	ACMS	8/DECchip 21164/350MHz
Digital	14,177	Sybase	Digital UNIX V3.2G	Tuxedo	10/DECchip 21164/350MHz

---

[5] Source: *The Transaction Processing Performance Council* (July, 1997). The TPC-C benchmark is measured in transactions per minute. You can look up the current numbers on-line at http://www.tpc.org.

Table 2-2. The Top 25 TPC-C Benchmark Results. (Continued)

Submitting Company	Throughput (tpmC)	Database	Operating System	TP Monitor	Qty/Processors/MHz
Digital	13,646	Informix	Digital UNIX V3.2D-2	Tuxedo	10/DECchip 21164/350MHz
SNI	11,503	Informix	Reliant UNIX V5.43C	Open UTM	8/R10000/200MHz
Sun	11,466	Sybase	Solaris 2.5.1	Tuxedo	12/UltraSPARC/167MHz
Digital	11,456	Oracle7	Digital UNIX V3.2D-1	Tuxedo	8/DECchip 21164/350MHz
Sybase	11,014	Sybase	Digital UNIX V3.2C	Tuxedo	10/DECchip 21164/300MHz
Unisys	10,666	MS SQL Server	MS NT Server 4.0	Tuxedo	6/Pentium Pro/200MHz
Digital	10,350	Sybase	Digital UNIX V4.0D	Tuxedo	4/DECchip 21164/466MHz
SNI	9,524	Informix	Reliant UNIX V5.43B	Open UTM	22/R4400MC/250MHz
Digital	9,414	Oracle7	Digital UNIX V3.2D-1	Tuxedo	8/DECchip 21164/300MHz
HP	9,198	MS SQL Server	MS NT Server 4.0	Tuxedo	4/Pentium Pro/200MHz
IBM	9,165	Sybase	AIX 4.2.1	Tuxedo	8/PowerPC 604e/200MHz

Transactional middleware also saves you money by being more efficient, thus requiring less hardware. Essentially, transactional middleware offloads the database server by multiplexing client requests. It acts as a funnel on top of whatever funnel the database may have already put in place. In addition, the TP Monitor's precompiled (and prebound) application code runs more efficiently than interpreted stored procedures.

Figure 2-11 shows you how dramatic some of these performance numbers can be—the benchmarks were run on the same hardware with an Informix database engine, both with and without transactional middleware. In addition to better performance, significant hardware cost savings can be achieved because you need fewer database resources to support a given workload.

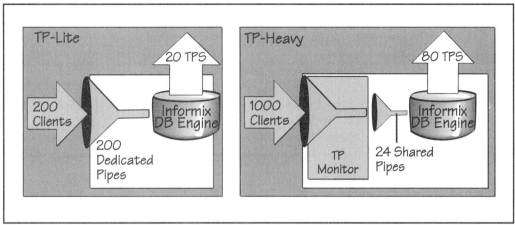

Figure 2-11. TP-Heavy Helps the Performance of TP-Lite. (Source: Unisys Corporation.)

TP MONITORS WILL MORPH WITH ORBS

TP Monitors are competing with distributed objects to become the application platform of choice for 3-tier client/server computing. So it should come as no surprise that the key TP Monitor vendors are introducing a new generation of TP Monitors built on ORBs (see the next Briefing box). For example, the *Microsoft Transaction Server* is based on DCOM. IBM is introducing its *Component Broker* technology, which is based on CORBA business objects. Finally, BEA is delivering its next-generation Tuxedo system (code-named *Iceberg*) on a CORBA distributed object foundation. Gartner Group calls these *Object Transaction Monitors*.

What do ORBs do for TP Monitors? ORBs will bring TP Monitors to the client/server mainstream. There, they will become the orchestrators of the *Object Web*—that is, the next-generation infrastructure that combines Web and object technologies to support Internet, intranet, and extranet applications. CORBA ORBs support a built-in transaction protocol called OTS.[6] This allows TP Monitors to work with transactional middleware provided by standard off-the-shelf ORBs. These ORBs will be incorporated into commodity desktop operating systems such as NT, OS/2, Windows 95, and Macintosh. In addition, ORBs will be distributed freely with Web browsers, where they will be used to provide a distributed object foundation for Java and intranets. For the first time, TP Monitor vendors will not have to provide all of the transactional communications environment themselves. TP Monitors will be able to work with commodity middleware, especially on the client.

---

[6] Most of the architects that defined CORBA's Object Transaction Service worked in TP Monitor development groups. So you can guess that OTS was designed to do two things: 1) be a really good implementation of the transaction processing principles collected from years of practice, and 2) allow TP Monitors and ORBs to be more easily integrated.

What Do ORBs Do?

Briefing

Object Request Brokers (ORBs) are object buses. They let objects transparently make requests to—and receive responses from—other objects located locally or remotely. The client is not aware of the mechanisms used to communicate with, activate, or store the server objects. The CORBA 1.1 specifications—introduced in 1991—only specified the IDL, language bindings, and APIs for interfacing to the ORB. So, you could write portable programs that run on top of the dozen CORBA-compliant ORBs on the market (especially on the client side). CORBA 2.0 specifies interoperability across vendor ORBs. CORBA 3.0 will provide server-side portability.

A CORBA ORB provides a variety of distributed middleware services. The ORB lets objects discover each other at run time and invoke each other's services. An ORB is much more sophisticated than alternative forms of client/server middleware—including traditional Remote Procedure Calls (RPCs), Message-Oriented Middleware (MOM), database stored procedures, and peer-to-peer services. In theory, CORBA is the best client/server communications middleware ever defined. In practice, CORBA is only as good as the products that implement it.

To give you an idea of why CORBA ORBs make such great client/server middleware, we offer the following "short" list of benefits that every CORBA ORB provides:

■ *Static and dynamic method invocations*. A CORBA ORB lets you either statically define your method invocations at compile time or dynamically discover them at run time. So you get either strong type checking at compile time or maximum flexibility associated with late (or run-time) binding. Most other forms of middleware only support static bindings.

■ *High-level language bindings*. A CORBA ORB lets you invoke methods on server objects using your high-level language of choice. It doesn't matter what language server objects are written in. CORBA separates interface from implementation and provides language-neutral data types that make it possible to call objects across language and operating system boundaries. In contrast, other types of middleware typically provide low-level, language-specific, API libraries. And they don't separate implementation from specification—the API is tightly bound to the implementation, which makes it very sensitive to changes.

■ *Self-describing system*. CORBA provides run-time metadata for describing every server interface known to the system. Every CORBA ORB must support an *Interface Repository* that contains real-time information describing the functions a server provides and their parameters. The clients use metadata to discover how to invoke services at run time. It also helps tools generate code on-the-fly. The metadata is generated automatically either by an IDL-language precompiler or by compilers that know how to generate IDL directly from an OO language. For example, the MetaWare C++ compiler generates IDL directly from C++ class definitions; Visigenic/Netscape's *Caffeine* generates IDL directly from Java bytecodes. To the best of our knowledge, no other form of client/server middleware provides this type of run-time metadata and language-independent definitions of all its services.

■ *Local/remote transparency.* An ORB can run in stand-alone mode on a laptop, or it can be interconnected to every other ORB in the universe using CORBA 2.0's *Internet Inter-ORB Protocol (IIOP)* services. An ORB can broker interobject calls within a single process, multiple processes running within the same machine, or multiple processes running across networks and operating systems. This is completely transparent to your objects. Note that the ORB can broker among fine-grained objects—like C++ classes—as well as more coarse-grained objects. In general, a CORBA client/server programmer does not have to be concerned with transports, server locations, object activation, byte ordering across dissimilar platforms, or target operating systems—CORBA makes it all transparent.

■ *Built-in security and transactions.* The ORB includes context information in its messages to handle security and transactions across machine and ORB boundaries.

■ *Polymorphic messaging*. In contrast to other forms of middleware, an ORB does not simply invoke a remote function—it invokes a function on a target object. This means that the same function call can have different results, depending on the object that receives it. For example, a *configure_yourself* method invocation behaves differently when applied to a database object versus a printer object.

■ *Coexistence with existing systems*. CORBA's separation of an object's definition from its implementation is perfect for encapsulating existing applications.

Using CORBA IDL, you can make your existing code look like an object on the ORB, even if it's implemented in stored procedures, CICS, IMS, or COBOL. This makes CORBA an evolutionary solution. You can write your new applications as pure objects and encapsulate existing applications with IDL wrappers.

For more information on CORBA and ORBs, please see *Instant CORBA*, by Orfali, Harkey, and Edwards (Wiley, 1997). ❏

The distributed object infrastructure provides TP Monitors with a myriad of standard services—including metadata, dynamic invocations, persistence, relationships, events, naming, component factories, versioning, licensing, security, change management, collections, and many others. And objects also make it easier for TP Monitors to create and manage rich transaction models—such as nested transactions and long-lived transactions (or workflow). TP Monitors will become frameworks for managing smart components.

So, what do TP Monitors do for ORBs? TP Monitors will be able to offer these independent components a broad array of mission-critical services—including transaction management, transactional workflow, load balancing, transactional queues, fault-tolerance, and life-cycle services. TP Monitors make it possible for ORBs to manage millions of objects.

Pure CORBA and DCOM implementations are totally anarchistic. Objects can appear anywhere at any time. Once they do, they stick around—no one knows how to stop them. This is not a good scenario for applications that could have millions of run-time objects. In contrast, TP Monitors do not like to be surprised. They like to be in control of their environment. Under the supervision of a TP Monitor, objects can be managed in a *predictable* manner. Instead of just loading and running an application, a TP Monitor will prestart components, manage their persistent state, and coordinate their interactions across networks. TP Monitors will make ORBs mission-critical.

Together, TP Monitors and components can literally perform magic. TP Monitors will become the coordinators of distributed components on the Internet and intranets. Instead of managing server classes, TP Monitors will manage JavaBeans, components, and CORBA business objects (see Figure 2-12).

CONCLUSION

There is a strange dichotomy in how enterprise IT shops deal with the middle tier. The same organizations that would never dream of building a database management system jump headfirst into building their own infrastructure for the middle tier. They tend to see it as a simple task—at least until the requirements start to grow exponentially. The result is that—according to Standish Group—IT shops spend 70% of their resources building infrastructure. These large, risk-prone projects probably contribute to the high project failure rate we discussed in Chapter 1.

TP Monitors provide a rich infrastructure for 3-tier client/server applications that is difficult to duplicate. After all, TP Monitor vendors spent hundreds of person-years building these systems in the first place. And they have had the added advantage of incorporating feedback from hundreds of production, mission-critical 3-tier applications.

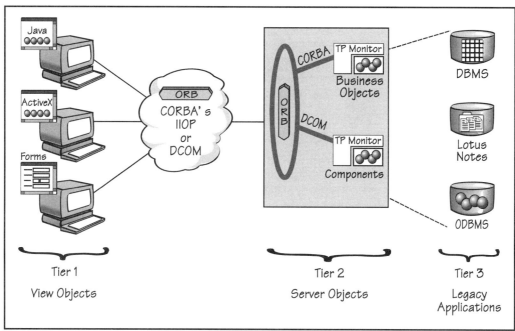

Figure 2-12. The Morphing of TP Monitors With ORBs.

So, when should you use a TP Monitor? Standish Group recommends that you use a TP Monitor for any client/server application that has over 100 clients, processes five or more TPC-C type transactions per minute, uses three or more physical servers, and/or uses two or more databases. We recommend that you use a TP Monitor for all of your client/server applications. Even though TP Monitors were originally introduced to serve very large mission-critical applications, the new versions are well-suited for handling client/server applications that span from a few to thousands of nodes.

TP Monitors put you in the healthy habit of writing 3-tier client/server applications. And they prepare you for the final destination: the world of distributed objects on the "SuperNet," where Internet, intranet, and extranet applications all use a common infrastructure—the Object Web—for maximum functionality, flexibility, and access. Now that some of the popular client/server tools have added support for TP Monitors, you can't use the excuse that they're too difficult to program. If you believe Standish Group, they save you money in the long run, so cost shouldn't be an issue.

Now that we've discussed the theory behind TP Monitors, we're ready to take a behind-the-scenes look at the leading open TP Monitor—Tuxedo—on which many of the applications in Part 2 are built.

Chapter 3

Tuxedo 101

BEA Tuxedo is the middle-tier platform used by most of the 3-tier client/server applications in Part 2. So before you "peak under the covers" into these applications, you'll need a crash course in the Tuxedo basics, which is the topic of this chapter.[1]

A BRIEF HISTORY OF TUXEDO

AT&T began developing Tuxedo in 1984 at Bell Laboratories to support their large-scale client/server applications. For a time, the fate of Tuxedo was interlocked with UNIX. AT&T transferred Tuxedo and UNIX to the UNIX System Laboratory (USL) when it was established in 1989—USL then made Tuxedo commercially available. Novell bought USL in 1993 to acquire UNIX— it got Tuxedo as part of the bargain. In 1996, BEA Systems acquired Tuxedo from Novell. BEA Systems was established specifically to market and support enterprise middle-tier platforms—so Tuxedo found a home at last. It is now the cornerstone of BEA's product family.

---

[1] For more information on Tuxedo, we strongly recommend *The Tuxedo System*, Andrade et al. (Addison Wesley, 1996).

THE WORLD'S SHORTEST TUXEDO TUTORIAL

Tuxedo provides a distributed middle-tier infrastructure that lets you write applications as a collection of *services*, each implementing a business function (see Figure 3-1). Tuxedo manages these services and coordinates their involvement in transactions. Services can access a variety of databases and be ensured of full transactional integrity. Tuxedo runs on over 50 different platforms—including NT, OS/400, MVS, Tandem's NonStop Kernel, and, of course, all flavors of UNIX.

Tuxedo also provides a variety of communications options that these services can use—including RPCs, conversations, queues, publish-and-subscribe, and broadcasts. Tuxedo extends this messaging environment to allow LAN- and Internet-based clients to call its services (through the use of *Tuxedo /WS* and *BEA Jolt*, respectively). Clients can define transaction boundaries; the management of the transaction is then handled by the server on behalf of the client.

Tuxedo services and clients can also communicate with IMS and CICS—and vice versa—using *BEA Connect*; it provides transparent access to existing mainframe applications.

Whew! Now that we've given you the whirlwind tour, let's catch our breath and go back over each of these functions in detail. The important thing to remember is that the services you write are first-class citizens in Tuxedo. Everything in Tuxedo is designed to cater to their needs—including the messaging infrastructure, mainframe access, Internet support, system management, and fault-tolerant features.

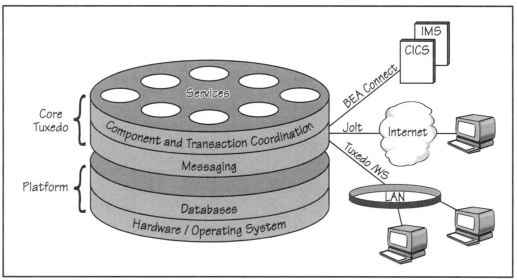

Figure 3-1. A Functional Diagram of Tuxedo.

PROGRAMMING TUXEDO APPLICATIONS

You design Tuxedo applications modularly as a collection of services that perform a single task—for example, *Buy_Book*, *Add_Customer*, and *Bill_Customer*. Each service has a logical name and well-defined input and output parameters—these form the *contract* that allows clients to invoke the service. Services can also call other services. Often, application designers define a pyramid relationship between services—where clients invoke a master service that uses other finer-grained services to implement sub-tasks (see Figure 3-2). By structuring applications in this modular manner, you maximize your potential to reuse services in a variety of situations.

Clients invoke services—so do other services, as we've indicated. They do this by calling the *Application-to-Transaction Monitor Interface* (*ATMI*) routines in the Tuxedo communications library. Today, Tuxedo provides C and COBOL versions of these libraries. Applications written in other languages—such as C++ and Small-talk—use these libraries, too. Tuxedo also has a client-side Java library (called *Jolt*) that lets Java applets call Tuxedo services. Tuxedo ensures that their message gets to the right service. Clients and services tell Tuxedo when business transactions begin and end—in between, they use Tuxedo to call the services they need to execute the transaction.

In addition to ATMI, Tuxedo provides a TxRPC interface—another X/Open DTP interface. This interface is patterned after DCE's *Remote Procedure Call* (*RPC*). With TxRPC, you define your service's interface using the TxRPC Interface Definition Language (IDL). The IDL compiler creates portable C code stubs for both the client and server sides of an application. The stubs are compiled and linked with the Tuxedo runtime library, which locates the right interfaces in your distributed system, performs the messaging exchanges, packs and unpacks the message parameters, and processes any errors that occur.[2]

Tuxedo provides a framework (known as *main* in C) that runs multiple services as a single executable program, which we call a *server class*.[3] Tuxedo starts, stops, distributes, and monitors these server classes. It dispatches clients' requests to the appropriate service within a server class. In addition to writing these services, you also write server initialization and termination routines that Tuxedo uses to open and close the resources—such as databases and other subsystems—your services need to access.

---

[2] By the time you read this, Tuxedo will also support CORBA objects that you define via CORBA IDL.

[3] As we noted in Chapter 2, Tuxedo refers to this as a "Tuxedo server." For purposes of clarity, we will call this a "server class" in this book—the standard industry term for this facility. To TP Monitors, a service class groups a set of services as a run-time unit. Don't confuse this concept with object-oriented "classes."

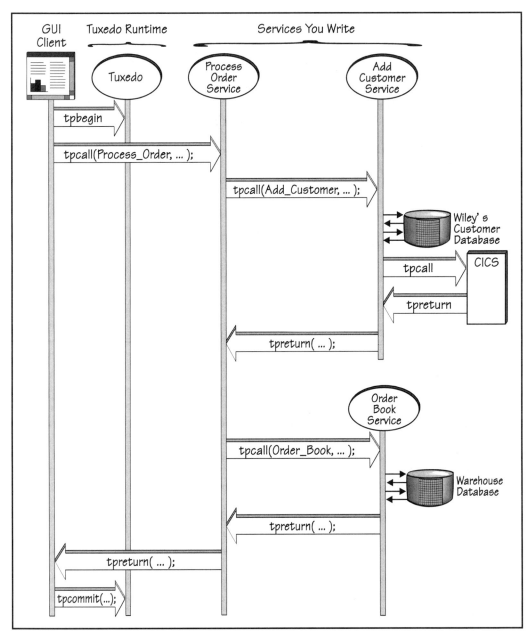

Figure 3-2. A Tuxedo Client Invoking Services to Execute a Business Transaction.

What You Don't Program

The best part about the Tuxedo programming model is the code you *don't* have to write. Tuxedo makes the following distributed processing issues transparent to your programs:

- **Network protocols and computer-specific interfaces.** Tuxedo applications can communicate over a variety of networks that use different protocols. They can run on a variety of computers. Your application remains blissfully unaware.

- **Service location.** Programs use logical names to access users, clients, databases, and services. You don't have to worry about where any of these are located in the production environment. You can relocate these application elements at run time without impacting your application. In addition, you can dynamically add and relocate elements to increase capacity or recover from system failures.

- **Implementation nuances.** Services are encapsulated—clients do not know how they are implemented. This means that you can modify a service without impacting clients. You can also write clients and servers in different programming languages.

- **The management infrastructure.** You don't worry about management consoles, failure recovery, transaction integrity, scale, and many more infrastructure issues. Tuxedo includes built-in mechanisms for handling these.

Development Tools

Many 3-tier client/server tools target Tuxedo as their run-time environment. These products come from vendors such as Dynasty, MagnaX, MicroFocus, NatStar, Passport, Prolifics, Seer, Supernova, and Texas Instruments.

For GUI development, you can use ActiveX GUI tools—such as Microsoft's Visual Basic and Sybase's PowerBuilder—via *BEA Builder for ActiveX*, an optional BEA product. For applet development, you can use Java tools—such as Microsoft Visual J++ and Symantec Visual Café—via BEA Jolt, the Tuxedo Internet commerce product. In both environments, you access all of your Tuxedo services—including mainframe-based applications that are accessible via BEA Connect— as if they were native objects. For example, when using BEA Builder for Active X, your *Update_Account* middle-tier Tuxedo service looks like an ActiveX; if you use BEA Jolt, it looks like a Java method. A common repository allows you to simultaneously develop ActiveX clients and Java applets that access the same Tuxedo services.

HOW TUXEDO MANAGES SERVICES

TP Monitors do for applications what databases do for data—they manage, organize, and protect them. To do this, they provide a set of system services that act as your application's unsung heroes, transparently keeping everything running smoothly. These system services include naming, application activation and deactivation, dynamic application configuration, fault management, communications management, transaction management, and security. Figure 3-3 depicts these in a distributed Tuxedo application.

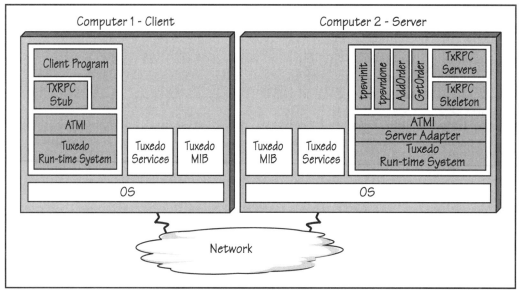

Figure 3-3. Tuxedo Services Running in a Server Managed by Tuxedo.

Naming Service

The naming service is responsible for providing service location transparency. When Tuxedo server classes are activated, they advertise their services in the Tuxedo *Bulletin Board*. The Bulletin Board maps these logical names to the server class's physical location. Clients ask for a service by name; Tuxedo then consults its name registry in the Bulletin Board to send the request to the appropriate service. The Bulletin Board maintains a memory cache to obtain ultra-fast performance. Each computer in a distributed application environment has a Bulletin Board; Tuxedo propagates name changes to all of them.

Tuxedo also provides *data-dependent routing*. Tuxedo can route a client's request to different services, depending on the contents of specific data fields. Data-dependent routing is often used to horizontally partition a database and balance loads.

For example, you can split a table's rows across several physical tables—even on different computers—and assign their management to different server classes.

Run-Time Management

Most operating systems are designed to start and run long-lived processes—like word processors, I/O drivers, and print servers. In this case, you can afford a long start-up time for each process. OLTP applications, on the other hand, require many quick interactions with a variety of services. The application must be able to service large numbers of bursty requests in very short-lived conversations. Tuxedo was designed to manage these types of applications.

Tuxedo must turn standard, run-of-the-mill operating systems into environments tuned for hit-and-run access. It must support high volumes of business transactions on demand. Tuxedo does this by acquiring resources from the operating system at system start-up and then reallocating them to meet the requirements of OLTP applications. It starts all of the components that are part of an application—including the application services, connections, and its own system services (to get an idea of the complexity of this job, see the next Details box).

 The Ups and Downs of Application Management

Details

Let's look at a real-world scenario to get a better appreciation for the value of application activation and deactivation. Imagine that you run a 24-by-7, mission-critical distributed application (some of you probably do). Your application could easily involve thousands of clients, hundreds of services, and a dozen server systems. Sometimes you may be faced with the task of upgrading a critical piece of software, such as your operating system, database, or communications software. First, you must gracefully shut the application down. This means that you need to allow existing connections to stop gradually as users complete their transactions. And you probably want new requests to be serviced by another node during the conversion—this keeps your application available for your users. After you do the upgrade, you must restart the application again. Don't forget that the time it takes to restart the application appears as downtime to your users—so you need to do this quickly, too.

As you can see, starting a distributed client/server application would be next to impossible manually. Tuxedo provides the services to do these tasks on-line. ❏

Dynamic Application Configuration

Change may be the only constant attribute in an environment with thousands of clients and many distributed servers. New users are added; others move. A user's security authorization changes. Application functions expand.

Tuxedo supplies several management tools that let you dynamically configure (and reconfigure) applications on-line. You can make these changes through either a Motif-based GUI or a Java-based Web console. Or, you can create a program or write an on-demand script to make a series of changes.

Fault Management

In a distributed client/server environment, thousands of independent processors and processes must cooperate to run the application. Lots of things can go wrong. Tuxedo keeps the application running in the face of failures by doing two things: 1) ensuring no single point of failure by providing replicas that can keep going when something breaks, and 2) restoring the running application to good condition after failures occur. Here is a list of things that can go wrong in distributed client/server applications and what Tuxedo does to recover from the problem:

■ *Clients terminate.* Clients join and quit applications—sometimes voluntarily, sometimes because of failures. While clients are part of the application, they use operating system and Tuxedo resources. Tuxedo tracks clients to tell if they leave the application abnormally (for example, because of failures). When clients quit applications for whatever reason, Tuxedo works with the operating system to release their resources.

■ *Server processes terminate.* Server class processes join and quit applications, too. This is a normal event that Tuxedo was born to manage. But sometimes a bug can cause a server class process to exit abnormally—or the server may crash. This is a much more serious problem than when a client fails—many clients and services may be dependent on the failed server class process. Tuxedo lets you define replica server classes that can take over the load. These server class processes can be on the same computer or different computers. When a server class process failure occurs, Tuxedo cleans up any in-process requests and sends a failure indication back to the client or service that originated it. If the failed server class process shares a queue with other server classes, the surviving server classes will simply pick the pending messages off the queue. Otherwise, Tuxedo will forward requests to a replica server class process. Tuxedo will also restart server class processes when they abnormally fail.

- **Computers crash.** When a computer crashes, you lose all unsaved data, open sessions, and running processes (except persistent resources like application queues). Clients that use the computer as an entry point to the network will hang. And network failures can make computers appear to have failed. These failures can be permanent or temporary (for example, caused by an overloaded computer or transient network problem). Tuxedo monitors the status of all the computers in its domain. You can specify back-up computers for groups of server classes. When computer failures occur, Tuxedo reroutes requests to replica server classes in these computers.

- **Maintenance requires planned outages.** Sometimes you need to take a computer out of service for maintenance. Tuxedo can migrate server classes gracefully to a back-up computer so that the primary computer can be turned off without impacting the running application.

- **Networks fail.** Networks can fail—they can also be so overloaded that they can appear to have temporarily failed. The larger the network, the more likely you are to encounter these failures. Network failures can disrupt a distributed application. During these failures, Tuxedo partitions (or divides) the network into two domains—one on either side of the failure. It then manages each half of the network separately. This lets the application continue to run despite the failure. When the network is fixed, Tuxedo reintegrates the distributed environment—it heals itself.

- **Transactions deadlock.** In a distributed environment, deadlocks can occur when two components have locked resources while they wait for each other's locks to release. In this situation, Tuxedo times out one of the transactions by rolling it back, thereby releasing its locks and breaking the deadlock condition.

Tuxedo can automatically recover from many failures. However, some failures—often the most serious ones—require operator intervention. This is because it is often difficult to determine what has actually failed. The operator can use tools Tuxedo provides to recover from these failures.

Communications Management

Tuxedo clients and server classes receive requests and send replies through *message queues* (see Figure 3-4). They can have private queues, or multiple server classes can share a queue so that free server classes process the requests next in line (it's like the waiting line for tellers in a bank). When server classes share queues, these queues act as a second form of load balancing—the first is when Tuxedo originally chose the queue for the client's request. Requests are handled on a priority basis—requests of a higher priority are processed first.

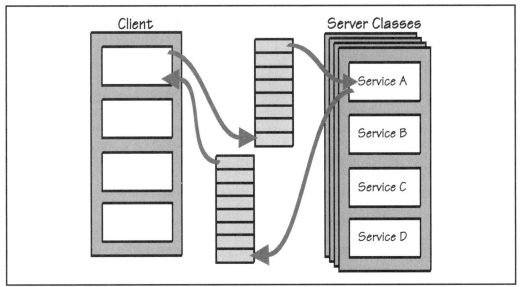

Figure 3-4. Tuxedo Routes Requests Between Clients and Servers Using Input and Output Queues.

Transaction Management

One of the most fundamental features of Tuxedo is transaction management. Tuxedo is responsible for applying the ACID properties—which guarantee data integrity—in a distributed, component-based client/server application. This is a heavy responsibility, to say the least. Tuxedo provides the following support for transactions:

■ It creates a *global transaction identifier* when a client or a service initiates a transaction.

■ It tracks the components that are involved in a transaction and, therefore, need to be coordinated when the transaction is ready to commit.

■ It notifies the resource managers—which are, most often, databases—when they are accessed on behalf of a transaction. Resource managers then lock the accessed records until the end of the transaction.

■ It orchestrates the *two-phase commit* when the transaction completes, which ensures that all the participants in the transaction commit their updates simultaneously. It coordinates the commit with any databases that are being updated using X/Open's XA protocol. Almost all relational databases support this standard. In addition, Tuxedo uses OSI-TP to synchronize the transaction completion with other TP Monitors. Soon, it will also be able to coordinate transaction sychronization with transaction monitors—like CICS—that support IBM's APPC's sync_level 2 protocol.

■ It executes the *rollback* procedure when the transaction must be aborted.

■ It executes a *recovery* procedure when failures occur. It determines which transactions were active in the computer at the time of the crash. It then determines whether the transaction should be aborted or committed.

Security

The Tuxedo security service supports five incremental levels of authentication and authorization:

■ **Level 1: No authentication.** Neither clients nor servers are authenticated. This level of security is most often used in development environments or in physically secured environments.

■ **Level 2: Application password.** There is a single password for the entire application—clients must supply it when they log in.

■ **Level 3: End-user authentication.** In addition to the application password, clients must supply a user name and application-specific data (for example, their personal password).

■ **Level 4: Access control.** Some or all of an application's services may have an *access control list (ACL)*. Tuxedo will deny access to clients that are not part of a service's ACL. Authenticated clients, however, can use any service that doesn't have an ACL. ACLs can also be defined for application queues and events.

■ **Level 5: Mandatory access control.** Clients cannot access services that do not have an ACL—only other services can access them.

In addition to authorization, Tuxedo supports link-level encryption using RSA's RC4 algorithm on all intercomputer communications—including between Tuxedo domains, between clients and servers, and over the Internet.

Tuxedo Domains

Tuxedo lets you define administrative *domains* to manage large distributed environments. It also lets you federate separate applications. A domain is the unit of monitoring and administration for Tuxedo: it manages a domain's computers, service classes, and queues as a single unit. If a domain grows too large, Tuxedo must spend a considerable amount of time managing it. Therefore, large distributed environments are almost always broken down into multiple domains to streamline administration. You can assign domains based on application function, security needs, or geography. All of the Tuxedo management consoles let you manage a single domain or multiple domains.

TUXEDO MESSAGING

Tuxedo allows clients and services to communicate using any of the following five messaging mechanisms:[4]

- ■ **Request-response.** In request-response communications, a client issues a request to a service and then waits for a response before performing other operations. Services fulfill each request independently—so each request must contain all the information the service needs. Tuxedo offers several variations of the basic request-response protocol (see Figure 3-5). One variation is called *asynchronous request-response*; it allows the client to issue a request and then continue doing other tasks while it checks periodically if the response has been received. The client can, in parallel, issue other requests—this is called *fan-out parallelism* because it enables multiple requests to be outstanding at the same time. Another type of request-response is called *pipeline parallelism*; it enables a server to forward a client's request to another server. The second server in the pipeline can then respond directly to the client instead of sending the request back through the first server. In addition, many clients' requests can be queued for completion.

- ■ **Conversational.** When a client and a service must conduct prolonged exchanges, they can use conversations. Unlike request-response, each request in a conversation goes to the same service; the service maintains information (called *state information*) about the client between requests. The advantage of conversations is that clients don't have to send state information with each request. Its disadvantage is that it locks up a service for the duration of the conversation—no other client can access it. So conversations are not as resource-efficient as request-response. Because of this, designers tend to use conversations sparingly.

- ■ **Application queues.** Queues provide time-independent communications for applications that do not need to communicate interactively. Queued messages are stored on disk for fault tolerance. Clients can even use queues to communicate among themselves—no servers need to be involved. You set ordering criteria for each queue, which determines the order in which the requests are processed. These can be first-in-first-out (FIFO), last-in-first-out (LIFO), by assigned prior-

---

[4] Note that services can be "clients" from a communications perspective.

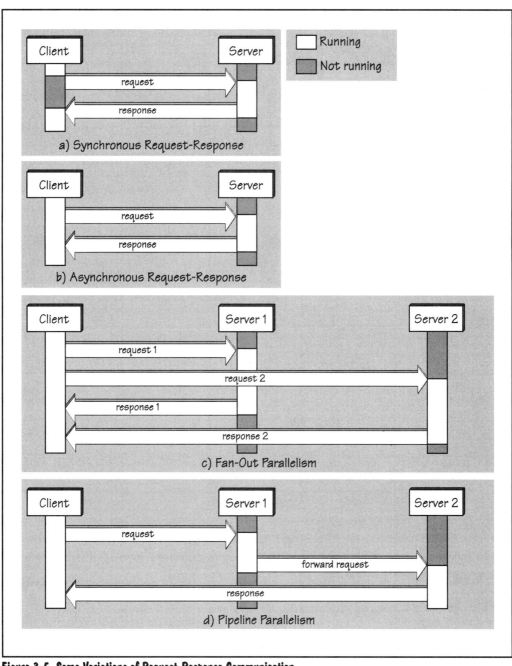

Figure 3-5. Some Variations of Request-Response Communication.

ity, or by a timestamp that indicates the earliest time you can access the message (called the *birthtime*). You can also use a variation of queued communication, called *forward*; it dequeues messages and sends them to a service via request-response communications.

■ *Publish-and-subscribe.* The Tuxedo event manager, called the *EventBroker*, provides a publish-and-subscribe communications mechanism. Any client or service can subscribe to an event—and any client or service can post an event. Event names are the rendezvous points for subscribers and publishers. Subscriptions define which of the following actions must be done when a particular event occurs. Tuxedo can 1) send an unsolicited message to the subscriber, 2) send a request to a named service, 3) enqueue the posted data to an application queue, or 4) execute an operating system command.

■ *Broadcasts and other unsolicited communications.* Services or clients can send unsolicited messages to client programs. They can either send broadcasts to groups of clients, or they can send a notification to a specific client.

CONNECTING TO CLIENTS AND OTHER SERVERS

The middle-tier never lives in isolation. It has clients to manage, other transactional and non-transactional servers to communicate with, and legacy applications to integrate. To handle these requirements, Tuxedo provides a modular set of connectivity products and features, which we describe in this section. With all these products, Tuxedo makes service development easier by handling the differences in protocols and environments transparently: your services access all other components in the environment as if they were other Tuxedo services.

Client Support in Tuxedo

A client/server environment wouldn't be complete without client support. /WS manages client communications in Tuxedo environments over TCP/IP networks. /WS consists of three modules:

■ *The Workstation Listener* acts as a client's single point of contact on the servers. When clients connect to Tuxedo, they first call the Workstation Listener; it assigns them a communications port and a Workstation Handler to use. This allows Tuxedo to balance client loads across servers and processes.

■ *The Workstation Handler* is a multi-threaded process that manages client communications. It monitors their status, routes their messages to Tuxedo, and acts as their surrogate for delegated transactions. There are typically many

Workstation Handlers in large environments; they can be spread across multiple physical servers.

- *The /WS Client* handles the communication session with the server on behalf of the client application.

/WS supports RSA-compatible encryption and compression between the clients and servers.

Java Applets and Internet Applications

BEA Jolt allows Java applets to access Tuxedo services across the Internet. Applets can begin and end transactions—and call a variety of services in between. Jolt includes a repository that lists Tuxedo services as Java methods so that Java-based development tools can create client/server Internet applications. It also includes a state manager so that applets can have sessions with particular services. Tuxedo access control lists provide access authorization for the Java applets. In addition, Jolt can encrypt the Internet communication session.

Using Tuxedo With Legacy Applications

BEA Connect allows Tuxedo clients and services to call—and be called by—IMS and CICS applications via standard Tuxedo communications interfaces. IMS applications use their standard queuing mechanism to receive and transmit requests. CICS applications use IBM's CPI-C or DPL communications interfaces. BEA Connect can use either SNA or TCP/IP networks.

Using Tuxedo With DCE

Tuxedo can serve as a high-volume, secure application server in DCE networks. It provides a gateway to DCE networks, which enables standard DCE services to call Tuxedo services, and vice versa. With the TxRPC API, you program applications using a transactional superset of DCE's standard RPC interface.

COMING NEXT: TUXEDO DOES MISSION-CRITICAL CORBA

Distributed objects are quickly becoming the standard for 3-tier client/server programming. They are also becoming a foundation technology for the Internet and intranets. For example, Netscape is bundling a CORBA ORB with all of its browsers and Web servers. In these type of environments, objects provide many advantages over procedures, including:

- A clean separation between an object's interface and its implementation
- Standard multi-language bindings
- A distributed component infrastructure for communicating across operating systems, languages, and networks
- Interface inheritance
- Built-in standardized support for transactions
- Standard security and firewall access
- Built-in mechanisms for packaging and advertising components
- Built-in introspection for dynamically discovering components interfaces

Iceberg to Manage Millions of Objects

By the time you read this, BEA will have shipped Project Iceberg (at least, the Software Developer's Kit). Iceberg integrates Tuxedo with BEA's *ObjectBroker* CORBA ORB. In this way, Iceberg gives you the advantages of CORBA distributed objects, while retaining the robust Tuxedo features we described in this chapter. This is not an easy job. While there may be a thousand object classes in a large mission-critical application, there are potentially millions of stateful objects in a CORBA environment. For example, think of a banking application. Each customer will likely be represented by several objects (for their checking account, savings account, customer information, and so forth). Clients assume that these millions of objects are active all the time—just waiting to service their requests. But because objects are a combination of data and state, it is impossible to have all these objects active all the time. The infrastructure must manage these objects in and out of memory efficiently, and with integrity. The thousand objects in memory this second will be different from the thousand objects in memory during the next second.

Iceberg provides this capability by morphing ObjectBroker's CORBA infrastructure with the management and transactional features of Tuxedo (see Figure 3-6). The result is an environment for building and deploying mission-critical 3-tier applications based on distributed objects. As we noted in Chapter 2, Gartner Group calls this new type of middleware *Object Transaction Monitors (OTMs)*. OTMs have been called the "holy grail" of middleware because they combine the functions of TP Monitors, ORBs, and MOMs.

How Iceberg Works

You develop Iceberg applications as standard CORBA objects, using IDL or visual tools. These objects communicate with other objects (including those running on

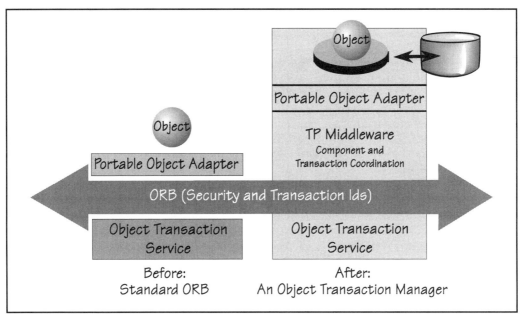

Figure 3-6. Standard ORB Architecture Compared With Iceberg.

clients) using ObjectBroker's CORBA IIOP protocol.[5] But the run-time server environment is "Tuxedo on steroids." It provides:

- **Scale and load balancing for server-side CORBA applications with millions of objects**. Iceberg manages classes and instantiates objects, thus enabling your distributed applications to scale effectively across multiple servers.

- **Performance similar to today's Tuxedo.** Iceberg prestarts and manages object pools and instantiates object state to provide the same high level of performance Tuxedo achieves in the current service-based TPC-C benchmark results.

- **Support for thousands (or tens of thousands) of clients.** Iceberg uses the funneling and switching mechanisms from Tuxedo to support thousands of clients over standard IIOP connections.

- **Frameworks that simplify server-side programming.** Iceberg provides pieces of pre-built function (called *frameworks*) that automate many tasks that were previously the developer's responsibility—including management of transactions and application state. Frameworks allow you to program by exception: they call you when they need something from you. In doing so, they codify many

---

[5] Iceberg also interfaces with other ORBs and with ActiveX clients.

of the good design practices that were previously the trade secrets of application architects.

Iceberg is built on the management infrastructure of Tuxedo, so all of the features we've described in this chapter are available to you in this distributed object environment—including failover, load balancing, system management interfaces, and legacy application access. In addition, procedural services can call Iceberg objects, and vice versa. This eases the transition to distributed objects for current Tuxedo users. Because these calls can be within the scope of a single transaction, the ACID properties can span these environments. It also enables architects to use both procedures and objects in the same application.

CONCLUSION

Tuxedo provides an off-the-shelf infrastructure designed for 3-tier client/server computing. It helps you create, administer, maintain, and extend your applications. Tuxedo is used every day to run millions of transactions in thousands of applications. Part 2 introduces you to seven of these production applications. The applications in the eighth case study use ObjectBroker.

Part 2
3-Tier
Client/Server
at Work

An Introduction to Part 2

Now that we've given you an overview of the architectural concepts that underlie 3-tier applications, we're ready to look at real-life, hard-working client/server implementations. This is a rare treat—after all, mission-critical applications are the lifeblood of companies, and few organizations are willing to openly share information about the applications that bolster their competitive advantage. So we're extremely grateful to these architects and their enterprises for taking us on this behind-the-scenes tour of their applications and projects.

Are you ready for your grand tour? We're about to lead you on an excursion of eight of the world's most demanding distributed applications to show you how 3-tier client/server systems are really architected, built, and deployed. The applications we've included in Part 2 vary in a number of dimensions:

- **Industries**—they include healthcare, telecommunications, banking, government, and manufacturing.
- **Organizations**—they come from corporations, governments, and software vendors.
- **Breadth of application**—some are single applications; many are suites of applications.
- **International reach**—there are European, Canadian, American, and multinational applications.
- **Architectural infrastructure**—most of the applications use Tuxedo as their infrastructure (we had a large and expanding base of production Tuxedo applications to draw from). We also include Wells Fargo's home-banking application. It is based on BEA's ORB, ObjectBroker.

We found the similarities between the applications even more enlightening than the differences—they illustrate the "best practices" of 3-tier applications. These are the lessons we will emphasize in Part 3. In this part, we describe these aspects of each case study:

- **The application**—what it does and why it was undertaken.
- **The architecture**—the design of each tier and cross-tier subsystem (such as security and system management).
- **The project**—how the application was defined, implemented, tested, and moved into production.
- **The outcome**—how the application turned out.
- **The future**—what other projects are planned to expand the application.
- **Advice**—tips and techniques for successful 3-tier applications from the chief architects.

So without further ado, let's meet the 3-tier client/server architects and their projects.

Chapter 4

U.K. Employment Service Rolls Out 3-Tier in Record Time

The UK Employment Service has the largest distributed application in Western Europe. It runs 6.8 million transactions a day—419 transactions a second.

> — **Phil Mullis, Technical Services Team Leader**
> **Information Technology Services**
> **U.K. Employment Service**

Imagine that you were told to plan, develop, and roll out a nationwide client/server system with more than 1000 server machines and over 20,000 PCs in two or three years. Is your blood pressure rising? Now imagine that you had just 12 months to complete this massive project. Have you run for the door yet? In June 1995, the United Kingdom's Employment Service was told to do just that. The U.K. government passed the *Job Seekers Allowance* legislation to encourage people to get jobs and move off benefit payments faster. To comply with this new program, the Employment Service's staff—in 1,100 offices—quickly needed a top-notch application. They were now required to monitor the progress that 2.45 million unemployed people were making toward finding work. The IT department at Employment Service rose to this mammoth challenge. It rolled out a major new application— called the *Labour Market System*—in record time. It is one of the largest operational client/server systems in the world.

THE APPLICATION

Employment Service is an executive agency of the Department for Education and Employment in the U.K. Its branch offices are located throughout England, Scotland, and Wales. The agency's main business is to help people without jobs find work. Currently about 2.45 million people have registered as being unemployed.

Before the government passed the Job Seekers Allowance (JSA) legislation, unemployed people received benefit payments if they had previously made unemployment insurance payments, or if they requested income support. JSA added additional requirements. To keep receiving benefit payments, Employment Services clients have to sign and comply with a Job Seekers Agreement. This agreement makes them promise to apply for a certain number of jobs within a particular time period. Staff members at the employment offices have to log their clients' Job Seekers Agreement and job-seeking activities. As a last resort, they can recommend that benefits payments be docked if clients aren't making progress.

The Existing Non-Integrated Systems

JSA required an application that let staff members record the relationship between job seekers and job vacancies, as well as access the benefits system. The Employment Service's existing applications weren't designed to do this—they also couldn't be enhanced to do this. They had been implemented as three separate systems that staff members accessed using different terminals:

■ *OSCAR* logged the meetings between the employment office staff and the people coming in to seek jobs. OSCAR was a local application—each of the 1,100 Employment Services offices kept its own data.

■ *SVACS* showed the vacancies available for jobs in the U.K. The SVACS data resided in nine regional databases.

■ *The Benefits Payment System* tracked payments of unemployment benefits and allowances.

So the JSA legislation required an application that could combine the data that was kept in the local offices using OSCAR with the job vacancy information that SVACS tracked. The application would also need to let the staff access the benefit payment system.

Since the late 1980s, Employment Service had dreamed of replacing these separate systems with an enterprise database accessed over a single network with a PC-based office infrastructure. The existing systems were limiting its ability to help its clients.

For example, OSCAR recorded the jobs individual clients sought and whether they were hired. But without integration between OSCAR and SVACS, the Service couldn't determine how many clients applied for a particular vacancy. In 1994, they had even developed a prototype of the new system. Unfortunately, there was no funding for this major undertaking. So, while JSA placed the department on an incredibly tight deadline, it also gave the Employment Service the mandate—and the funds it needed—to upgrade its systems. There was a silver lining to this JSA cloud.

The Labour Market System

With LMS, we moved to an integrated system infrastructure that lets the Employment Service staff access all our applications from a single terminal.

— Phil Mullis

Now that they had the funding and the mandate, the IT department of Employment Service had the awesome challenge of making their integrated system a reality. They did this by creating the *Labour Market System (LMS)*. LMS is an N-tier client/server application. The LMS user interface provides Employment Services staff with an integrated view of clients, potential employers, job openings, caseloads, and other information that makes their jobs easier. The LMS databases contain nationwide information about job vacancies, as well as records for every unemployed person looking for work in the U.K.—information that was formerly kept separately in OSCAR and SVACS.

The benefits payment system was not integrated into LMS, but users can access it through the LMS PC. It has been upgraded to support the JSA legislation, and is now called the *Job Seekers Agreement Payment* system *(JSAP)*.

LMS allowed the Employment Service to kill two birds with one stone—meeting the JSA requirements while meeting its own goals. Employment Service workers can now access all their on-line functions from a single interface on a single PC.

The Demanding Job Ahead

In just one year, the Employment Service development team met a number of challenges that would make most reasonable people turn around and run the other way:

■   They developed a major new client/server application (LMS) from scratch.

- They revamped another major application (the benefits payment system).

- They replaced dumb user terminals with 21,000 PCs running the LMS client application and the upgraded payment system.

- They installed 1,100 LMS servers in local employment offices.

- They converted the existing OSCAR data at each of these local employment offices to the LMS repository in 16 weekends—this meant successfully migrating about 100 new offices and 1,500 new users every week.

- They consolidated the nine SVACS databases into two LMS data centers.

- They replaced the proprietary SVAC servers—which were coming to an end of their life and incurring high costs—with UNIX systems.

- They replaced an X.25 network with a dedicated 64 Kbps wide area network (WAN) to handle the heavier data traffic. This extended corporate network is now the largest routed WAN in Europe.

- They achieved their performance and reliability goals. The system completes 95% of all transactions within three seconds and achieves 99.5% availability for every user.

- They trained more than 30,000 users.

THE 3-TIERED ARCHITECTURE

3-tier provides greater flexibility: we can respond to change without modifying the application.

— Phil Mullis

With an initial application rollout that targeted 21,000 users in 1,100 offices, the Employment Service needed a highly scalable architecture that could manage large transaction volumes. To accomplish this, they designed a multilevel, multitier architecture that not only consolidates connections from the offices, but also provides users with fast response time and high availability.

LMS' Multilevel Physical Architecture

To meet their performance requirements, the development team designed a multi-level physical infrastructure (see Figure 4-1). This architecture allows some amount

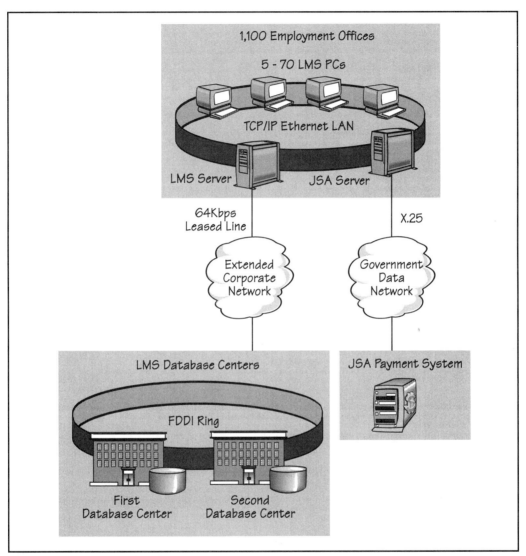

Figure 4-1. The LMS Physical Architecture.

of processing and data storage to remain in the local offices. Information that must be accessible on a nationwide basis is managed in centralized data centers. This multilevel architecture improves the system's overall performance (see the next Details box). Because Tuxedo acts like a multiplexer, database calls from the PCs in each office are merged into a single stream. As a result, even with 21,000 PCs, each of the four back-end database servers only supports between 300 and 400 local LMS servers—and typically only about 300 simultaneous connections.

21,000 Clients Spell 3-Tier

Details

In their first pilot, the developers tried a 2-tier architecture that connected the clients directly to the databases via IngresNet. Each client required a separate connection, and this proved to be overwhelming.

As a result, the team started looking for a TP Monitor to replace IngresNet. Tuxedo emerged as the top contender due to its excellent site references and its inherent capability to manage and route a large number of connections. The team also needed Tuxedo domains, which at the time was only a promise. Luckily, this promise was fulfilled in time for the project's launch—a single domain would never have been able to encompass 1,100 servers. ❑

In the Employment Offices

Each employment office provides PCs for its staff. These PCs are connected over a LAN to two Intel-based Siemens-Nixdorf servers:

■ A local LMS server accesses the LMS application. This server holds some data specific to the office (including data about users) and some static data (such as standard industrial and occupational classifications).

■ A JSAP server accesses the benefits payment system.

In the LMS Database Centers

Each LMS server connects to one of four primary LMS database servers. These servers are located in two database centers in Sheffield, England. Each center also maintains a backup database server that plays a dual role; the Employment Service staff uses it as a training server, too. The centers are connected together by a FDDI ring.

Each database server actually consists of a pair of servers (see Figure 4-2). They communicate via a Tuxedo bridge. In this paired-server architecture, the front-ends manage communications, allowing the back-end database server to focus on processing requests. They are connected to four 240-GB disk subsystems via an extended bus.

There are a number of high-availability features built into the physical design of the database centers:

■   The wide area network allows the local LMS servers to use a number of physical routes to access the data centers—they can usually find a path around a network failure.

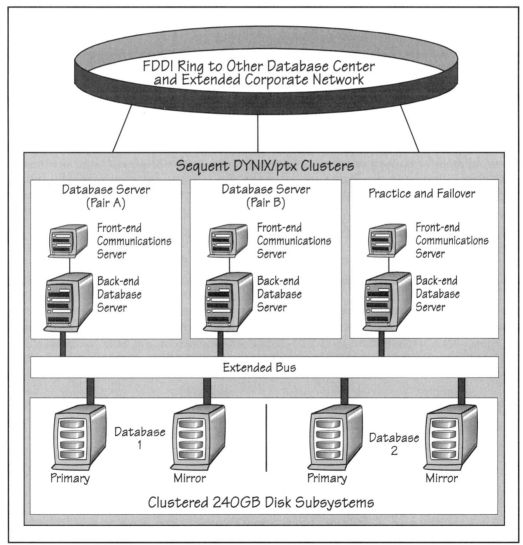

Figure 4-2. Detailed View of One LMS Database Center.

■ Sequent's DYNIX/ptx clustering software runs across the three pairs of servers in each data center to allow them to back each other up.

■ Each of the server pairs acts as an individual Tuxedo domain. This makes LMS more manageable and further reduces the system's single points of failure.

■ Two of the disk subsystems provide primary storage for the two regional databases in each center—the other two subsystems mirror this data.

■ Because all the database servers connect to all the disk subsystems via the extended bus, the third database server in each center can take over the workload of either of the other servers if a failure occurs.

An Overview of the LMS Logical Tiers

It was clear from the start that LMS required a 3-tier architecture to meet its performance and scale requirements: a 2-tier architecture wouldn't work. 3-tier made it easier to control and maintain the system. And a 3-tier architecture would provide the flexibility the Employment Service wanted to be able to handle future requirements more easily.

The three tiers of LMS are as follows (see Figure 4-3):

■ *Tier 1* consists of the client software and Tuxedo /WS running on the PCs in the employment offices.[1]

■ *Tier 2* is spread across multiple servers. Local users log in to the LMS servers in each office. These servers run Tuxedo services that access locally cached, static data. Tuxedo also routes requests to the data center servers. There, the front-end communications servers manage the incoming connections and route requests to services running in the back-end servers.

■ *Tier 3* consists of four regional Ingres databases.

These tiers work together to handle requests:

1. When the user signs on, Tuxedo /WS opens a connection from the client to the local office's LMS server.

---

[1] /WS is not shown in Figure 4-3—and you won't find it in any of the other case studies' logical diagrams. This is because we want to focus your attention on the application's components. But it is necessary because it provides the client's interface to the server-side Tuxedo Workstation Listener and Handler.

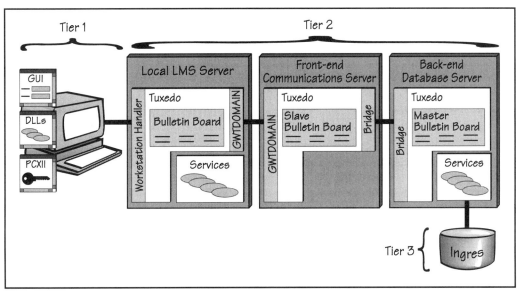

Figure 4-3. The LMS Logical Layers.

2. The client GUI calls DLLs on the PC to access or update data. This initiates a call to the local LMS server.

3. Tuxedo Workstation Handler running on the local LMS server checks the Bulletin Board to see where the requested service resides—of course, this check is transparent to the user and application. Requests to access the locally cached data are handed to a service running on the office's LMS server. The majority of requests, however, are routed out to a database center through GWTDOMAIN—the Tuxedo gateway-to-domain facility.

4. The request comes into the data center through the communications server for that office's region. The communications server passes the request to its paired back-end database server through a Tuxedo bridge.

5. Tuxedo on the database server checks the Master Bulletin Board and routes the request to the appropriate service. These services are written in C and use embedded SQL commands to access Ingres.

6. The response is then sent back to the client.

Tier 1: The LMS Client

Early in the project, the Employment Service decided to use PCs to give their users better performance, an attractive GUI, and—most importantly—single-terminal access to the applications they use. The PCs replaced dumb terminals in the employment offices. They run the LMS client application, Tuxedo /WS, and PCXII (a security application).

The LMS client application was created using CA/Ingres' *OpenRoad* 4GL. Open-Road was selected as the client tool because of its tight integration with the Ingres database. The LMS client application is divided into specific work areas that users access via the menu bar (see Figure 4-4). It displays forms and information for each of these entities:

■ Clients
■ Client advisors
■ Workflow
■ Caseloads
■ Employer/job providers
■ Vacancies and opportunities
■ Management information

The office staff also needs to access the JSAP benefits payment system to make changes in benefit allowances based on each client's job-seeking efforts. They do this by opening a terminal emulation screen on their PCs to connect to the JSAP server.

	View Client Details - C BLACKMORE	

File **Edit** **Function** **Documents** **Help**

| New | Amnd | More | IntHist | Prmpts | Actns | SOC | Conv | Case | Sub | Hist | Spec | Keep | Save | Close |

Advisor: None   Diary   Status: Inactive

Nino: AB333000A   Title: Mr   Address: C.Blackmore Home

Forename: CEDRIC   C.Blackmore Crescent

Surname: BLACKMORE   C.Blackmore Estate

DOB: 01/01/1953   Age: 42   YP: No   Cblackmoreton

Tel No: 0 114   2599333   Sex: Male   Postcode: AB3 3AB

Oth No: PWD: No

Emp Stat: Unemployed, Not Claiming   Input By: T WATKINS

Figure 4-4. The LMS Client Application.

The development team chose Windows 3.11 as the client operating system. At the time, they didn't think Windows 95 was stable enough. While Windows 3.11 had limitations, they couldn't chance a shaky operating system with tens of thousands of PCs to roll out. Employment Service doesn't plan to upgrade its client operating system—its top priority now is to continue to expand the user base itself. It is currently moving up to 26,000 users.

Tier 2: The Server Side

The Employment Service architecture distributes middle-tier functions across many machines. Hundreds of local UNIXWare-based LMS servers run Tuxedo and roughly 30 C-based Tuxedo services to provide access to locally cached data. These local office servers support an average of 15 connected clients—large offices can have as many as 70 clients. By running Tuxedo, they reduce the load on the database servers in two ways:

- In-office services access cached static data to handle some of the clients' requests locally.

- Tuxedo concentrates communication between the clients and the back-end database servers, streamlining the connections.

The back-end database servers run about 200 Tuxedo services. These services were written in ANSI C. To interface with the Ingres database, the Tuxedo services use either embedded SQL or call stored procedures—or a mixture of the two if necessary. At the moment, server classes are not prioritized, although the developers are looking to support this feature to further improve performance.

Tier 3: The Database

> *Our system data grew at a phenomenal rate, increasing across the four databases by five-to-six gigabytes every two-to-three weeks during rollout. My bet is that it will grow to 100-to-120 gigabytes, probably by the end of this year.*
>
> *— Phil Mullis*

The Employment Service had already standardized on Ingres—so there was one less technology decision for the designers to make. But it also added a new challenge. LMS required the IT department to consolidate the previous nine regional SVACS job vacancy databases. This turned out to be too much data to put in a single Ingres database. So they decided to create four separate databases—one for each region. The North and South database servers reside in one data center, and East and West database servers reside in the other. Each database server manages a disk subsystem.

The size of the databases still posed a bit of a problem. The databases were so large it wasn't clear that a backup was achievable during off-hours. The largest database is the North database, at about 16 GB; it handles around 132 transactions per second (tps). The other databases run about 14 GB for the East and South and about 10 GB for the West. Employment Service had to do considerable work to get the North database to run well. Sequent helped them tackle this challenge by running key functions in parallel—such as writing the logs out to tape.

The total volume of data is still growing fast—at over 5 GB every six weeks. This makes it not only one of the largest Ingres databases in the world but also one of the fastest growing. All the data is being kept indefinitely—so to bring this growth under control, the team is now thinking about purging some of it.

Security

To accommodate the needs of the payment system, the client PCs run PCXII, a security product that replaces the Windows Program Manager. It prompts the user for a user name, which involves swiping an ID card, and then asks for a password. PCXII then validates each PC at log-in by calling the JSA Terminal Controller. If the log-in is valid, the PC downloads a desktop configuration with icons for programs the user has access rights to use. This authorization is used for both the benefits payment application and LMS. Users employ a separate LMS log-in if the JSAP payment system is down.

System Management

BMC's *Patrol* is used for system management of the data center. Patrol provides a central mechanism for managing the computer systems, and it has a built-in interface to system management interfaces in Tuxedo to manage the application. System managers also rely on Cabletron's *SPECTRUM* for network management. An in-house product lets the staff log in remotely to the LMS servers in the employment offices to upgrade their software.

The LMS application also supports some reporting features. For example, it checks and reports on each local server's processing capacities: if usage exceeds 80%, the LMS server sends a message to the system administrator. This lets the administrator resolve the situation before it becomes a problem.

The team is now looking at extending system management to the local offices. But with the system providing 99.5% availability to the users, this is a low priority.

THE PROJECT

We had a prototype in the works, and planned to roll out a new system in 1998. Then the government said in June 1995 that we would have to deal with the new JSA agreement by April 1996. That didn't give us a lot of time for design and development.

— Phil Mullis

The team knew it was in for a challenge. After all, the government had asked them to develop and roll out a nationwide information and transaction processing system in ten months, by April 1996 (see the next Details box). When the JSAP team began to face difficulty meeting that timeframe, the government pushed it out to October 1996, but it still required LMS to be ready in June. This let the Employment Service fully stabilize the new system infrastructure before the JSAP rollout.

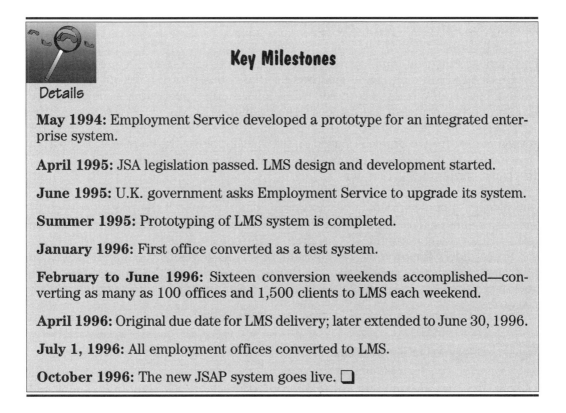

Key Milestones

Details

May 1994: Employment Service developed a prototype for an integrated enterprise system.

April 1995: JSA legislation passed. LMS design and development started.

June 1995: U.K. government asks Employment Service to upgrade its system.

Summer 1995: Prototyping of LMS system is completed.

January 1996: First office converted as a test system.

February to June 1996: Sixteen conversion weekends accomplished—converting as many as 100 offices and 1,500 clients to LMS each weekend.

April 1996: Original due date for LMS delivery; later extended to June 30, 1996.

July 1, 1996: All employment offices converted to LMS.

October 1996: The new JSAP system goes live. ❑

The LMS development team clearly faced a beast of a schedule. To add to their problems, it was difficult to find people already trained in the products they were using. So, in addition to racing the clock, they undertook their own training. In the end, all of the development was done in-house; the team only hired a few contractors who were experts in the products.

Partners also assisted in easing this workload. Siemens-Nixdorf and Sequent worked with BEA Systems to install the new server hardware and software. Siemens Network Systems, Siemens, and ICL assisted with installation of the PCs. And Cisco, British Telecom, and Cabletron helped with the network.

The Design Phase

The IT development team's primary goal was to design a new system that combines the OSCAR and SVACS data and functionality in one system. In addition, the Employment Service wanted to provide access to JSA from the LMS client PC.

Deriving the Design From a Prototype

The IT department at Employment Service had already created a prototype of a system like LMS in May 1994. This was used as a basis for the design of the LMS system. Four staff members worked to develop the concepts tested in the prototype system and to document the project's requirements. To do so, the team used the *Structured Systems Analysis and Design Methodology,* a U.K. standard for government software projects. Based on this methodology, the team developed a set of system and user requirements. Next, they defined the 3-tier architecture we described earlier in this chapter.

One problem the development team experienced throughout the project was shifting requirements. The team worked with a group of employment office users to gather requirements. But the JSA program required new functionality, so sometimes the users didn't know what they would need. As a result, business processes continued to change and evolve as the team developed the application. This obviously required considerable flexibility in development (not to mention a positive attitude).

Key Technology Selection Decisions

After the design was complete, the team needed to select the technology they would incorporate into the system. The following describes how some of the key purchasing decisions were made:

■ **The TP Monitor.** When it became apparent that IngresNet just couldn't cope with the size of the system, two team members began looking for an open TP

Monitor. They evaluated products, including Tuxedo and Encina. The middleware companies were asked to provide a copy of their software, which the team then tried to run in the prototype. Tuxedo was by far the easiest to work with and had the best reference sites, so it was chosen as the LMS TP Monitor.

- **GUI development tools.** Other members of the design team started to look at GUI front-ends. They created a prototype of a screen by working with office users. The team chose CA/Ingres' OpenRoad 4GL as the GUI development tool because of its price and its integration with the back-end Ingres database. The team, however, needed to figure out a way for the 4GL-based GUI to interface with the 3GL-based Tuxedo services. They solved this interface issue by having the GUI call 3GL routines residing in DLLs on the PCs.

- **PCs**. Employment Service and the Department of Social Security had a joint PC purchasing contract in place with Siemens—so the bulk of the client PCs were purchased from them. An additional 3,000 PCs were bought from ICL.

- **The local LMS servers.** The LMS team decided on the local LMS server hardware later in the design process. After determining how many users they would want each LMS local server to support, they asked suppliers to bid on what they felt could do the job. A few team members then visited the various suppliers to view demonstrations of Tuxedo working on their servers. Siemens-Nixdorf proved that its servers were up to the job—it also helped that there was an existing contract with them. As a result, the team chose Siemens boxes for the local server in each employment office.

- **The Data Center servers.** The vendor for the back-end servers wasn't chosen until October 1995. The team knew it wanted to use open systems, but at the start of the project, the hardware to support such a system just wasn't a reality. The original prototype was built using a Pyramid box; but it wasn't meeting the performance requirements. As a result, the team decided to also have Sequent enter the bidding process. A consultant was brought in to assist in the definition of what the servers would need to do. Then the team asked each vendor to demonstrate what they had. In the end, Sequent came through with the best solution, and thus became the provider for the back-end servers.

Development

Once the team nailed down the basic parts of the system's design, it quickly organized development groups:

- **The Tuxedo services group.** Nine developers began to work on the Tuxedo services and the PC-based DLLs that would call them.

■ **The database group.** Four developers started to develop the LMS database structure and define the necessary database procedures.

■ **The GUI group.** About twenty developers began to develop the LMS client using OpenRoad. The client group used rapid prototyping to develop the GUI; they painted screens in OpenRoad and then showed them to users for sign-off.

The GUI group notified the Tuxedo services group when it needed a new service. The Tuxedo group then determined if such a service had already been implemented. If not, the group consulted with the GUI staff to write the new service.

After the various pieces of the system were fairly well developed, the team attempted to integrate the entire system. They assembled an integration lab that included a full copy of the equipment that would exist in each local office and a small Sequent box for use as the back-end database server. Some integration issues arose, primarily between the back-end and the front-end client. These, however, were quickly resolved.

The developers had a functional system in place by January 1996. Now, the first office could be converted. This installation was used as a test bed, running a minimal version of the application. The developers were able to quickly fix bugs and introduce new functionality. The application was then rolled out to the other offices.

Testing and Documentation

Considerable testing was done throughout the development process, including:

■ User assurance testing
■ Benchmarking
■ System testing
■ Performance testing
■ System integration testing
■ Service delivery testing
■ Stress testing
■ Piloting

Halfway through development, the team began to stress the data center server using in-house load-testing software—called *Target* and *Injector*. They loaded the largest database onto a Sequent machine. They also installed Target and a standard configuration of the LMS software on it. Injector ran on another Sequent box. It simulated the traffic from 400 local offices, sending the transactions to the Target test system. This method is now used to test each new application release.

Going Into Production

The rollout of the LMS system was a model of efficiency. The team put an eight-week conversion process in place that each of the 1,100 local offices followed. The IT department successfully converted all of the offices over a 16-week period between February and June 1996. Table 4-1 shows the steps taken for each office. As many as 100 offices were converted each weekend (see the next Details box).

Table 4-1. The LMS Eight-Week Conversion Cycle for Each Local Office.

Timeline	Activities Completed
Eight weeks before conversion weekend	Users trained.
Seven weeks before conversion weekend	Hardware and software installed, including PCs, routers, and local LMS server.
Six weeks before conversion weekend	Users given access to LMS training application for practice.
Four weeks before conversion weekend	OSCAR data cleaned up.
Two weeks before conversion weekend	SVACS data cleaned up.
Thursday night before conversion weekend	OSCAR and SVACS-resident data for the office is dumped to tape and brought to LMS data center. Developers in the data centers convert the data into the appropriate LMS database.
Friday before conversion weekend	No access provided to OSCAR and SVACS data.
Conversion weekend	SVACS and OSCAR access removed. LMS access added. LMS server and PCs go live.
Monday following conversion weekend	Users begin to use LMS.

Siemens-Nixdorf played a large roll in putting the necessary hardware in place, installing more than 20,000 PCs and 1,100 LMS servers in the employment offices over eight months. This required more than 3,500 engineering visits.

Out of the Employment Service's 48,000-member staff, more than 30,000 staff members were trained over six months. Users in the employment offices were given two to three days of training eight weeks before the team converted their office. To support this, the Employment Service set up 300 training sites throughout the U.K., using an LMS server running both the LMS application and the Ingres database. In addition, they held special training sessions for managers, system administrators, and support center staff.

Data conversion was probably one of the most difficult aspects of the rollout. As offices were migrated to LMS, their data needed to move from their local OSCAR databases to the LMS data center. In addition, their data in the regional SVACS databases had to be moved into LMS. Because this data wasn't previously integrated, cross-checking the information coming from these two systems was very complicated. For example, clients could be registered in OSCAR by National Insurance (NI) number; SVACS just tracked this information by name, instead. As a result, it was often impossible to match the names listed in SVACS with those in OSCAR. In another example, Robert Jones could be listed as Bobby Jones in SVACS, but as Robert Jones in OSCAR. LMS now identifies each person by NI number or by name and birthdate.

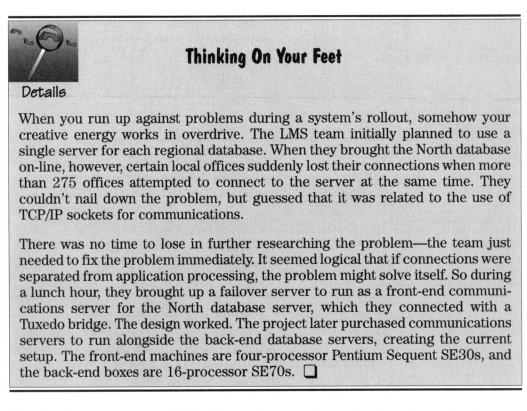

Thinking On Your Feet

Details

When you run up against problems during a system's rollout, somehow your creative energy works in overdrive. The LMS team initially planned to use a single server for each regional database. When they brought the North database on-line, however, certain local offices suddenly lost their connections when more than 275 offices attempted to connect to the server at the same time. They couldn't nail down the problem, but guessed that it was related to the use of TCP/IP sockets for communications.

There was no time to lose in further researching the problem—the team just needed to fix the problem immediately. It seemed logical that if connections were separated from application processing, the problem might solve itself. So during a lunch hour, they brought up a failover server to run as a front-end communications server for the North database server, which they connected with a Tuxedo bridge. The design worked. The project later purchased communications servers to run alongside the back-end database servers, creating the current setup. The front-end machines are four-processor Pentium Sequent SE30s, and the back-end boxes are 16-processor SE70s. ❑

The developers converted the Doncaster employment office in early January 1996—they were the first. Once the initial system bugs were fixed, the other office conversions began. They completed the conversions on schedule each weekend. Only one office experienced trouble converting the data. Performance issues typically emerged the Monday or Tuesday after a conversion. The IT staff would find out about the problems Wednesday, fix them Thursday, and be ready Friday for the next conversions. The conversions became more complicated as more offices came on-line (see the next Details box). But by Monday, July 1, 1996, every employment office in the U.K. was live with LMS. The JSAP developers brought the revamped benefits payment system on-line on October 7.

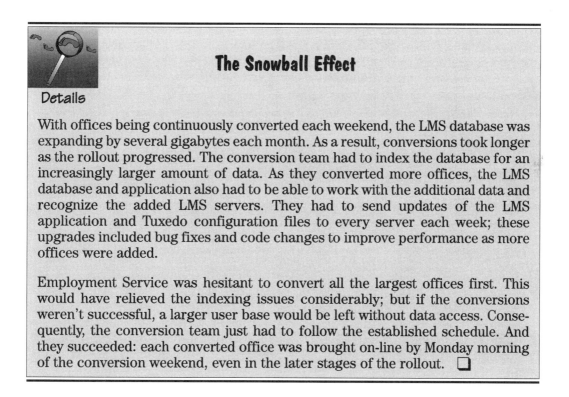

The Snowball Effect

Details

With offices being continuously converted each weekend, the LMS database was expanding by several gigabytes each month. As a result, conversions took longer as the rollout progressed. The conversion team had to index the database for an increasingly larger amount of data. As they converted more offices, the LMS database and application also had to be able to work with the additional data and recognize the added LMS servers. They had to send updates of the LMS application and Tuxedo configuration files to every server each week; these upgrades included bug fixes and code changes to improve performance as more offices were added.

Employment Service was hesitant to convert all the largest offices first. This would have relieved the indexing issues considerably; but if the conversions weren't successful, a larger user base would be left without data access. Consequently, the conversion team just had to follow the established schedule. And they succeeded: each converted office was brought on-line by Monday morning of the conversion weekend, even in the later stages of the rollout. ❑

In Production

Initially, LMS experienced some performance problems. The developers addressed these issues by fine-tuning the back-end database. The system now meets its performance requirements. But performance is an ongoing challenge as users continue to ask for more functionality and the system becomes more widely used. LMS now services most of its 6.5 million daily transactions within two seconds and provides 99.5% availability to every PC.

When users first started using LMS, they had many questions—far too many for the existing Help Desk staff to handle. Users were having to wait as long as five minutes before their calls were answered. To solve this, Employment Service quickly beefed up its support department to 30 people. A software program is being installed at the central Help Desk to better track calls and to link the help system to the system management environment. This is especially important because there is no system support staff at the employment offices. When problems occur, the Help Desk attempts to fix them remotely over the network. If this isn't possible, a staff member is dispatched to the office.

A team traveled to the various offices after LMS went live to get users to tap into more of the application's functionality. They provided additional training and encouragement. Following the rollout, the developers sent out upgraded application software to fix bugs and add extra functions every week. These updates are now sent out to the offices via the network every two to three weeks. They mostly add function.

THE OUTCOME

The hardware and maintenance costs of LMS will run about 232 million pounds over a 10-year period.[2] Over the same period, the Employment Service expects to save 448 million pounds—an excellent return on investment.[3] The savings will result from reduced maintenance and support costs, as well as staff savings.

The LMS users are pleased with the application. As they become more comfortable with LMS, they continue to ask for more features; so the developers continue to add to the system's functionality. In fact, the system is a victim of its own success—the development team continues to have to tune performance to keep up with its increasing transaction volume. The load is increasing for three reasons: 1) LMS is constantly adding more functionality, 2) as the users get more comfortable with the application, they are using it more frequently, and 3) more users are added to the system all the time.

The Employment Service's IT department clearly pleased the government by meeting its deadline and enabling the JSA legislation to become reality on schedule. Employment Service now has a top-notch open system infrastructure it can leverage for future projects.

THE FUTURE

The IT department continues to focus on supporting the rapidly growing number of LMS users. In addition, the department is looking at a number of enhancements to the application, which include:

---

[2] For our readers in the United States, this is more than $460 million given the exchange rate in effect when we went to press.

[3] About $900 million.

- **Replacing the four databases with a single logical database.** This would allow job vacancy information for all parts of the U.K. to be available to all applicants from a single database.

- **Replacing paper manuals in the local offices with on-line documents.** This would give all users immediate access to documentation and procedures.

- **Implementing more ways to broadcast job openings.** LMS client PCs could be set up at locations outside Employment Services offices—for example, in libraries—to let people more easily research job openings. A pilot has been set up at one site that lets people search for jobs through use of touch screens. The Employment Service may tap the Internet to provide increased access to job seekers.

- **Placing LMS clients on employer premises so that they can key job postings.** This would make it easier and quicker to gather information on job openings.

The U.K. is also involved in a Europe-wide project to share job openings—the interested countries are looking at LMS as a prototype system. This is an exciting idea; but for the near future, the efforts of the LMS development team will primarily focus on just trying to stay ahead of the burgeoning system usage and the requests for enhancements. They continue to work hard, but they can breathe a little easier now that they have successfully met the government's staggering demand.

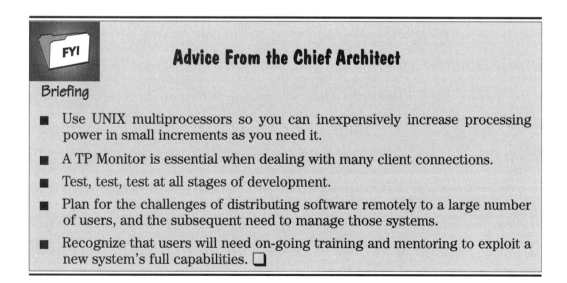

FYI   **Advice From the Chief Architect**

Briefing

- Use UNIX multiprocessors so you can inexpensively increase processing power in small increments as you need it.

- A TP Monitor is essential when dealing with many client connections.

- Test, test, test at all stages of development.

- Plan for the challenges of distributing software remotely to a large number of users, and the subsequent need to manage those systems.

- Recognize that users will need on-going training and mentoring to exploit a new system's full capabilities. ❑

Chapter 5

PeopleSoft Moves Applications to 3-Tier

We're heading down the path of not only 3-tier, but N-tier. We want to have any number of clients talk to any number of application servers.

— Rick Bergquist
Vice President of Technology, PeopleSoft

With revenues of $450 million in 1996, PeopleSoft has built a successful business delivering 2-tier client/server applications that run their customers' core business functions. While these are enterprise-class applications—mostly used by Global 2000 customers—they are typically installed as departmental applications that support a few hundred concurrent users.

But PeopleSoft recognized that its customers were changing the way they were using their applications. With the arrival of the Internet, many of PeopleSoft's customers began launching initiatives to let all their employees—and, at times, their partners—access the applications. In addition, many of these customers were using several PeopleSoft applications together; this created a growing requirement for better inter-application integration.

So the future looked very different from the past for PeopleSoft and its customers. Instead of a few hundred users in a department accessing a particular application, tens of thousands of concurrent users will be using an entire suite of applications. Given these emerging trends, PeopleSoft had to 1) improve performance, 2) expand scalability, and 3) increase the interoperability between its applications. To get ready for this exciting—but very different—future, PeopleSoft moved its entire product line to 3-tier. Its challenge was to do it in a way that didn't disrupt its customers—or slip its aggressive feature delivery schedule. It devised an ingenious approach to address this problem.

THE APPLICATION

PeopleSoft provides a series of integrated application modules that run its customers' core business functions. These applications are often used by Global 2000 customers. Eighty percent of PeopleSoft's 1,500 customers fall in this category; they have more than 1,000 employees and make revenues exceeding $100 million annually. These customers often use several of PeopleSoft's horizontal applications—including manufacturing, distribution, financial, human resource, and materials management. The remaining 20% of PeopleSoft's customers are small businesses, higher education institutions, and federal, state, and local governments in the United States and Canada. These customers use PeopleSoft's vertical applications for health care, higher education, and government.

Why 3-Tier?

PeopleSoft migrated its application suite to 3-tier to support its strategic direction, and the needs of its customers. Here are the primary advantages that 3-tier delivered:

- Increased performance and reduced network traffic by replacing SQL requests with remote procedure calls. Reducing the number of messages the applications use is necessary to enable user access over wide area networks, like the Internet.

- Support for a variety of user interfaces by separating the user interface from the application. For example, PeopleSoft has added Web/Java clients to their applications.

- Upward scale by integrating a TP Monitor to funnel client requests, manage server loads, and distribute the application across any number of servers.

- Better inter-application communication using publish-and-subscribe.

THE 3-TIERED ARCHITECTURE

To facilitate its migration to 3-tier, PeopleSoft integrated Tuxedo with *PeopleTools*, the rapid application development environment it uses to build all its applications. PeopleTools automatically generates Tuxedo-based 3-tier applications. Because of this technique, all of the PeopleSoft applications have transparently become Tuxedo-enabled, allowing PeopleSoft to move seamlessly to 3-tier. The applications retain their traditional PeopleSoft look and feel—the PeopleTools-generated GUI didn't change. Another benefit of this approach is that PeopleSoft developers don't need to be aware of the intricacies of implementing a 3-tier architecture—the tool takes care of all the details automatically.

The Architectural Evolution of PeopleSoft

PeopleSoft created a three-phase delivery model for its upgrade to 3-tier. This approach ensures a painless—and optional—evolution for its existing customer base. The following describes these three product releases (see Figure 5-1):

■ ***PeopleSoft 6***—the first release to bundle Tuxedo—used 3-tier to migrate many previously batched functions to on-line, middle-tier services. For example, PeopleSoft has a batch process for calculating employee checks. With the new on-line service, a human resources manager can now interactively request that a single check be cut for an employee who is leaving the company. PeopleSoft 6 implemented a combination 2-tier/3-tier architecture—some special functions were implemented as middle-tier services, but the bulk of the functions were still processed 2-tier style; clients sent their requests as SQL messages directly to the database. This release allowed PeopleSoft and its customers to get their feet wet with 3-tier computing while providing some very useful new features.

■ ***PeopleSoft 7*** moves all application processing to 3-tier. PeopleTools is the enabler for this release; as we mentioned earlier, all of PeopleSoft's applications are generated using this visual tool. The new release of PeopleTools *(PeopleTools 7)* directly generates Tuxedo services which its clients invoke. This allows PeopleSoft developers to transparently create new 3-tier releases of their applications. Customers who use PeopleTools—it ships with every release of PeopleSoft—can also easily create new 3-tier applications or migrate their existing applications. However, PeopleTools also retains the ability to generate 2-tier applications. Consequently, customers can decide when to move to 3-tier.

■ ***PeopleSoft N*** (due to be released in 1998) will add support for Tuxedo's publish-and-subscribe messaging; PeopleSoft will integrate EventBroker with PeopleTools N. EventBroker will act as a server-to-server asynchronous message bus to support inter-application communication. In addition, it will let companies

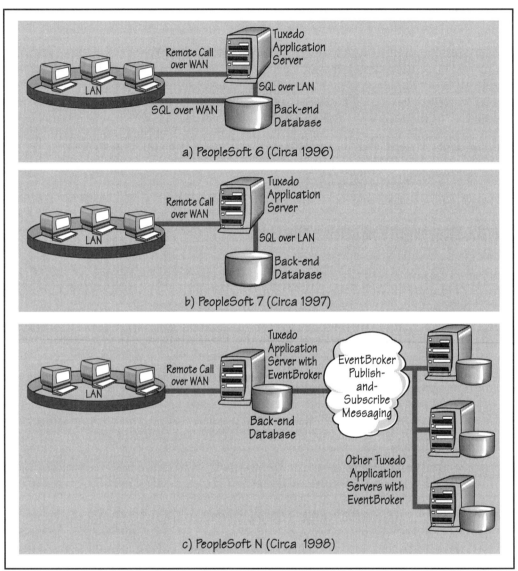

Figure 5-1. The Evolving Multilevel Physical Architecture of PeopleSoft.

partition applications by content or geographical location. The publish-and-sub-scribe system will eliminate the need for database replication that is used by the current 2-tier implementations (see the next Details box). PeopleSoft N will support different versions of PeopleSoft applications running simultaneously in a single environment. This will eliminate the need for customers to simulta-neously upgrade all of their systems to a new version of PeopleSoft.

As a result of this phased approach, PeopleSoft can offer a dramatic restructuring of its architecture as an evolutionary—rather than revolutionary—change for both itself and its customers.

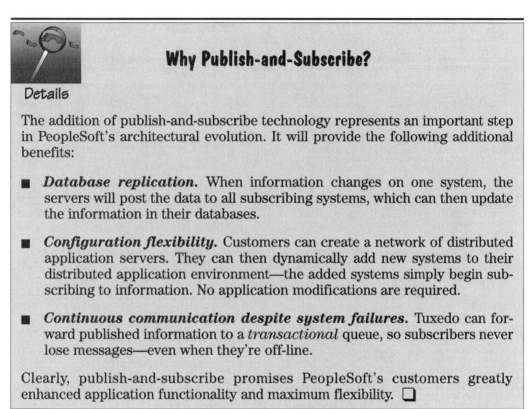

Why Publish-and-Subscribe?

Details

The addition of publish-and-subscribe technology represents an important step in PeopleSoft's architectural evolution. It will provide the following additional benefits:

- **Database replication.** When information changes on one system, the servers will post the data to all subscribing systems, which can then update the information in their databases.

- **Configuration flexibility.** Customers can create a network of distributed application servers. They can then dynamically add new systems to their distributed application environment—the added systems simply begin subscribing to information. No application modifications are required.

- **Continuous communication despite system failures.** Tuxedo can forward published information to a *transactional* queue, so subscribers never lose messages—even when they're off-line.

Clearly, publish-and-subscribe promises PeopleSoft's customers greatly enhanced application functionality and maximum flexibility. ❑

An Overview of the PeopleSoft Logical Tiers

Figure 5-2 illustrates how PeopleSoft's 3-tier software architecture is evolving with each new release. Here is how the tiers are being partitioned:

- **Tier 1** consists of PCs running the PeopleSoft client application, Tuxedo /WS, and Jolt.

- **Tier 2** consists of application servers running Tuxedo services for handling transactions (see the next Briefing box). The middle-tier application servers can either run on a stand-alone machine or on the same hardware as the back-end database. Supported operating systems include all major UNIX platforms, NT, VAX/VMS, AS/400, and MVS.

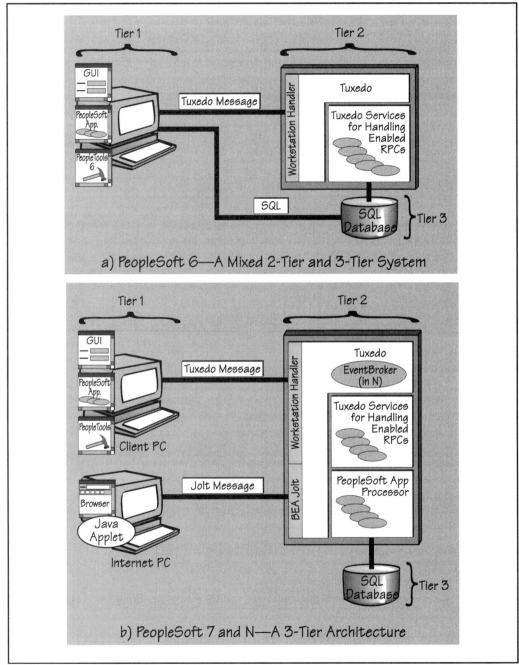

Figure 5-2. PeopleSoft's Evolving Logical Layers (with 3-Tier Mode Enabled).

■ *Tier 3* is the SQL database. PeopleSoft supports a broad range of databases—including Informix, Oracle, Microsoft SQL Server, Sybase, and multiple flavors of DB2.

FYI PeopleSoft's Demanding Middleware Requirements

Briefing

PeopleSoft chose Tuxedo because it met all of its middleware requirements. These requirements were extensive, including:

■ Support for multiple messaging metaphors (request-response, publish-and-subscribe, conversations, and so on)

■ Data-dependent routing to partition applications

■ High availability and reliability, with automatic failover and recovery features

■ Load balancing for application scalability

■ Transactional integrity of both database changes and publish-and-subscribe messages

■ Security, including authorization and encryption

■ Administration and monitoring features

■ Broad support for the hardware, databases, and operating systems that PeopleSoft supports

The middleware also had to be scalable, efficient, and completely trusted by customers. PeopleSoft evaluated a number of messaging and TP Monitor products. Tuxedo provided both the messaging requirements and transaction monitoring features it was looking for. Tuxedo also offered stellar references—with 1,500 sites in production. ❑

Tier 1: The PeopleSoft Client

PeopleSoft's client applications are built using PeopleTools. With the release of PeopleSoft 6, the clients are now 32-bit, and support Windows 95 or NT. Applications range from human resource management to materials management, but the client GUIs share a common "look and feel," as shown in Figure 5-3.

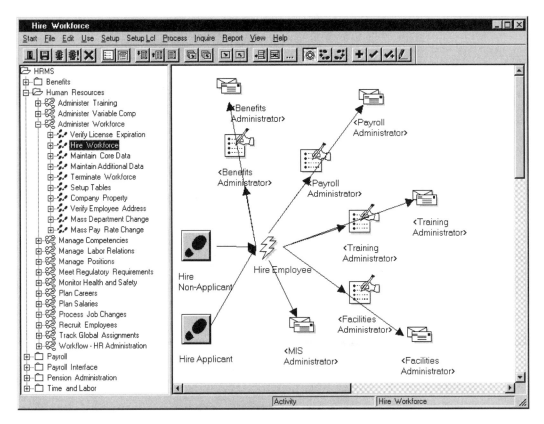

Figure 5-3. User GUI for PeopleSoft 6 Human Resource Application.

When customers install PeopleSoft 6 using the 3-tier model, the clients also run Tuxedo /WS. This enables the applications to invoke PeopleSoft 6's new interactive middle-tier services. All other functions are still handled by sending SQL directly to the database, 2-tier style, or by batch processes.

In addition to the new interactive services, PeopleSoft added other features to PeopleSoft 6:

- A Navigator interface provides a graphical view of business processes in addition to the more traditional Windows hierarchical menus.

- New tools—including *Business Process Designer*—let users quickly design, build, and then navigate through business processes.

- Improved integration with ActiveX applications lets clients now manage ActiveX objects at the desktop by invoking OLE Automation.

In PeopleSoft 7 and N, the build and save logic—which retrieves data from the database and updates the database after entering changes—resides on the application server rather than on the client. This makes the client much thinner.

PeopleSoft 7 adds support for Macintosh clients. In addition, it supports Java clients via BEA's Jolt software, which PeopleSoft includes with all its applications. This lets PeopleSoft's users access applications across the Internet (see the next Details box).

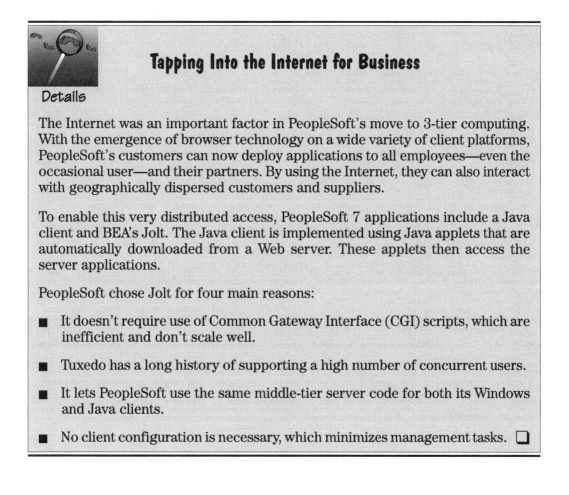

Tapping Into the Internet for Business

Details

The Internet was an important factor in PeopleSoft's move to 3-tier computing. With the emergence of browser technology on a wide variety of client platforms, PeopleSoft's customers can now deploy applications to all employees—even the occasional user—and their partners. By using the Internet, they can also interact with geographically dispersed customers and suppliers.

To enable this very distributed access, PeopleSoft 7 applications include a Java client and BEA's Jolt. The Java client is implemented using Java applets that are automatically downloaded from a Web server. These applets then access the server applications.

PeopleSoft chose Jolt for four main reasons:

- It doesn't require use of Common Gateway Interface (CGI) scripts, which are inefficient and don't scale well.

- Tuxedo has a long history of supporting a high number of concurrent users.

- It lets PeopleSoft use the same middle-tier server code for both its Windows and Java clients.

- No client configuration is necessary, which minimizes management tasks. ❑

Tier 2: The Server Side

Why would we want to go through the process of reinventing the wheel? That wouldn't be an efficient use of our time. So, we decided to license the Tuxedo technology from BEA.

— *Peter Gassner, Product Manager*
PeopleTools Application Server

As we explained earlier, the middle tier of PeopleSoft's applications will evolve as the company releases its 3-tier upgrades. PeopleSoft 6 enabled specific functions to run as RPC-enabled Tuxedo services. All other requests are still 2-tier—clients send SQL to the database. Table 5-1 shows the remote service calls that were added to the PeopleSoft 6 modules.

Table 5-1. Remote Service Calls Available in PeopleSoft 6.

Module	On-line Services
Payroll	Create paysheet, calculate check, confirm check, reverse check, delete check
General Ledger	Edit and post
Billing	Tax calculations, verify addresses using Vertex or Taxware
Receivables	Generate accounting entries
Inventory	Reserve stock, ship and issue, post journals on-line
Treasury	Update treasury positions
Student Administration	Course enrollment

The 3-tier architecture lets PeopleSoft 6 improve system responsiveness by reducing the number of requests a client makes to access data. In its traditional 2-tier design, PeopleSoft clients make as many as 27 remote requests to access data—with the new 3-tier architecture, this can drop to as few as three.

By making 3-tier pervasive, PeopleSoft 7 further reduces the number of messages going across the network. The remote calls that were added in PeopleSoft 6 continue to be handled by specific Tuxedo services. All other on-line client requests are made as remote calls to a special Tuxedo server class, called the *PeopleSoft Application Processor*, which moves all build and save logic from the client to the application server. The middle tier in PeopleSoft 7 can run on one node or across multiple nodes. Here's how it works:

1. Calls come from Tuxedo /WS on the client over a network to the PeopleSoft Application Processor.

2. The Application Processor builds the appropriate panel—for example, an "order" panel.

3. The Application Processor issues all of the necessary SQL calls to retrieve the needed data from the database.

4. Finally, the Application Processor sends a single message back to the client that includes all of the necessary data.

PeopleTools 7 transparently generates both SQL and Tuxedo requests as the application is developed. If a customer installs PeopleSoft applications in 3-tier mode, the Application Processor runs under Tuxedo. All functions then result in Tuxedo calls. If Tuxedo is not loaded, all functions run in 2-tier mode using SQL requests.

PeopleSoft's Message Agent API provides a uniform interface to the business rules and logic. This published API lets other applications interact with the PeopleSoft applications and data. In PeopleSoft 6, the Message Agent runs on Windows 95 and NT clients—so only applications on these platforms can call it. With PeopleSoft 7, it moves to the application server, making it available on additional platforms.

PeopleSoft N: The Arrival of Publish-and-Subscribe

With the release of PeopleSoft N, the PeopleTools environment will add support for Tuxedo's EventBroker. EventBroker will act as a message bus for handling communications between application servers, using publish-and-subscribe messaging.

By using publish-and-subscribe messaging and Tuxedo's data-dependent routing, companies will be able to partition applications or data across different systems. Partitioning can be done geographically or by data content. For example, a company could set up a server for North American inventory and another for European inventory. Tuxedo will route the data appropriately and let the servers share common information through publish-and-subscribe. Here's an example of how this middle-tier publish-and-subscribe message bus will work:

1. Pricing for a product changes on Machine A.

2. Machine A saves the change in its database and "publishes" this event.

3. All subscribers to price change messages then automatically receive the update.

This enables systems to store accurate and timely data. It also reduces network traffic by eliminating the need for each system to poll for updated data.

Another feature of PeopleSoft's publish-and-subscribe messaging implementation is simplified system management. When a company adds a system, administrators set it up as a message publisher to—and subscriber of messages from—the other systems it needs to be synchronized with. The administrator does not need to change existing servers to recognize and interact with the new system. PeopleSoft applications also use two-phase commits when updates need to be synchronized across multiple systems.

PeopleSoft as a Component Suite

As part of this publish-and-subscribe release, PeopleSoft N applications will also provide standard business components that can be reused across applications. By breaking functionality at the business component level, a shipping component, for example, can use publish-and-subscribe messaging to communicate with an invoice component. Business components will also improve data sharing—for example, a component can publish data that is subscribed to by a data warehouse. They can also accommodate a variety of resource managers—various data servers could subscribe to the same published data, but store it in different forms. Remember, the components are creators of information.

PeopleSoft's business components will be built with PeopleTools. It will allow customers to modify components to meet their specific business needs and build new ones. The components will be able to interface with both DCOM and CORBA applications when Tuxedo adds support for these in Iceberg.

Tier 3: The Database and Legacy Applications

PeopleSoft's applications support a wide variety of databases—including Oracle, Informix, Sybase, Microsoft SQL Server, DB2/UNIX, DB2/400, and DB2/MVS. The databases typically range in size from 300 MB to 300 GB; third-party tools let customers partition the data across systems if necessary. With the arrival of PeopleSoft N, the applications themselves will support database partitioning via EventBroker's publish-and-subscribe messaging and Tuxedo's data-dependent routing.

PeopleSoft also allows customers to integrate their legacy data with its applications through one of several methods. One basic method is to import flat files, bringing them into the PeopleSoft system through interface tables. Customers can also set up EDI environments to integrate legacy data on a continual basis.

Security

PeopleSoft applications provide three layers of security:

1. *Authentication* requires users to enter a user ID and password to gain access to the application.

2. *Authorization* controls what functions and specific data users can access based on their log-in. In addition, applications use Tuxedo's security mechanisms to prevent messages from unauthorized systems.

3. *Encryption* safeguards messages and data that is transmitted across the network. This is implemented via Tuxedo's built-in, RSA-compatible encryption technology.

System Management

PeopleSoft 6 and 7 applications use Tuxedo's management capabilities to administer applications and monitor messages. PeopleSoft N augments these system management features by monitoring application-specific status data—including the active users, running applications, and functions being performed. This data can then be published using the EventBroker.

THE PROJECT

Although 2-tier has worked well for us to this point, we knew going forward that to meet our customers' basic objectives, we had to move to 3-tier.

— Rick Bergquist

PeopleSoft made the decision to move to a 3-tier architecture in the summer of 1995 as part of its development of a long-term corporate strategy. Rick Bergquist, vice president of technology, headed the planning exercise. A number of factors affected the company's decision, including performance issues in a 2-tier environment and the new functionality customers demanded—such as support for Internet and data warehousing.

The development schedule for the deployment of the new design was ambitious—PeopleSoft announced its plans to integrate Tuxedo in June 1996; the company shipped PeopleSoft 6 in November of the same year (see the next Details box). PeopleSoft 7 applications will arrive in September 1997, three months ahead of schedule. PeopleSoft attributes this fast delivery to the reuse it has gained by relying on the PeopleTools foundation. Design and development for PeopleSoft N is being done concurrently—PeopleSoft expects it to ship 12 to 15 months after the release of PeopleSoft 7.

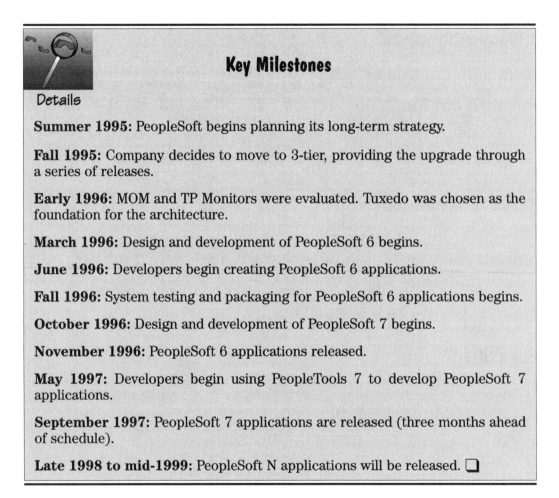

Key Milestones

Details

Summer 1995: PeopleSoft begins planning its long-term strategy.

Fall 1995: Company decides to move to 3-tier, providing the upgrade through a series of releases.

Early 1996: MOM and TP Monitors were evaluated. Tuxedo was chosen as the foundation for the architecture.

March 1996: Design and development of PeopleSoft 6 begins.

June 1996: Developers begin creating PeopleSoft 6 applications.

Fall 1996: System testing and packaging for PeopleSoft 6 applications begins.

October 1996: Design and development of PeopleSoft 7 begins.

November 1996: PeopleSoft 6 applications released.

May 1997: Developers begin using PeopleTools 7 to develop PeopleSoft 7 applications.

September 1997: PeopleSoft 7 applications are released (three months ahead of schedule).

Late 1998 to mid-1999: PeopleSoft N applications will be released. ❏

Design

A team of four strategists and developers—headed by Peter Gassner, PeopleSoft's Application Server product manager—put together PeopleSoft's architectural plan. The team looked at where the markets in which PeopleSoft played were heading. Then they forecast their customers' future needs. Several key technical requirements emerged:

■ Better support for massively scalable transaction volumes

- A component-based architecture to support a long-term Internet strategy
- Better application-to-application communication
- Database and application partitioning

Because of these requirements, the team quickly realized that a 3-tier environment was the only way to go. By the end of 1995, they had nailed down the three-phase release plan, selected Tuxedo, and settled on the migration path to 3-tier via PeopleTools. The team then convinced the rest of the company to buy into the strategy. Table 5-2 describes the specific goals for each release.

Table 5-2. Functionality Targeted for Each Release.

Release	Functionality
PeopleSoft 6	■ Reduce network traffic. ■ Incorporate specific RPCs using Tuxedo to bring low-volume batch processes on-line. ■ Move portions of the processing to the middle-tier application server. ■ Support 32-bit clients.
PeopleSoft 7	■ Provide complete Tuxedo support for all on-line functionality at the application server level. ■ Eliminate SQL generation at the client by moving build-and-save logic to the application server. ■ Add Tuxedo's Naming Services and dynamic load balancing. ■ Integrate the Web into all applications through use of Jolt and a Java client.
PeopleSoft N	■ Incorporate Tuxedo's EventBroker for publish-and-subscribe messaging. ■ Create business components, such as an order object, to ease application development and data sharing. ■ Enable applications to run in a mixed environment of PeopleSoft releases. ■ Use Tuxedo message prioritization.

Development

After nailing down the initial design target for each release, PeopleSoft began development of the upgraded PeopleTools environment and consequent applications. The process of delivering upgraded applications follows these steps:

1. In the strategy organization, a small design group of about four people first designs the upgraded release.

2. They pass their specifications to a larger tools team, which develops the upgraded PeopleTools.

3. The tools team then delivers the upgraded PeopleTools environment to PeopleSoft's application developers so that they can create the upgraded applications.

For PeopleSoft 6, the tools and application developers first decided which batch processes could benefit most from coming on-line. Because one of the primary design goals was to reduce network traffic, functions that required considerable SQL traffic were closely examined. For example, a task such as course enrollment—part of PeopleSoft's higher-education application—generates a long string of SQL commands. The process would be much more efficient via an RPC-enabled service that generates SQL on the server.

Next, the tools development team built the remote service calls for these functions into PeopleTools. Then, about ten developers created the services by wrapping existing COBOL code so that Tuxedo could invoke it. About 200 other developers worked on adding application functionality to the PeopleSoft 6 release. Because these developers relied on PeopleTools 6, they didn't need to know anything about writing in Tuxedo. The development environment transparently provides support for the hybrid 2-tier and 3-tier modes, depending on what calls the client makes.

Client and server specialists work together to develop the upgraded applications. They decide what the GUI should look like and how it should function following the company's standard for user interfaces.

The tools development team had already analyzed the messaging patterns of the existing applications; their goal was to minimize the number of messages going across the network. So they recommended to the application development groups which functions would benefit most by being re-architected as middle-tier services. PeopleTools 6 accessed these new services transparently; application developers just continued to build their applications as usual.

As we go to press, the company is preparing to release the PeopleSoft 7 application suite. The tools team has created PeopleTools 7, which transparently builds an application that can function in either a 2-tier or 3-tier mode. The development organization has also started designing PeopleSoft N. While the company's goal is to allow customers to continue to choose between a 2-tier and 3-tier architecture, it's not clear whether this flexibility will continue to be possible in the PeopleSoft N release.

Testing

Each time PeopleTools is upgraded, it goes through a series of tests before being passed on to PeopleSoft's application developers. Then, once an application has been written using the upgraded development environment, it is tested separately. Standard testing includes performance testing and regression testing to ensure compatibility among PeopleSoft applications. The development teams do extensive usability testing to ensure that the GUI is both easy to use and attractive.

Going Into Production

After application testing completes, the programs are packaged and released to customers, along with the associated PeopleTools and product documentation. Any customer that is part of PeopleSoft's maintenance program—which includes virtually all of its customers—automatically receives the upgraded tools and applications. Tuxedo and Jolt are bundled with each release.

In Production

Customers receive support for all PeopleSoft products through the company's hotline. PeopleSoft delivers maintenance releases as needed to fix minor bugs. For major releases, the company delivers upgraded PeopleTools and PeopleSoft applications at the same time.

THE OUTCOME

PeopleSoft's customers have responded enthusiastically to the company's technical strategy. PeopleSoft 6 and 7 provide them with many added benefits. PeopleSoft's customers can also start to prepare now for partitioned applications with the release of PeopleSoft N. At that time, they will need to decide if they want to take advantage of the publish-and-subscribe messaging feature and business components.

The architectural evolution of PeopleSoft's product line supports its business goals well. The company can now deploy its applications to more people within the enterprise. It can deliver more sophisticated Internet solutions to meet customers' growing needs for electronic commerce.

THE FUTURE

Replication is not sufficient for tomorrow's applications.

— Rick Bergquist

PeopleSoft 7 sets the foundation for PeopleSoft N. Here the ultimate goal is multiple application servers communicating with each other—and with various database repositories—in an N-tier environment through publish-and-subscribe messaging. PeopleSoft is also planning to build data warehouses and related tools for the specific vertical marketplaces that it currently serves. It will use publish-and-subscribe messaging to synchronize the content of the data warehouse with a customer's OLTP system. At this point, Tuxedo becomes the engine for active data warehousing.

Clearly, PeopleSoft is well on its way toward delivering a 3-tier environment that will support its customers' needs for more scalable, faster systems, as well as improved inter-application communications. And by consistently integrating more 3-tier features, they have accomplished this in an evolutionary—not revolutionary—manner.

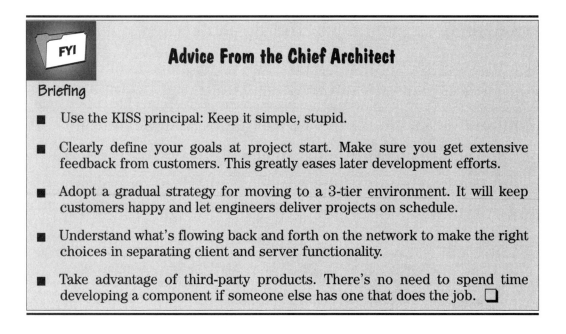

FYI

Advice From the Chief Architect

Briefing

- Use the KISS principal: Keep it simple, stupid.

- Clearly define your goals at project start. Make sure you get extensive feedback from customers. This greatly eases later development efforts.

- Adopt a gradual strategy for moving to a 3-tier environment. It will keep customers happy and let engineers deliver projects on schedule.

- Understand what's flowing back and forth on the network to make the right choices in separating client and server functionality.

- Take advantage of third-party products. There's no need to spend time developing a component if someone else has one that does the job. ❑

Chapter 6

Wells Fargo Leads the Way to Internet Banking

Financial services is, inherently, an information-intensive industry. Therefore, an organization's agility in transforming its information systems to meet changing business needs becomes a critical competitive success factor.

— Erik Townsend, President
The Cushing Group[1]

It was once simple to understand the difference between a bank, a brokerage house, a mutual fund company, and an insurance company. They offered fundamental products, and there was little overlap. Today, the differences have become blurred as financial institutions of all types compete for investors' funds. Leadership in the financial services industry now requires that an organization be able to quickly adapt to a changing market, offering new products and services to its customers in a timely and efficient manner.

---

[1] This case study is based on "A Case Study: Distributed Object Technology at Wells Fargo Bank," Copyright © 1997, The Cushing Group, Inc. The authors are Erik S. Townsend, Chief Technical Officer of The Cushing Group, and Michael L. Ronayne, Vice President of Information Systems Consulting and a principal in The Cushing Group.

Wells Fargo Bank has become a technology leader in banking, thanks in part to its pioneering use of distributed object computing technology. This technology has helped the company achieve several business objectives, including changing the way bank employees work with computers to become *customer*-focused rather than *account*-focused. Innovations made possible through the use of this technology also enabled Wells Fargo to become the first major bank to offer its customers secure on-line access to account balances through the World Wide Web.

THE APPLICATION

In the 1980s, competition for investors' funds—traditionally kept in banks—expanded to include brokerage and insurance companies. To remain competitive, banks began offering products such as mutual funds and brokerage accounts—products historically outside the purview of traditional banking. By the late 1980s, a growing trend was *compound statement banking*, where customers expected to receive a single, unified statement listing the balances and transactions for all of their accounts—including checking and savings, mortgage, credit card, brokerage, and retirement accounts. Customers wanted their banking activities to be structured in terms of their overall relationship with the bank instead of a single account.

Enabling a Customer Focus

Wells Fargo realized that to meet new customer demands, it needed to change from an account focus to a customer focus. By using BEA's ORB, *ObjectBroker*, the *Customer Relationship System* (*CRS*) accomplishes just that. Now, when customers who own several accounts call the bank, they no longer need to know their account numbers. They just need to provide their Social Security Number (SSN)—or Employer Identification Number (EIN) in the case of business accounts. The bank service agent can then see a complete view of each customer's overall relationship with the bank, including all accounts owned and their balances and statuses.

CRS allows a service agent to retrieve a comprehensive profile of customer account information simply by entering the customer's SSN. The system then interrogates several systems of record, including IBM MVS/CICS-hosted applications, an application running on a Digital VAX/VMS system, and a UNIX-based system. Finally, CRS returns to the user an organized, coordinated view of the customer's relationship with the bank; this is presented through a Windows GUI. It includes a list of the customer's accounts as well as their current balance, status, and so on.

Wells Fargo named the application *Customer Relationship System* to reflect its function of presenting all accounts in a customer's relationship with the bank. The application was developed by a project team that included Wells Fargo represen-

tatives, Digital staff members, and Cushing Group consultants, who acted as the primary consultants for the project.

Challenges the CRS Development Team Faced

To accomplish its shift to a customer focus, Wells Fargo faced a number of challenges. Like most banks, Wells Fargo's computer systems were optimized for account processing instead of providing integrated customer data. Direct deposit accounts were managed by mainframe computers; mutual funds were tracked by a Digital VAX/VMS system. Meanwhile, brokerage account processing was out-sourced to a vendor who used a Tandem system.

As a result, bank employees were required to log in to several different computer systems; each one had a character-oriented user interface. A simple customer question such as *"How much money do I have in all my accounts combined?"* could require an employee to navigate through three or more disparate data systems; none of these offered a GUI. This became an impediment to efficient customer service.

Wells Fargo began to seek out remedies to this problem. It was clear that re-engineering all of the bank's systems of record to embrace client/server—or any other technology—would neither be practical nor cost-effective. Too much investment already existed in the legacy systems. Instead, Wells Fargo needed a way to overcome the inherent disparity among its existing systems. It needed to seamlessly integrate the systems' functionality and deliver the integrated results through a GUI. The primary feature missing from the existing systems was the ability for an agent to specify the identity of a customer (by SSN, name, and so on) and then see a complete view of that customer's overall relationship with the bank.

CRS solved this. The project team decided to use ObjectBroker—then owned by Digital—to build CRS. The ObjectBroker-based solution is fully integrated and automated. It provides real-time connectivity to the actual systems of record. The application proves the viability of distributed object technology for complex, disparate systems integration. In addition, the robustness of the Internet Banking Solution serves to prove that Wells Fargo has achieved its goal of being the technology-leading bank.

Branching Out to More Applications

CRS was Wells Fargo's first application based on ORB technology. Fueled by its success, additional projects emerged for using ObjectBroker to deliver innovations to Wells Fargo customers. These include the following:

- ***Wells Fargo's Internet Banking Solution*** provides customers with real-time access to account balances via the Web.

- ***An interactive voice response unit (IVRU)*** provides automated service to customers calling in over telephone voice lines. Its user interface is based on touch-tone dialing equipment. For instance, the automated answering system could ask you to "Press 1 for customer service, 2 to check balances, or 3 to transfer funds."

- ***Automated teller machines (ATMs)*** provide access to customers' brokerage account balance information via a connection through the mainframes.

- ***A stock market data application***, purchased from Quotron, makes stock quotes and other data available to any application in the Wells Fargo network through a simple ObjectBroker client request. This delivers stock quotes to customers through several channels because the application is encapsulated and exposed as an ObjectBroker server. The application, hosted on an IBM RS/6000 platform running AIX, receives real-time feeds of stock market data from exchanges via a network provided by Quotron.

Through these projects, several new services were delivered to Wells Fargo customers. But perhaps more importantly, the bank's object model was refined, which results in a robust library of truly reusable business object services. These encapsulate the bank's core systems of record. Wells Fargo is now poised to fully exploit the principal benefit of distributed object technology: reuse of business object services to satisfy a new business need at a fraction of the cost and time to market that would be required using a traditional, ground-up approach to solving the same problem.

WELLS FARGO'S 3-TIERED ARCHITECTURE

Wells Fargo now bases most development of software systems that support direct, electronic customer access to account information on an object model that relates the bank's business processes, products, and services to a set of reusable modular software components (see the next Details box). Several different application systems can access and share these software components—or *business objects*—through the company's TCP/IP network.

Wells Fargo, however, first needed to develop a technique for integrating mainframe-based applications into a CORBA-based system, despite the absence of an ORB on the mainframe. (The MVS version of ObjectBroker was not available until after the completion of the initial release of CRS.) For CRS, ObjectBroker provides communication between applications on all platforms *except* the IBM mainframe, which runs MVS. Although the *Account* and *Customer* business objects are implemented by application "systems of record" which mainly run on a mainframe, the

Wells Fargo's Transition to Distributed Objects

Details

Distributed object computing offers a means of interfacing disparate computer systems with one another. It can result in reusable software components—or *business objects*—that can be combined in a variety of ways to meet changing business requirements. Wells Fargo has been using distributed object technology since 1993, and has put in place large-scale production systems based entirely on CORBA-based ORBs. The bank has, in fact, become one of the most successful users of this technology.

Distributed object computing and the CORBA standard were relatively unknown in 1993 when Wells Fargo began using the technology. Recently, both have been widely heralded as major direction-setting factors in the software industry. This is evidenced, in part, by Netscape's "ONE" architecture, which portrays CORBA as a key component in the evolution of Internet/intranet technologies to widespread use in the large business enterprise. Wells Fargo's early adoption of this leading-edge technology serves as further evidence of the company's commitment to technology leadership in banking.

However, the technology itself is just an enabling factor. Wells Fargo's success is primarily due to the company's willingness to commit itself to technology leadership and to reshape part of its IT organization to focus on creating reusable software components. The company has developed management techniques for structuring an organization to benefit from object technology, which serve as a reference model for other companies. ❑

CORBA object implementations for *Account* and *Customer* run on the HP 9000 platform. To implement the business function, the CORBA objects communicate with one or more mainframe applications using non-CORBA mechanisms (see Figure 6-1).

Here are the results of this architecture:

■ The semantics of communication between the Microsoft Windows client and the HP-UX object server are based on a CORBA interface definition. This interface was built to provide the client with a logical, consistent interface to customer information that is unrelated to how that data is stored in a given application.

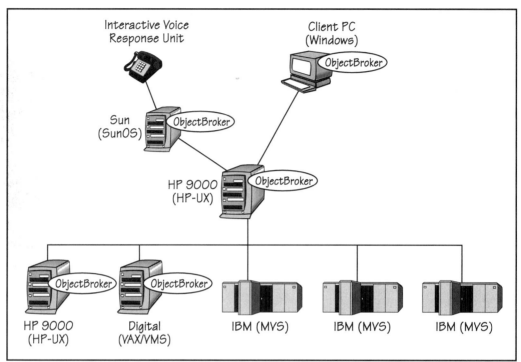

Figure 6-1. Simplified Diagram of the CRS Application.

■ The back-end IBM mainframe applications are not forced to change their semantics to conform to the new object interface definition. Rather, they simply expose the semantics of their original design (see the next Soapbox).

■ Inconsistencies and disparity between the back-end applications are hidden by the middle-tier server—the CORBA object implementation—running on the HP-UX platform. In fact, a primary purpose of this layer is to translate and hide complexities of the back-end systems and expose a single, logical, consistent interface to the client applications. Thus, if the back-end application topology changes, the middle-tier server must be modified, but client software need not be changed.

■ The mainframe programming environment remains unchanged. The paradigm shift to distributed object technology is made on the UNIX platform. Mainframe programmers must expose their applications' functions for remote access, but this is done with conventional and well-known mechanisms supported by the MVS platform.

■ The integration rules are separated from the systems of record. For a business object like Customer, whose functionality is implemented by several different systems of record, there are really two distinct sets of business logic: the logic

in the systems of record themselves and the business rules that dictate how the functions of various, disparate systems of record must be combined into an overall solution. In CRS, the latter type of business logic—the integration rules—are separated from the systems of record themselves.

- The back-end systems are completely hidden from the semantics of the client's communication with the CORBA server. The systems of record could, in theory, be completely rearchitected and even re-implemented on a different platform without modifying or recompiling the client applications.

Don't Touch That Mainframe!

Soapbox

The project team developed Wells Fargo's technique for integrating main-frame-based applications into a CORBA-based system out of necessity. In 1993, when CRS was developed, no commercial ORB was available for IBM main-frames. The Cushing Group believes that this approach—which doesn't use CORBA to communicate with the back-end IBM mainframe-based data tier—has significant merit and should be considered today, even when the chosen CORBA middleware product is available for the mainframe.

The primary counter-argument from proponents of mainframe-hosted ORB servers is that this approach appears to require an extra "hop" in the network. Both the mainframe and the UNIX server must process a client's request before a response can be returned. This is entirely true. However, this does not necessarily result in a noticeable performance penalty.

For many applications, direct implementation of CORBA objects on the main-frame is appropriate and desirable—but it is not the only option. The alternative indirect wrapping approach discussed here may, in some cases, actually be preferable. As a general guideline, if the objective is to eventually move the application off the mainframe platform, indirect wrapping is likely preferable. For applications that are intended to remain on the mainframe indefinitely, a direct CORBA-on-the-mainframe approach is more likely to be appropriate. ❑

Tier 1: The Client

Wells Fargo developed a Windows-based client application to provide its service agents with a graphical user interface (see Figure 6-2). The client gives the agent a list of all of a customer's accounts, as well as data such as account balances and

Product	Lock	Account #	Date	Type	Bal
Sav/MRA		6007454010			
Cr Line		7342222222			
Sav/MRA		6538888888			
Sav/MRA		6538000118			
Checking		0538000118			
MstrCd		505012332222****			
Visa		404067855****			
Checking		0008005407			
Checking		0008000275			
Sav/MRA		6007454028			

Customer Relationship System – [Detail: Other]

File Actions Preferences Window Help

Customer
○ SSN   008-00-5407
○ EIN
Mr. David An Goliath

Contacts
<PBM data not available>
<PFO data not available>

Figure 6-2. The End-User's View of the CRS Application.

statuses. GUI elements—for example, color and icons—organize the display and highlight certain conditions, such as overdrawn or frozen accounts.

In the first phase of the CRS project, it wasn't practical to provide a GUI for all of the possible functions a user might want to perform on the accounts themselves after identifying them. Although those features came with time, both schedule and funding constraints dictated a retrieval-only scenario for the first version. However, Eric Castain, Vice President and Manager of Wells Direct Systems, devised a very powerful extension to the initial client release.

When users wanted to actually perform transactions on an account, they simply double-clicked that account on the screen. CRS then activated a terminal emulator

window connected to the appropriate system of record. CRS then "drove" the terminal emulator to navigate to the appropriate screen in the mainframe application, enter the account number, and bring up the account. The users then took over, using the mainframe application they were already familiar with. CRS took the legwork out of the process and put them directly in the screen they needed—a major improvement. Given the complexity and difficulty of migrating away from legacy systems, this approach offered a reasonable alternative to the "Big Bang" tactic of replacing legacy systems.

Later projects moved more functionality into the GUI. This eliminated the need for users to double-click into the mainframe application's character-oriented user interface. These projects included Wells Fargo's Internet Banking Solution, which enables customers to check account balances via the Web (see Figure 6-3). The bank also added its IVRU as another client access channel.

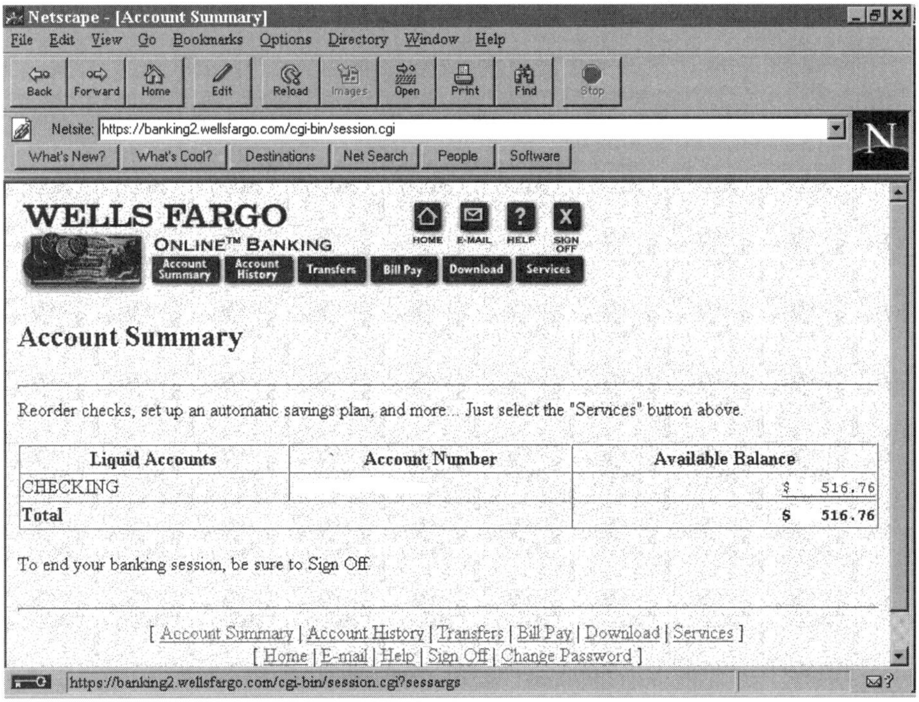

Figure 6-3. Wells Fargo's Internet Banking User Interface.

Tier 2: The Server Side

Wells Fargo considers detailed content of its banking object model to be highly confidential and proprietary. After all, it is the model that directly enables the integration of systems—this gives Wells Fargo a significant advantage over its competitors. Figure 6-4, however, provides a simple example of what an object model looks like—the actual object model used by Wells Fargo contains much more detail than is included here. The diagram shows how a bank's products relate to one another. Products consist of *accounts*, which can be owned by a customer, and *services*, such as bill payment, which can be used by a customer. The model defines a set of possible functions (or "operations" in CORBA's parlance) that applications can perform on the objects. Each of these operation definitions includes a set of input and output arguments, which must be specified by the client of the object. This is similar to the definition of a callable function in a procedural programming language.

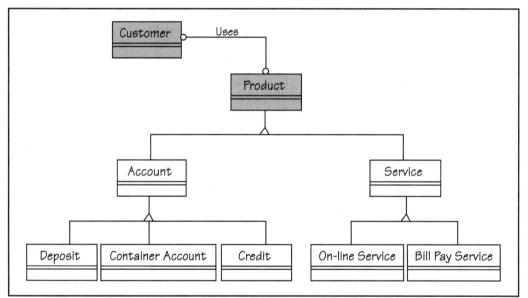

Figure 6-4. A High-Level Model for Banking Business Objects.

Also defined in the model is the definition of attributes, or data values stored to describe an object. For instance, a *CheckingAccount* object might include attributes such as *LedgerBalance* and *OverdraftLimit*. The model further describes relationships between object types, as is suggested by the depicted relationship between the *Customer* and *Product* object types in the diagram.

A company's object model is an extremely valuable asset. If companies want to be successful in building object-based applications, they should give it the care and attention it deserves (see the next Briefing box).

The Enterprise-Wide Object Model

Briefing

An object model defines the reusable software components—or business objects—in a distributed object system. The model specifies what the objects are and stipulates the semantics they use to communicate with other software. In a banking system, for instance, examples of objects are *CheckingAccount* and *RetailCustomer*. For each object, the model needs to define the following:

- ***Its relationship to other objects.*** For example, a *RetailCustomer* object may be capable of owning one or more *CheckingAccount* objects.

- ***The data associated with the object that is made available to other applications.*** For example, a *CheckingAccount* object might have a current balance, an overdraft limit, and so on.

- ***The functions the object can perform.*** A *CheckingAccount* object might support *Deposit*, *Withdraw*, and *Transfer* functions, while a *RetailCustomer* object might instead support functions such as *ChangeAddress*.

The model must be shared among the groups of developers who seek to integrate software. So if group A has one object model and group B has a similar but different object model that addresses some of the same functions, their software will be incompatible. If the long-term objective is to achieve seamless, enterprise-wide integration of systems, enterprise-wide coordination of the modeling effort is necessary. This doesn't mean that there must be a single model developed by one person. Different organizations should use their subject-matter expertise to develop object models within their functional domain. But when two groups overlap in their efforts and define slightly different semantics for the same object types, problems arise. To solve this, several different groups or individuals should contribute to the development of a coordinated, enterprise-wide object model.

For an organization to be successful using distributed object technology, the model must be well-designed, consistent, and based on proper object-oriented design methodology. The Cushing Group believes that the single largest factor in the failure of companies' efforts to use CORBA as a systems integration technology is that they fail to invest in (or realize the need for) a proper object model. Many companies who think they are developing distributed object systems are actually using CORBA-based middleware as a glorified RPC mechanism. The resulting applications will likely provide useful point solutions, but will not integrate with one another to deliver a unified solution. ❑

Tier 3: The Database and Legacy Applications

As noted, CRS interrogates several systems of record. These include:

- IBM MVS/CICS-hosted applications
- An application running on a Digital VAX/VMS system
- A UNIX-based system

The CRS client then presents the data retrieved from the systems to the service agent—or, in the case of the Internet Banking Solution, to the customer. ObjectBroker provides this seamless integration of the existing systems' functionality.

Security and System Management

Security is of primary importance to a bank. As a result, Wells Fargo's applications rely on user authentication and authorization checks. In addition, the bank uses a firewall to protect its internal network from outside customers that are accessing account information via its Internet Banking Solution.

Wells Fargo now depends on its CORBA-based infrastructure as a key component of its operational systems environment. Like other mission-critical systems, the ORB servers support the bank's ability to conduct business. Service outages are simply not acceptable.

To support such mission-critical use, the run-time environment must be managed and controlled. Here are the features it must support:

- Automated mechanisms must monitor the status of ORB servers running on several different computers.

- If a server process fails, an automated mechanism must respond by restarting the server, perhaps on a different network node.

- The failed server's clients must be redirected to an alternative server.

- The system needs to be able to alert someone about problems that can't be automatically resolved and require human intervention.

- Client demand for servers must be load-balanced across several network nodes, and their usage must be tracked.

- Instrumentation must be maintained on the overall system to identify bottlenecks and allow the overall run-time environment to be tuned for optimal efficiency.

The Cushing Group evaluated the commercial ORBs using these requirements. At the time, none of them provided these necessary features. As a result—and out of necessity—Wells Fargo designed its own *ORB System Management* facility (OSM). OSM is a complete management tool that augments ObjectBroker to provide:

■ Run-time instrumentation
■ Dynamic run-time management of server processes
■ Load-balancing management
■ Exception handling
■ Complete reporting of performance metrics to facilitate tuning

OSM is an internally maintained add-on subsystem. It is a distributed application based on ObjectBroker's CORBA implementation. It provides a mechanism to manage Wells Fargo's distributed object applications in its production environment.

THE PROJECT

The CRS project began in early October 1993. The goal was to develop a more customer-focused application. The initial target users were the customer service agents who support the "mass-affluent" market—those customers who typically have several accounts and significant financial assets. Wells Fargo set an aggressive timeframe for implementing CRS—90 days! Of course, it would have been impossible to re-engineer the systems of record in that time. But the company felt that ObjectBroker was powerful enough to encapsulate and integrate the existing systems into a working application in that time.

The CRS application was placed in pilot in late December 1993 and in full production use in January 1994—104 days after design began (see the next Details box). The team feels that several last-minute additions of functionality—not to mention the winter holidays—justified the slip to 104 days.

Design

In the fall of 1993, Wells Fargo began to evaluate approaches that could graphically present integrated data from several systems of record at a practical cost. A key objective was to deliver the integrated functionality through a native Microsoft Windows user interface.

The bank began working with several companies, including Digital's San Francisco office. They discussed the concept of an integrated, PC-based application to allow agents to be more focused on customers. Digital then worked with Wells Fargo to refine the functional requirements for such an application and relied on engineering groups at Digital's headquarters on the East Coast to help determine what technologies could be used to meet Wells Fargo's needs.

An engineering group at Digital's headquarters was familiar with The Cushing Group and referred the consulting company to Digital's San Francisco office.[2] The Cushing Group first met with Castain in October 1993. Castain was not one to waste time, and in the course of a full-day meeting the newly formed team managed to scope and define a three-month project (see the next Briefing box for more about object-oriented design). The goal was to provide the customer service agents with a more integrated, intuitive, and easier-to-use interface to customer account information.

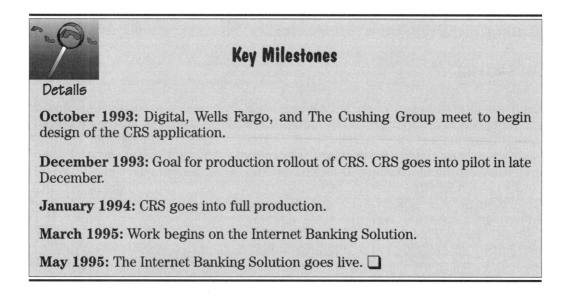

Key Milestones

Details

October 1993: Digital, Wells Fargo, and The Cushing Group meet to begin design of the CRS application.

December 1993: Goal for production rollout of CRS. CRS goes into pilot in late December.

January 1994: CRS goes into full production.

March 1995: Work begins on the Internet Banking Solution.

May 1995: The Internet Banking Solution goes live. ❏

Defining the CRS Requirements

Castain shared with The Cushing Group his vision for a solution to the customer service agent requirements based on the description of the problem he was given by the Telephone Banking group. The discussion began with the assertion that the team should "forget about account numbers as the key focus in this effort." As anyone familiar with banking systems knows, account numbers are the primary index keys for just about everything, so this was a bit unsettling at first. Castain

---

[2] Erik Townsend, the Chief Technical Officer of The Cushing Group, and Michael Ronayne, Vice President of IS Consulting and a principal at the group, had previously worked with Digital to help design its ObjectBroker product. It was named ACA Services then. ObjectBroker was acquired by BEA Systems in early 1997.

explained that when customers who own several accounts call the bank, they should not be required to know their account number. Customers may wish to do business based on their account number—or they may want to transact business based on an overall relationship with the bank, which might involve several different accounts and, perhaps, transfers between them.

CRS was designed from the end-user's point of view using rapid prototyping of the GUI components of the application as the drawing board. As the application was intended for use by customer service agents, the design team enlisted two agents to participate in the design sessions. There were also a number of other participants from the business side of the organization involved from day one. In fact, the ratio of business participants to IS participants was close to 2:1 throughout the effort— a factor that contributed heavily to the project's overall success.

Setting the Architecture

The team quickly confirmed the feasibility of using a 3-tier client/server architecture to deliver a rapid solution with production-grade quality. The group decided to use ORB technology to meet the goals. Object request brokering offers a way to construct distributed application systems using object-oriented semantics to define an application-level communication protocol between client and server programs. They had considered two options for the client and the server relationship management—DCE or CORBA. Both options were new technologies, so the primary consideration was software availability and stability. The long-term technical direction was also very important. The team recommended Digital's ObjectBroker ORB—it was stable and met Wells Fargo's needs.

FYI

Adopting an Object Mindset

Briefing

Ever since computers have been used for business information systems, the software development paradigm has been one in which a business problem is identified, then a solution is built—essentially from the ground up. Advancements such as database management systems have provided useful platforms on which to build business applications, but these are technology infrastructure platforms. The business application logic has always been built, in its entirety, to support a given problem.

Component-based software development, on the other hand, involves building *business solution components*—chunks of reusable software that solve some aspect of a business problem. These components are combined in new and different ways to solve each business problem that arises. This means that the design process doesn't begin with "What software will solve the business problem at hand?" but instead with how the business problem at hand can be decomposed into smaller, more generic subproblems. A successful team must also consider how they can define the requirements of these subproblems in a way that results in reusable components that can solve the problem at hand, and be used later to solve a different problem.

Simply put, this is counterculture for most IS organizations. The emphasis on solving the problem at hand often drives these organizations to a "quick-and-dirty" approach that will never yield reusable components. Wells Fargo—like any company that implements object-based technology—had to avoid this traditional development approach to develop a successful object model it could leverage in future projects. ❑

Although the Digital product was originally based on a proprietary design, Digital and several other companies had already joined forces to define a standard for ORB technology—CORBA. The Digital ORB product was already moving toward the then loosely defined CORBA standard. The selection of Digital's ORB set the direction for the effort within Wells Fargo, which would evolve to become what is now almost certainly the world's largest CORBA-based application development effort. This technology would later enable Wells Fargo to become the first bank to offer Web-based access to account balances, not to mention several other innovations.[3]

CRS could have been developed using message-oriented middleware, remote procedure calls, or any other similar approach. But the difference between distributed object technology and other approaches centers on the *reusability* of the business object services. No such services exist before the application is built, so little value is perceived until a second application is developed. If the first application is well-architected, the cost to develop other applications should be reduced through the reuse of components built for the original application. That is exactly what occurred at Wells Fargo, and it is probably the principal reason that Wells Fargo has been successful with this technology.

---

[3] Neither The Cushing Group nor your author are aware of another CORBA-based application in production use that rivals the size and scope of the ORB-based applications at Wells Fargo. However, many organizations working with this technology have avoided public disclosure of their efforts for competitive reasons. If any project of a similar scale exists, its secrecy has been well guarded.

Development

A team was formed to build the CRS application:

- The leader was Eric Castain, who has since become the bank's principal champion of ORB technology.

- Three Cushing Group consultants brought ORB and distributed systems experience to the team.

- Digital provided the ORB product itself as well as a consultant who was an expert in PC GUI design and development.

- Several Wells Fargo employees provided knowledge of the existing applications and participated in the overall development.

While the GUI expert from Digital worked with the users, the other consultants from The Cushing Group concentrated on defining the business object model. They mapped the model to the transactions of existing legacy applications and developed the UNIX-based methods that would implement the business objects. This initial project relied heavily on screen-scraping technology to gain access to the functions and data in the existing environment. Screen scraping is a technique for transforming an application's human user interface into an API by capturing data from a 3270 terminal session.[4]

As the object model took shape, the developers mapped each operation to the corresponding mainframe application screen, and identified the data fields that would have to be accessed to perform a function. Once this information was specified, a consultant from OpenConnect Systems of Dallas, Texas, implemented the required screen-scraping routines. A Cushing Group consultant then incorporated the screen-scraping routines into the ORB server program. The resulting application provided Wells Fargo's telephone customer service agents with a Microsoft Windows-based GUI for accessing customer relationship information. The only necessary input from customers is their Social Security Number.

Home Banking in Record Time

When Wells Fargo developed the CRS application in 1993, the World Wide Web existed, but it was essentially still a tool only used by research and development

---

[4] Although screen scraping is a very effective rapid application development technique, it is suboptimal in terms of reliability, maintenance, and performance. The screen-scraping software was replaced in a later version of CRS with software that communicated with the mainframe using a messaging-based protocol developed internally at the bank.

companies. By March 1995, the Web and the Internet had taken on an entirely different function. Consequently, management at Wells Fargo funded an effort to offer electronic banking to its customers through a Web server on the Internet. Wells Fargo wanted to deliver on-line electronic banking services to customers over the Web, instead of limiting the site to product literature, as was common at the time.

Sixty days later, Wells Fargo was on-line with real-time access to account balances via the Web. By delivering its Internet Banking Solution, Wells Fargo became the first truly Internet-accessible bank. The amazingly short 60-day project cycle was directly enabled by the reusable business object services developed for CRS and other applications. The legacy systems that needed to be integrated had already been exposed through distributed object interfaces. Most of the necessary functions were already available on the network. If not for security issues, the project would have involved little more than hooking up a Web server as an ObjectBroker client and using a CGI script in the Web page to escape to C code to make the ObjectBroker client request. But security is of paramount importance to a bank, so the customer authentication and authorization checks, firewall protection, and so on became a significant task.

The goal for the 60-day effort was to deliver on-line access to account information. Like other successful CORBA-based projects, the team went on to deliver numerous other banking functions to customers through the Web interface. These newer, more expansive Internet banking capabilities are also built entirely on top of a CORBA-based internal software integration architecture. Wells Fargo's Web site can be found at http://www.wellsfargo.com. The pages that actually access account data through the CORBA infrastructure are—of course—available only to Wells Fargo customers. IT professionals evaluating use of CORBA in their own organizations have actually opened Wells Fargo checking accounts solely for the purpose of being able to use this unique Web site.

How Development Was Organized

Instead of organizing a separate group for each business problem in the more traditional development manner, Wells Fargo found that a better approach is to structure the organization in terms of one or more ORB Server Engineering groups whose sole purpose is to create servers. They don't write client programs, except perhaps simple ones to test their servers. Their customers are one or more groups whose charter is to develop client programs to solve a particular business need. These groups submit their requirements to the ORB Server Engineering group. In this model, the manager of an ORB Server Engineering group is motivated to aggressively work to discover overlaps and commonalities in functional requirements and to develop the most generic and reusable components possible. This

simple technique has worked very well for Wells Fargo and appears to have helped create their success with ObjectBroker.

Developing Wells Fargo's Object Model

As we previously noted, success in object reuse is directly related to the quality of the object model. Wells Fargo's initial development of its object model was adversely affected by the following issues:

■ To meet the very aggressive schedule of the CRS project, the team intentionally let the object model be less than perfectly object-oriented.

■ The team didn't test the object model against use cases outside the immediate functional domain of CRS.

■ Digital's ORB became fully CORBA-compliant, impacting the model's definition.

Wells Fargo eventually rearchitected the object model that supported CRS to accommodate the needs of other client applications. The object model now eliminates the previously mentioned deficiencies, but at some cost—Wells Fargo learned from experience about the importance of a well-designed object model.

To ensure that a high level of object reuse continues at Wells Fargo, the bank created an ORB Coordination Group (see the next Details box). This group reviews all server objects being proposed by a particular client application team with other groups to ensure that it is appropriate for them as well. This lengthens the specification time for an object definition, but it also means that the object will be reusable. So far, this process has worked exceptionally well at Wells Fargo, with only a small handful of operations having to be reworked to make them more general.

Making Object Reuse a Reality

Details

Reusable software components have no inherent benefit over any other kind of software—unless the organization that owns them is successful in reusing them. This may seem obvious and self-explanatory, but real experience has proven that developing a library of reusable components—and then actually realizing a dramatic reduction in cost and time to market as a direct result of such reuse—is more difficult than one might guess.

Traditional management structure doesn't create an incentive for people to reuse existing components. Consequently, developers often create new, redundant components, which adds to the disparity between systems. Monolithic, redundant, dysfunctional legacy applications are replaced with redundant, dysfunctional distributed systems. Each distributed system consists of components that are theoretically reusable except that they are never actually reused.

Wells Fargo's success in reusing objects is not because of any technology or software function. It is a result of the following:

■ A willingness to modify and adapt its managerial approach to actively promote the reuse of software components among different groups of developers.

■ An investment in developing a well-architected enterprise object model. Wells Fargo recognizes the object modeling process as an essential component of ongoing application development. Therefore, enhancements to the model are funded as required.

■ A commitment to maintaining, extending, and using the object model as effectively as possible.

As with any other distributed computing middleware, a programmer can hack out a CORBA IDL file based on knowledge of what the application must do. This can be done in just a few minutes. The programmer might then go on to build client and server applications using that IDL. *This is exactly what must be avoided.* The IDL defines the interface through which an object is used—or reused. An object interface whose design is based solely on contemplation of the requirements immediately at hand may fail to make information or functionality available that another future application will need. For example, when defining the interface to a *BankAccount* object type, you must consider not only what functions and data the client program that plans to use that object may require but also what other functions and data future applications may require.

In addition, almost invariably programmers will write their own IDL to define a given object instead of using one that already exists. So you must ensure that objects are well-designed in the first place and that they are used effectively thereafter. Furthermore, when a function that does not exist is needed, you must carefully try to fit it into an appropriate, existing object definition before creating a new—and perhaps overlapping or redundant—object type. Wells Fargo recognized these needs and put organizational structures in place to manage them.

Wells Fargo commissioned an ORB Coordination Group. Essentially, the function of this small group of people is to be the keepers of the Enterprise Object Model. Instead of allowing anyone so inclined to simply define, build, and use object interfaces, all development groups using the object middleware are required to work with the ORB coordinator to ensure their object definitions are not incompatible, overlapping, or redundant. The ORB coordinator is *not* a dictator who stipulates the content of the object model—one person cannot have sufficient subject-matter expertise to know what the overall object model for a large organization must contain. Instead, the ORB coordinator's role consists of:

- **Being the librarian.** The coordinator knows what object interfaces different groups are working with and coordinates joint efforts. For instance, in response to a request to add a new *NoLoadFund* object to inherit directly from the existing *Account* object, the ORB coordinator might respond by encouraging the requestor to instead work with the group already building a *MutualFund* object, extending its semantics to cover no-load funds.

- **Playing the facilitator.** Another aspect of the job is to identify areas where different developers or groups have inconsistent views as to how the object model should be used. The coordinator tries to reconcile these inconsistencies.

This coordination may sound obvious, simple, and trivial. The truth is that it is of paramount importance, and most organizations don't make the investment.

Because the success of CRS led to several follow-on projects that added functionality and incorporated additional business processes, Wells Fargo's object model is constantly evolving. It takes more than two full-time senior developers to support this evolution. Wells Fargo has also adopted Rational Corporation's Rational Rose object-modeling tool to assist in maintaining the object model. Rational Rose makes it possible to keep the model—which is now quite large—well-documented and easily maintained. With the software, a staff member can design an object model graphically; a CORBA IDL can then be generated. ❑

THE OUTCOME

Wells Fargo invested in:

- The product licensing of Digital's (now BEA's) ORB technology
- 47 person-weeks of consulting services from The Cushing Group and Digital
- The personnel cost of approximately three full-time Wells Fargo employees

The result is a working solution that significantly changed the way users interact with the bank's core system of record. The bank's success is largely attributable to its willingness to explore different management approaches to create an environment conducive to successful reuse of application software components.

The Users' Perspective

Wells Fargo's Internet Banking Solution is a success. By the summer of 1997, the Web-based banking service grew to more than 400,000 enrolled customers. And more applications have come on-line. Wells Fargo's ObjectBroker servers are processing as many as 900,000 business object invocations per day in the production environment. The ObjectBroker ORB is actually handling more than 3,000,000 CORBA method invocations daily (each business transaction consists of several object interactions.) Wells Fargo anticipates continued aggressive growth in the transaction volumes.

CRS has also been successful from an end-user perspective. CRS users—the bank's customer service agents—are located in Concord, California, some 25 miles east of Wells Fargo's downtown San Francisco offices where the application was developed. The GUI interface and simplicity of the application induced a group of end users to travel to San Francisco to thank the developers, take them to lunch, and present them with an award. One bank executive was quoted as saying that although this was not the first time end users have gone looking for the programmers, it was probably the first time the purpose of such a visit was positive and complimentary.

A Key Success Factor: Getting the Organization Ready

Organizational readiness is a key factor in Wells Fargo's success. Distributed object computing is more than just the middleware tools that provide communication between applications. Instead, it embodies an entirely new approach and methodology for application software design. In support of its use of distributed object technology, Wells Fargo made the following investments:

- *Formal training.* Since 1993, The Cushing Group has trained over 100 Wells Fargo employees in the use of CORBA and ObjectBroker.

- *Mentoring.* Both Cushing Group consultants and experienced Wells Fargo employees have formally mentored other groups within the bank on the design of ORB-based applications and how to take advantage of ObjectBroker features. This ensures that the technology is applied in a uniform and consistent manner.

- *Formal reuse coordination.* A key success factor at Wells Fargo has been the ORB Coordination Group.

In the spring of 1996, Wells Fargo commissioned KPMG Peat Marwick LLP to conduct an in-depth evaluation of the prudence of using CORBA as a tool for high-volume transaction processing. KMPG conducted an in-depth analysis of the systems that have been developed, considered various risk factors, and interviewed

most of the bank employees, consultants, and contractors involved with the ORB-related work. The study was completed in August 1996. KPMG found that Wells Fargo's selection of CORBA-based object-oriented systems integration was sound. After evaluating the risks and benefits, KPMG recommended continued use of CORBA. And, after evaluating several competing products, KPMG also found that ObjectBroker was a proper choice at Wells Fargo.

THE FUTURE

Wells Fargo has already become expert with CORBA, and it is likely that the bank will continue to use its investment in CORBA-based, reusable business objects to offer customers new and innovative products and services. Wells Fargo and a handful of other pioneering organizations have also proven the merits of distributed object computing. It therefore comes as no surprise that the software industry on the whole has now begun to embrace distributed object computing as the mechanism that will allow Internet/intranet and "component" technologies to interface with enterprise-scale business information systems.

Wells Fargo's technologists, meanwhile, continue to:

■ Identify new, innovative ways to exploit their existing investment in CORBA-based business objects.

■ Explore emerging technologies.

■ Determine how the new technologies can be used to help Wells Fargo offer the best possible products and services to its customers.

According to Eric Castain, the bank's goal for 1997 is to add significant new features every 6 weeks. They are currently installing new releases every 4.5 weeks. He expects to eventually be installing new functions every week. The bottom line is that the bank's reusable, middle-tier components are enabling the deployment of new functions at an unheard of pace. It differentiates Wells Fargo in the marketplace and enables them to attract new customers. In addition, they can offer existing customers a broader set of financial products and services.

Wells Fargo has clearly become a technology leader in banking. Distributed object technology has played a key role in helping the bank achieve this leadership position.

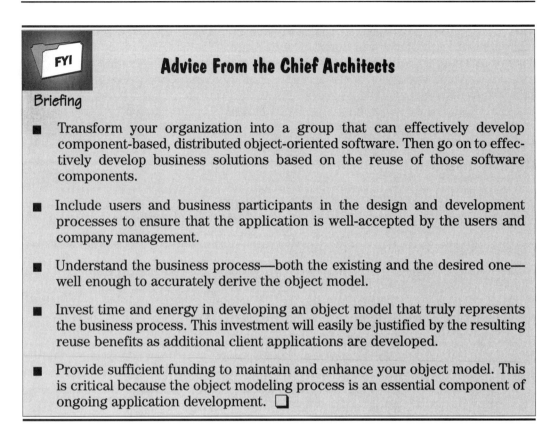

FYI

Advice From the Chief Architects

Briefing

■ Transform your organization into a group that can effectively develop component-based, distributed object-oriented software. Then go on to effectively develop business solutions based on the reuse of those software components.

■ Include users and business participants in the design and development processes to ensure that the application is well-accepted by the users and company management.

■ Understand the business process—both the existing and the desired one—well enough to accurately derive the object model.

■ Invest time and energy in developing an object model that truly represents the business process. This investment will easily be justified by the resulting reuse benefits as additional client applications are developed.

■ Provide sufficient funding to maintain and enhance your object model. This is critical because the object modeling process is an essential component of ongoing application development. ❑

Chapter 7

Apple Improves Ordering With a 3-Tier Upgrade

With a standard infrastructure in place globally, we gain cost savings and we leverage our development efforts and skills.

— Dean Rally, Senior Manager
Apple's Technology Integration Group

Apple Computer relies on its electronic ordering systems to give its authorized resellers and service providers an easy way to order computers and parts. This lets the resellers have greater control over the ordering process, and it offers Apple cost savings by minimizing administrative tasks. But when Apple decided to move to an SAP-based solution for all its corporate functions, it found that it also had to replace the existing ordering systems with a new one that could interoperate with SAP R/3.

To accomplish this, Apple developed a new worldwide ordering system based on a 3-tier architecture. The new system—called *AppleOrder Global*—serves as a front-end to SAP for processing electronic orders. It provides the scalable, on-line performance needed to service thousands of resellers around the world. AppleOrder Global is now up and running in Canada and Europe; U.S. resellers are due to come on-line in 1998.

THE APPLICATION

> *With AppleOrder Global, external Apple resellers and service providers can order finished goods and also inquire about their orders, invoices, and account history on-line. They don't need to call Apple anymore to get that information.*
>
> — *Michelle Pope, Apple Project Manager*

AppleOrder Global is Apple's new electronic ordering system—it will soon replace all of Apple's existing ordering systems. Until the advent of AppleOrder Global, the company supported five different electronic ordering systems in different regions around the world. These systems provided many benefits to Apple's resellers—and they saved the company a great deal of money by reducing data entry costs and consequent errors. The U.S. system alone saved Apple the equivalent of 50 staff members per year.

But the corporate move to SAP meant that Apple had a choice. It could either modify all of these systems to front-end the new corporate environment—or it could create a single new worldwide electronic ordering system to replace all of them. You're reading this case study on AppleOrder Global, so you've probably deduced that Apple decided to create a new, unified system.

Because the new system can't take away any existing features from the resellers, AppleOrder Global consists of the best features of all the current systems. As a result, everyone will have more capabilities than they have now. For example, AppleOrder Global was a great improvement over the system it replaced in the Canadian region. The old system relied on batch processing. In contrast, AppleOrder Global moved many functions on-line. Resellers now get better response times, more timely data, and the capability to confirm an order as soon as it is submitted. The change is even more dramatic for Europe, where most countries had no existing Apple electronic ordering system at all.

What AppleOrder Global Does

External Apple resellers around the world can login to AppleOrder Global to order finished goods—such as Macintoshes, monitors, and keyboards—and get information about the status of pending orders and shipments. They can access their account and invoice information. And they can access up-to-date product and pricing information—such as product availability. Authorized Apple service providers can also order parts on-line.

To provide these functions, AppleOrder Global must access the corporate systems that run SAP's suite of software applications. While SAP includes modules for

handling all aspects of running the company (see the next Briefing box), electronic order processing requires interfaces to only two of the SAP R/3 modules.

The rollout of AppleOrder Global is synchronized with that of the new SAP environment. As the regions upgrade to the SAP information systems, they upgrade to AppleOrder Global. As a result, resellers have uninterrupted access to an electronic ordering system while SAP R/3 rolls out.

A Rollout in Progress

AppleOrder Global is up and running in many countries. The Canadians were first; about 45 resellers used it to order finished goods. As this book went to press, Apple was completing the European rollout: 1,500 resellers and service providers in Europe are using the system to order finished goods and service parts. The 4,000 resellers and service providers in the United States will move to the upgraded system for finished goods ordering when Apple migrates the U.S. data to its SAP system.

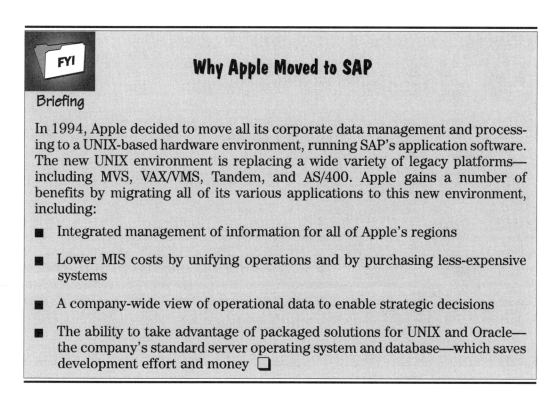

FYI

Why Apple Moved to SAP

Briefing

In 1994, Apple decided to move all its corporate data management and processing to a UNIX-based hardware environment, running SAP's application software. The new UNIX environment is replacing a wide variety of legacy platforms—including MVS, VAX/VMS, Tandem, and AS/400. Apple gains a number of benefits by migrating all of its various applications to this new environment, including:

- Integrated management of information for all of Apple's regions

- Lower MIS costs by unifying operations and by purchasing less-expensive systems

- A company-wide view of operational data to enable strategic decisions

- The ability to take advantage of packaged solutions for UNIX and Oracle—the company's standard server operating system and database—which saves development effort and money ❑

Subsequent releases of AppleOrder Global will let Apple complete the migration of all the regions. You may have noticed from the description in the previous paragraph that the U.S. and Canada are initially moving only their finished goods ordering to AppleOrder Global. The existing service parts ordering system will remain operational until AppleOrder Global has implemented additional features—such as warranty management.

The Demanding Job Ahead

To develop and roll out an electronic ordering system that would garner international acclaim—at least from Apple's resellers—the development team had to take on several tough assignments:

■ ***Develop a scalable system with interactive interfaces into SAP.*** Messages had to be translated into a format SAP recognizes. This required the developers to implement SAP R/3 remote function calls (RFCs) to invoke custom routines written in SAP's ABAP/4 programming language. This new SAP interface proved to be the developers' greatest challenge.

■ ***Support an international production environment.*** This meant providing real-time performance on a global scale. It also meant stringent availability requirements—after all, the worldwide resellers don't all go home at 6:00 p.m. Pacific Standard Time.

■ ***Ensure that AppleOrder Global offered all the functionality of all the existing systems***. Resellers wouldn't be satisfied with anything less. So the developers had to manage their feature development and rollout plans to make sure that they always matched the features of the ordering system they were replacing.

APPLEORDER GLOBAL'S 3-TIERED ARCHITECTURE

With a 3-tier architecture you have the ability to scale the servers and move them across machines. If you designed a system without that capability—such as a 2-tier database solution—you're limited to what a single database server can handle.

— *Tom Wilson, President*
IT Design USA

The AppleOrder Global 3-tier architecture front-ends Apple's SAP R/3 systems (see Figure 7-1). The clients are distributed around the world. Resellers access AppleOrder Global through a dial-up or leased-line connection over a dedicated network.

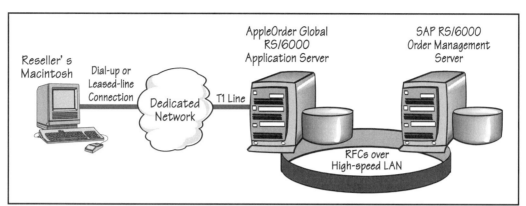

Figure 7-1. AppleOrder Global's 3-Tier Architecture.

This network is managed by CompuServe, a leading service provider. It supplies on-line access to the system without requiring Apple to manage the client connections.

The AppleOrder Global tiers are divided into the following components (see Figure 7-2):

■ **Tier 1** consists of the AppleOrder Global GUI and Tuxedo /WS. It runs on Macintosh clients and initiates calls to middle-tier services. Tier 1 is a multi-layered implementation that allows Apple to isolate the GUI from future infrastruc-

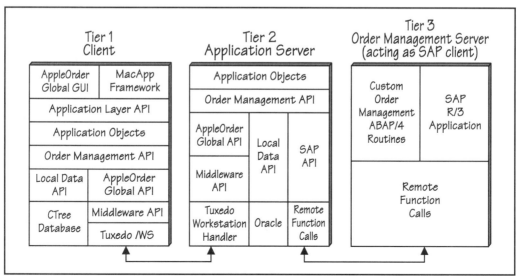

Figure 7-2. AppleOrder Global's Logical Layers.

ture changes. The client also manages a cache of local data that allows it to operate both off-line and on-line.

■ *Tier 2* runs on the AppleOrder Global application server. It consists of Tuxedo services running as application objects. They provide business functions and also interface to the back-end SAP systems.

■ *Tier 3* is the SAP R/3 Order Management application server, which in turn communicates with its finance module and its sales and distribution module.

The clients send TCP/IP requests through Tuxedo /WS, which communicates with the application server. Tuxedo consolidates these client connections and routes the requests to application objects on the middle-tier application server.

The middle-tier application objects work with an Order Management API to handle the requests in one of two ways:

1. If the request requires SAP data, an application object sends the request to the SAP API. The request is translated to text—creating an RFC that SAP can work with—and then sent to the Order Management server to access SAP data or, for example, to place an order.

2. If the request requires data held in the application server's local Oracle database, an application object invokes SQL requests via the local data API. The data stored in the local Oracle database includes the most recent product and pricing information as well as security data and messages for the clients.

When the Order Management server receives an RFC, it invokes custom ABAP/4 procedures to retrieve or enter data in SAP. In this way, AppleOrder Global acts as a front-end system for SAP to provide the following benefits to Apple and its resellers:

■ It supports a large network of resellers without adding a significant load to the SAP systems. Benchmarks showed that direct connections from Apple resellers to the SAP system would overload it. The AppleOrder Global 3-tier architecture lets Tuxedo handle the reseller network and offload the SAP systems.

■ It improves response system time for the resellers. It funnels client connections for better performance. It also caches functions in the front-end—like product and pricing information.

■ It provides resellers with tailored user interfaces.

Tier 1: The Client

Each authorized reseller and service provider runs the AppleOrder Global client on a Macintosh (see Figure 7-3). When a user logs in, AppleOrder Global first ensures that the client's local data cache is synchronized with the most recent data available. This cache is primarily product information, which the client downloads from the application server's Oracle database.

After logging in, the client also retrieves any messages waiting for it in the system's Message Board. These messages include notifications sent out by Apple, such as announcements of new product releases and updates, technical bulletins, and

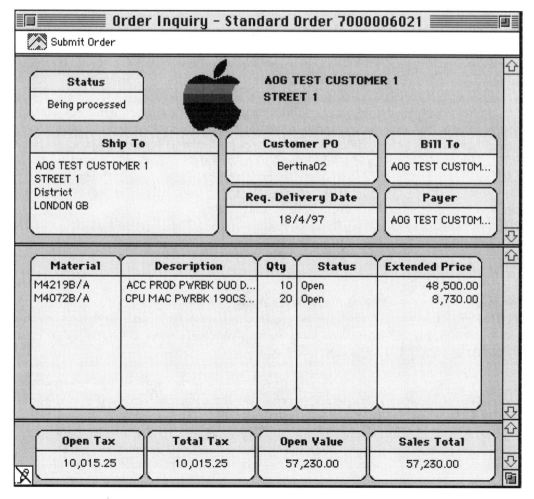

Figure 7-3. AppleOrder Global Client GUI.

service information. SAP also generates messages—for example, to inform resellers when orders ship. SAP generates these messages every 15 minutes.

Resellers can, of course, create orders on-line—or they can prepare the orders off-line against the local cache. Today, all pricing is done on-line to ensure that it is the most current information available. But this will have to change because the existing U.S. system supports off-line pricing. So, the developers will have to modify AppleOrder Global to support this feature before the U.S. rollout.

When resellers are on-line, they have access to a large volume of useful information—including order status, product prices, product availability, and invoice and accounting information. Product and partner information is cached on the client, so resellers have access to this information even when they are off-line.

To create the user interface, the developers first evaluated the GUIs on all of Apple's existing electronic ordering systems. They chose the one they considered to be the best as their starting point for AppleOrder Global—the winning GUI came from the Pacific Region's electronic ordering system.

The client is completely object-oriented. For example, the order form is associated with a local order object. These client-resident application objects communicate with either the local client data cache or the middleware API to send Tuxedo service calls to the application server. An Order Management API handles the routing. Note that Apple uses layers of APIs to insulate the various components of the system from each other and from the infrastructure products they use. This lets them change and add new components of the architecture more easily.

Tier 2: The Server Side

The Macintosh clients communicate—via Tuxedo /WS—with the AppleOrder Global application server, where the bulk of application services reside. In designing this middle tier, Apple again took a modular approach: it uses a variety of APIs to separate the functional layers (see Figure 7-4).

Tuxedo routes the incoming requests to one of about 30 application objects. The application objects provide specific services—such as *insert_order*, *get_order*, and inquiry functions—as well as management services. The application objects run in Tuxedo server classes. Tuxedo runs multiple instances of each Tuxedo server class—the exact number varies depending on the expected usage of the service calls in a particular Tuxedo server class. Each Tuxedo server class has its own queue.

Depending on the request, these objects then work with an Order Management API to either access the SAP system or the local Oracle database. To interface with

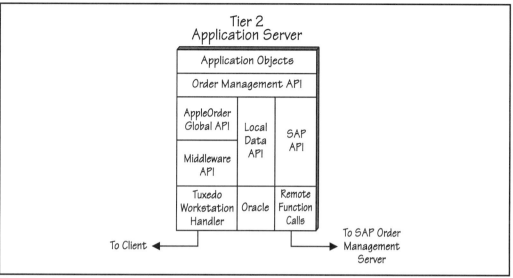

Figure 7-4. Logical Layers of AppleOrder Global's Middle Tier.

SAP—for example, to place an order—the application follows these steps in the middle-tier:

1. The Tuxedo service call invokes the *Order* application object to insert an order.

2. The Order object triggers a call through the SAP API. It translates the message structure into the text format SAP expects and then invokes an RFC.

3. The message is sent via the RFC to the Order Management server, where a custom ABAP/4 routine is invoked. The ABAP/4 routine accesses SAP and inserts the order.

4. A message is returned to notify the client of the order completion.

Application objects can also interface with the local data API, which then invokes SQL calls to read the replicated data from the local Oracle database. The middle-tier Oracle database is refreshed by the SAP system every two hours. By replicating the product information on the application server, AppleOrder Global provides resellers high-performance access to this important data.

The middle tier runs on an RS/6000 under AIX. In anticipation of the increased user loads, the single-processor server was loaded with 768 MB of RAM and 86 GB of disk space. It must store the continually refreshed reference data, security data, and client messages. If the server fails, Apple uses its test server as a backup. Resellers can also continue to work off-line, submitting the orders when Apple restores the system. As AppleOrder Global expands, it is likely that additional RS/6000 application servers will be brought in. Apple may then use IBM's HACMP—High-availability Cluster Multiprocessing—to provide failover support for the AIX servers.

Tier 3: The SAP System

Apple uses many of SAP's packages—including finance, accounting, and sales and distribution. AppleOrder Global only has to access two of these: the finance module and the sales and distribution module. This data resides in Oracle databases. Apple has standardized on Oracle to provide a consistent architecture, cut costs, make systems management easier, and leverage skills. Apple transferred data from their legacy systems to the SAP R/3 region by region. (You'll remember that AppleOrder Global's rollout was synchronized with this migration plan.) Eventually, all Apple data will reside in the SAP system, and the legacy systems will be retired.

The SAP software runs across ten clustered RS/6000 servers in Apple's data center. One of the servers in the SAP R/3 cluster is the *Order Management* server; the AppleOrder Global application server communicates with this server. The Order Management server acts as a client to SAP, which has its own 3-tier architecture. It provides access to the data handled by the finance module and the sales and distribution module. Like the application server, this RS/6000 also runs AIX and has two processors with 1 GB of RAM and 13.2 GB of disk space each. As more regions are ported to SAP, additional back-end servers will be added to provide support for increased numbers of AppleOrder Global resellers.

Security and System Management

In a sense, AppleOrder Global acts as a firewall that separates the Apple resellers from the internal corporate network. To access the AppleOrder Global system, clients log in to: 1) the dedicated network, 2) Tuxedo, and 3) AppleOrder Global, which accesses the middle-tier Oracle database to validate the user. If the log-in is successful, the user gains access only to the AppleOrder Global application server. The entire system is monitored in the data center using NetView.

THE PROJECT

The client and database portions of the project were a given. We wanted to maintain the same client interface from the previous system. And, obviously, SAP was the third tier. But we had to architect the middle tier.

— *Dean Rally*

The AppleOrder Global development team had a very tight schedule and shifting requirements—a situation that is challenging, but seems to be becoming increasingly common. Apple began investigating AppleOrder Global in mid-1995, began development in mid-1996, and put it into production at the beginning of 1997 (see the next Details box). The initial target production rollout date for AppleOrder Global was September 1996, to coincide with the migration date of the European region to SAP. This was a good initial rollout location for the project—Europe had the fewest requirements for the system, so a Phase 1 release there made sense. The developers missed this deadline by only a month—they were ready in October. But in the meantime, Apple had decided to delay the rollout of SAP in Europe. The new target region for AppleOrder Global's initial rollout was changed to Canada. The developers went back to work to make the additional enhancements that were required for a Canadian rollout.

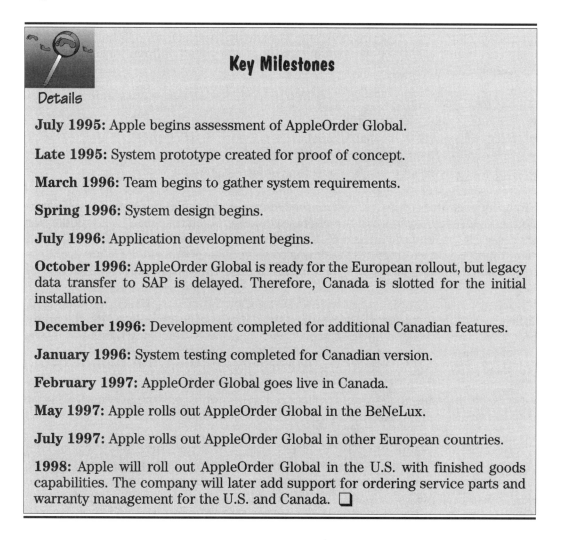

Key Milestones

Details

July 1995: Apple begins assessment of AppleOrder Global.

Late 1995: System prototype created for proof of concept.

March 1996: Team begins to gather system requirements.

Spring 1996: System design begins.

July 1996: Application development begins.

October 1996: AppleOrder Global is ready for the European rollout, but legacy data transfer to SAP is delayed. Therefore, Canada is slotted for the initial installation.

December 1996: Development completed for additional Canadian features.

January 1996: System testing completed for Canadian version.

February 1997: AppleOrder Global goes live in Canada.

May 1997: Apple rolls out AppleOrder Global in the BeNeLux.

July 1997: Apple rolls out AppleOrder Global in other European countries.

1998: Apple will roll out AppleOrder Global in the U.S. with finished goods capabilities. The company will later add support for ordering service parts and warranty management for the U.S. and Canada. ❏

To get a head start in creating AppleOrder Global, the developers leveraged the designs of the existing electronic ordering systems. The project also got a boost from IT Design, the consulting company Apple selected to develop the application. IT Design had developed the Pacific Region's existing electronic ordering system. This meant that IT Design thoroughly understood the application requirements. Its developers also had considerable experience working with the project's key technologies—including object-oriented design and development, the Macintosh platform, SAP R/3, and Tuxedo. As a result, Apple was able to quickly deliver AppleOrder Global to the resellers.

Design

In July 1995, a small group of people started to assess the requirements for an upgraded electronic ordering system. Obviously, AppleOrder Global needed to match the functionality of the existing systems. They also defined these objectives for the new application:

- Improve system response time.
- Add additional user features.
- Base the system on reusable objects.
- Use open systems to be more cost-effective.
- Ensure the system could scale to thousands of users.

From the very start of the project, three aspects of AppleOrder Global's configuration were already a given: 1) the clients would be Macintoshes, 2) the middle-tier database had to be Oracle, and 3) the corporate information system was SAP R3 running on UNIX. So their next task was to solve this pivotal riddle: What architecture would let them use these technologies to meet their objectives?

They considered simply using the SAP system, but they were concerned about its ability to handle the scale of the application. They also contemplated downloading SAP data to an Oracle application server each night and then using batch processes to enter the resulting orders into SAP. This scenario wouldn't have provided real-time processing for users. Also, it could have left Apple with synchronization problems between the Oracle database and SAP. So this concept was rejected. A 3-tier solution using a TP Monitor emerged as the only feasible alternative. 3-tier could provide both improved response times and better scalability.

After evaluating various open TP Monitors, they decided on Tuxedo—it was proven at other production sites, and IT Design had experience working with it. The developers were initially concerned about whether the path-lengths through the system would impact user response times. After all, an order has to come from the client network, through the middle-tier server, and then into the SAP multilayered

system. But they have found that Tuxedo greatly streamlines the client connections, and the time to move requests through the Tuxedo services is almost immeasurable.

Once the developers defined the architecture and the remaining system components, they had IT Design create a prototype as a proof of concept. The prototype was successful, so development got underway.

Development

We wanted the benefits of a modular architecture, where services were designed without any dependency. This allowed us to develop the application using people skilled in different areas; they didn't have to know about the complex interdependency of the components.

— *Oisín Clarke, Senior Engineer*
IT Design Ireland

Once Apple management agreed to the project, IT Design began to build the system. A small group of developers began to gather specific user requirements—an ongoing process as Apple rolls out the system to new regions. They had to match the high-level application requirements with the functionality that the SAP system could support. To do this, they had to understand how Apple was planning to use SAP.

The developers used the Pacific Region's ordering system—called ARC—as the basis for their design. Because ARC's user interface was object-oriented, adding /WS to it turned out to be a straightforward exercise.

The developers then needed to figure out how to replace ARC's middleware. They wanted to reap the benefits of a modular architecture. They felt that this would let them more easily add new functionality, reuse components, and swap out pieces if necessary. To do this, they made liberal use of custom APIs and interface layers. As a result, the developers of the application objects aren't required to know anything about Tuxedo.

The entire application was developed with a relatively small team of six people. The architecture they had defined let the developers specialize in the areas of their particular expertise:

■ One or two developers (this varied) worked on modifying the user interface.

■ One developer worked on implementing Tuxedo functionality in both the client and application server.

■ Two developers wrote the C++ application objects and SQL for accessing the local Oracle database on the application server. The C++ application objects were developed using IBM's xlC compiler.

The developers quickly realized that the most complicated part of the development effort was the interface to the SAP system (see the next Details box). They had to create custom routines—written in SAP's ABAP/4 programming language—that SAP RFCs could invoke. So, they decided to hire an SAP consultant to develop the ABAP/4 APIs.

Oisin Clarke of IT Design Ireland—who was the project's lead architect—integrated the system components throughout the development process. He relied on his previous design specifications, revising them as appropriate whenever interface issues emerged.

A New GUI That Taps SAP

Details

AppleOrder Global's development team wanted to create an efficient and scalable system with a simple GUI. At the same time, they wanted to be fairly compatible with SAP's business process design to reduce the amount of code they needed in the middle tier. To accomplish this, they needed to develop custom procedures in SAP's ABAP/4 programming language that RFCs could then invoke. These procedures mimic functionality built into SAP screens. This layer of indirection allows the developers to create an easier-to-use custom GUI for the resellers while interacting with SAP on the back end.

Writing the custom procedures proved to be complicated, so the developers brought in an experienced SAP consultant for the job. The consultant used R3's development environment, which only provides support for text data types in RFC communications. As a result, they also had to develop code for converting the typed Tuxedo message content to text.

AppleOrder Global's RFCs and custom ABAP/4 routines now provide all the necessary functionality to the client. However, if SAP were to significantly modify its current interface in a new release, the developers could end up rewriting the custom ABAP/4 APIs. ❑

Naturally, AppleOrder Global—being an international system—is multilingual. Resellers can use English, French, German, or Spanish versions. Apple hired an outside company to handle these translations.

Testing and Documentation

Throughout the development cycle, IT Design worked on system integration testing and the project documentation. IT Design and Apple also worked together as a team to conduct comprehensive testing to ensure that the system worked as expected with SAP. In addition, the two companies conducted user acceptance testing to ensure that AppleOrder Global would meet reseller needs. IT Design developed a user manual for the system.

Going Into Production

Before Apple rolled out AppleOrder Global to its Canadian resellers, it sent information to them explaining the company's shift to SAP. Apple also required that resellers sign and return an agreement before they received the AppleOrder Global client software. When the SAP data was converted from the legacy systems, Apple mailed the resellers who had responded a CD-ROM with the upgraded electronic ordering application.

On February 10, 1997, the existing Canadian system was discontinued, and AppleOrder Global was brought up. All electronic ordering now must be done using AppleOrder Global—the data is no longer accessible through the previous system. The European rollout is very similar to Canada's. Most European resellers never had access to electronic ordering before. So Apple added a one-day training course for resellers and service providers. The first European installation went on-line on May 12, 1997.

In Production

A Help Desk located in Napa, California, handles all system-support phone calls from Canadian resellers. European users can contact Apple Assistance Centers, which are located throughout Europe. If the Assistance Center is unable to handle a problem, they forward the call to Napa. Depending on the nature of the problem, Help Desk staff members either notify IT Design or internal Apple folks. A problem-tracking software program—called *Espresso*—logs each call as a ticket and records the escalation of the problem. This not only improves customer service in handling problems but also keeps resellers and service providers well-informed.

THE OUTCOME

Canadian reseller reaction to the system has been positive. AppleOrder Global offers them better response times and an improved GUI—not to mention the required access to the SAP data. The application is also being successfully received in Europe.

From a corporate standpoint, the system saves Apple money by reducing administrative tasks and data entry errors. The system also processes orders more quickly. And Apple is experiencing constantly decreasing costs—they will have a single system to manage instead of five.

THE FUTURE

Apple is thinking about extending AppleOrder Global with a Java client—the Java applets would communicate with the application server via BEA's Jolt. This would let resellers use any type of client. By making AppleOrder Global available through the Internet, any customer—such as an individual, a school, or a business—could place orders for Macintoshes directly with Apple. The system's 3-tier architecture gives Apple the opportunity to expand AppleOrder Global to meet this goal—or any number of future needs.

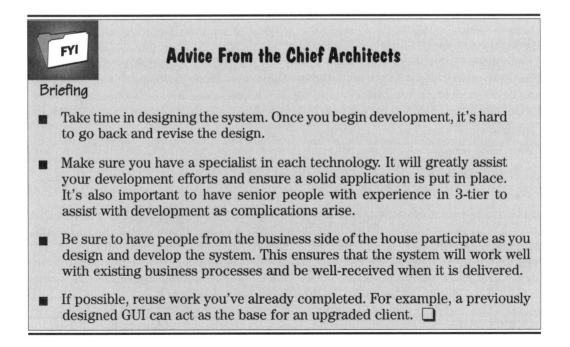

FYI   Advice From the Chief Architects

Briefing

- Take time in designing the system. Once you begin development, it's hard to go back and revise the design.

- Make sure you have a specialist in each technology. It will greatly assist your development efforts and ensure a solid application is put in place. It's also important to have senior people with experience in 3-tier to assist with development as complications arise.

- Be sure to have people from the business side of the house participate as you design and develop the system. This ensures that the system will work well with existing business processes and be well-received when it is delivered.

- If possible, reuse work you've already completed. For example, a previously designed GUI can act as the base for an upgraded client. ❑

Chapter 8

MCI: A Client/Server Framework for Data Services

Why recreate an infrastructure when you can buy one? Our client/server framework now lets us focus our efforts on the value-added portion of an application.

— Victor Koliczew
Senior Member, Technical Staff
MCI Network Services Engineering

With the demand for data services growing at a rapid pace, telecommunications companies can gain a competitive edge by providing their commercial customers with service perks. MCI Telecommunications Corporation is doing just that—it delivers a transaction monitoring system to make its data service more attractive than competing products.

The *Customer Transaction Monitoring System (CTMS)* puts MCI's large commercial customers in the driver's seat—well, maybe the front passenger seat—to ensure that all is well with the network that handles their mission-critical transactions. CTMS gives these customers a window from which they observe their transactions as they flow through the MCI data network. This creates a partnership between MCI and its largest customers. They can work together to make sure the network provides the highest quality of service.

THE APPLICATION

MCI's *Transaction Transport Service* provides a communications network for mission-critical information, such as credit card transactions. It is primarily used by banks and other financial institutions. The service is typically sold as a package; MCI also provides voice telephony services for these customers. Obviously, MCI monitors its transaction transport network as a whole. But, CTMS lets MCI's commercial customers monitor their *own* transactions; it's as if they have a private network. It lets customers do the following:

- *View real-time transaction statistics*. The CTMS client runs on a PC at the customer's site. The client polls the CTMS server for transaction statistics. Customers can view these statistics in multiple windows. This lets them monitor all their transactions at once, or focus on specific transactions. For example, a customer may want to know the volume of transactions handled by a particular 800 number over the weekend.

- *Track network performance*. For example, a customer can monitor a destination port to look for spikes in transaction traffic during a ten-minute period.

- *Receive notifications via alarms when problems occur.* CTMS comes with standard system alarms that notify customers when the network or the CTMS application experiences problems. Customers can also define their own alarms to monitor the network for particular events. For example, they can create an alarm to notify them if too many transactions fail over a set period of time.

In effect, CTMS turns MCI customers into consumer watchdogs for the services they receive. It gives them greater control over the network their business depends on. Although MCI remains responsible for addressing any network problems, customers can ensure that the network performance is acceptable—and they can encourage MCI to solve network issues that affect their transactions. Because MCI's customers are more aware of what is happening with their network traffic, they have the ability to contact their own customer base before a network problem starts to affect their business.

THE CTMS 3-TIERED ARCHITECTURE

CTMS acts as the seed for a number of other projects that require the same type of framework.

— *Victor Koliczew*

CTMS is the first in a series of MCI applications built on a new 3-tier platform that is designed to reliably support substantial transaction volumes. CTMS already handles 90 transactions per second—or 324,000 transactions per hour. This transaction volume doesn't come from its GUI clients—their requests are fairly light. Instead, the majority of transactions originate from software that gathers network statistics.

How CTMS Works

To understand how CTMS works, you need to understand not only how transactions flow through the Transaction Transport Data Service, but also how CTMS interacts with it. We've illustrated this in Figure 8-1. Here's an example of how a credit card transaction uses the network:

1. The transaction begins when someone uses a credit card to purchase an item. A store employee swipes the card through a card-reader. This results in a call to one of the credit card issuer's 800 numbers at MCI.

2. The transaction travels over the public telephone network until it enters a node in MCI's Transaction Transport Network.

3. From there, the transaction moves on to the credit card issuer, where it is approved or denied.

Now, let's look at how CTMS gathers information about this transaction as it moves through the MCI network:

1. MCI maintains two *Statistics Gathering* servers on the Transaction Transport Network to collect information about transactions on behalf of the billing and accounting systems. This information includes details on each transaction—such as network traversal time and path taken.

2. In addition to gathering data for billing and accounting, the servers also forward this data to a local CTMS process, called the *Transformation Client*.

3. The Transformation Client converts the information into CTMS format, packages the statistics into a Tuxedo message, and then sends it over an Ethernet LAN to the CTMS server.

4. The CTMS server maintains two versions of the data: one is cached in memory, another is stored in an Oracle database. Customers use the CTMS client to access this information.

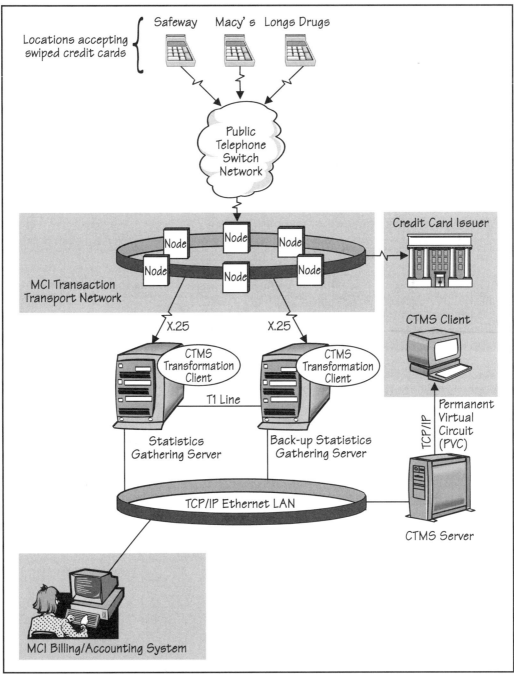

Figure 8-1. Physical Diagram of MCI's Transaction Transport Network and CTMS.

An Overview of the CTMS Logical Tiers

The logical tiers of CTMS are composed of the following (see Figure 8-2):

- *Tier 1* includes three types of clients. Two are GUI clients; the third is the GUI-less Transformation Client software that runs in the Statistics Gathering servers.

- *Tier 2* consists of the CTMS software services that record the information sent from the Transformation Client and answer requests from the CTMS clients. Tuxedo manages these services and the interfaces between the tiers.

- *Tier 3* is an Oracle database. It maintains statistics for a 48-hour period.

The CTMS software services, Tuxedo, and the Oracle database run on a Sun SPARC 20 server.

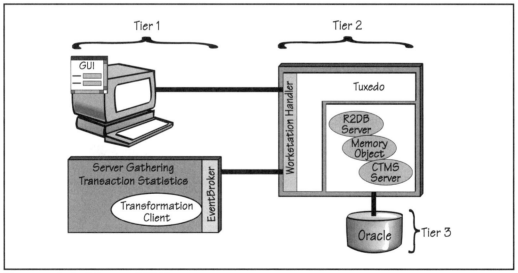

Figure 8-2. Logical Diagram of CTMS.

Tier 1: The Clients

The system has three kinds of clients: 1) a CTMS client for MCI's Transaction Transport Service customers, 2) a modified version of the CTMS client that the network administrators use, and 3) the CTMS Transformation Client.

The CTMS Client for MCI Customers

The CTMS client lets MCI customers monitor their transactions (see Figure 8-3). The client is typically connected to MCI via a permanent virtual circuit (PVC). It communicates with the CTMS server through Tuxedo /WS.

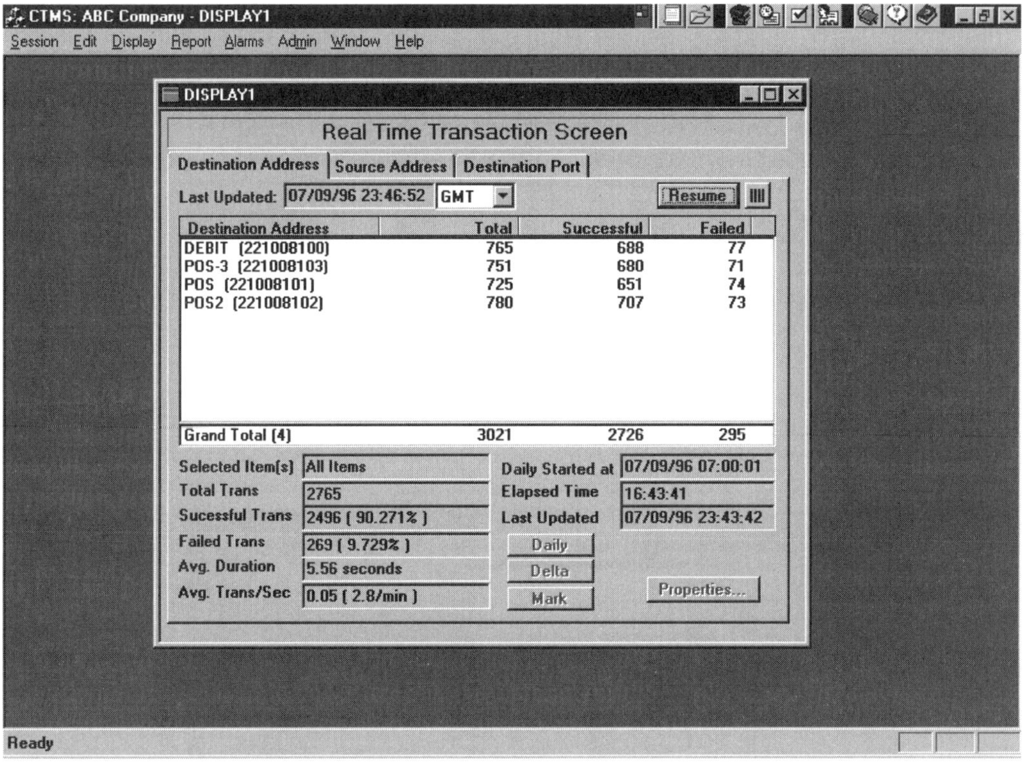

Figure 8-3. Viewing Transaction Statistics With the CTMS Client.

The client polls the CTMS server every 30 seconds—or at a user-defined interval—to collect statistics. The CTMS server returns the statistics that match the client's profile (i.e., customers can only view their own statistics). Users can also customize the client to change screens and views. The CTMS client contains built-in alarms to warn users if the server goes down or if there are problems with the network. Customers can also set custom alarms. All of the alarms are logged in a PC file on the client so that users can review anomalies at any time.

The client was written in C++ and developed using the Microsoft Development Studio and Foundation Classes 4.0. The design team hadn't worked with objects before, but thought it would save development time—not to mention the added bonus of gaining experience in working with cutting-edge technology.

The Administrator's Client

MCI network administrators also monitor the data network's transactions using CTMS. The network administrator's GUI is a modified version of the standard CTMS client. It extends the management of the network by letting operators at the MCI control center look at the transaction statistics of any customer or node. Operators can also initiate CTMS administrative transactions, such as adding a user or provisioning a customer.

The Transformation Client

A copy of the Transformation Client resides on both the primary and back-up Statistics Gathering servers (see the next Details box). Its job is to grab statistics, transform them into CTMS transactions, and then send them to the CTMS server via Tuxedo /WS service calls. The Transformation Client was coded in C. It is called a "client" because it invokes services. However, it has no GUI.

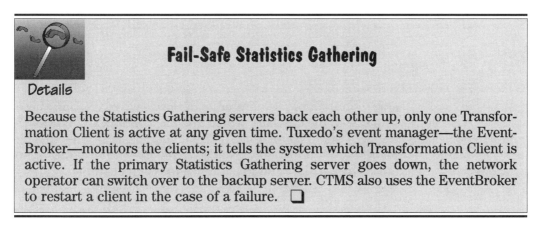

Fail-Safe Statistics Gathering

Details

Because the Statistics Gathering servers back each other up, only one Transformation Client is active at any given time. Tuxedo's event manager—the Event-Broker—monitors the clients; it tells the system which Transformation Client is active. If the primary Statistics Gathering server goes down, the network operator can switch over to the backup server. CTMS also uses the EventBroker to restart a client in the case of a failure. ☐

Tier 2: The Server Side

The second tier of CTMS consists of two Tuxedo server classes and a special component that provides an in-memory 24-hour information cache, called the *Memory Object*. Here is what they each do:

■ **The R2DB (record-to-database) server class** receives the statistical data from the Transformation Client, updates the Memory Object data, and stores the data in the database. It's an extremely active server; the data network generates more than 90 transactions per second. MCI expects this data traffic to double this year as they enlist new customers for the service.

■ ***The CTMS server class*** handles requests from the user client for statistics. The CTMS server class consists of about 50 services, which were developed in C. When clients request an update of their statistics—remember that they typically poll the server every 30 seconds—the CTMS server class then goes to the Memory Object to retrieve the most recent statistical information. Because the Memory Object only keeps information for a 24-hour period, the CTMS server must access the Oracle database to create reports that involve longer periods.

■ ***The Memory Object*** provides clients with instant response time by managing an in-memory cache of the most recent data. The CTMS server does not have to query the database each time a client polls for statistics. To keep it to a manageable size, the data in the Memory Object is cleared daily.

Almost all the client/server communication in the CTMS application is synchronous. Only the reporting service breaks this rule; its long report takes several minutes to generate, so CTMS uses file transfers to ship the results to clients when they are ready.

Tier 3: The Database

Transaction statistics are continuously generated at a very fast rate. If all these statistics were stored and saved, the database would grow astronomically. So CTMS maintains 48 hours' worth of statistics in a 4-GB Oracle database. It does this by using a database function that automatically truncates the size of the tables. The database has 29 common tables—plus additional tables for each customer.

Security

To enforce the privacy of the data, MCI's customers must follow a number of steps to view their CTMS statistics. The user logs in to the system by entering a user log-on, password, and unique company identifier. This information is sent to the CTMS server for authorization. The company identifier is used to look up a profile that defines the data a customer can access.

MCI network managers, on the other hand, can look at transaction statistics for any customer—they use a profile that authorizes access to all data.

System Management

CTMS is monitored via Tuxedo's Log Manager. The logs are displayed in real time and are also posted in a log file. If the application experiences problems, operators can access the log messages from any authorized device. If additional management is needed in the future, MCI's Network Control Center will monitor the application from its network management console. Events can be routed to the console using SNMP.

THE PROJECT

The CTMS development team received the green light for the project in September 1995. A very important MCI customer needed the transaction monitoring capability quickly; the customer was very disenchanted with the existing third-party system. Once the project got rolling, the customer became impressed with the development team's plans. As a result of the customer's enthusiasm, MCI fully funded the in-house development project.

The five-member development team was asked to deliver CTMS to the customer by May 1, 1996—just nine months later. Incredibly, they met the date—delivering a product that satisfied the customer's needs and cost only 25% of the third-party system's price tag (see the next Details box).

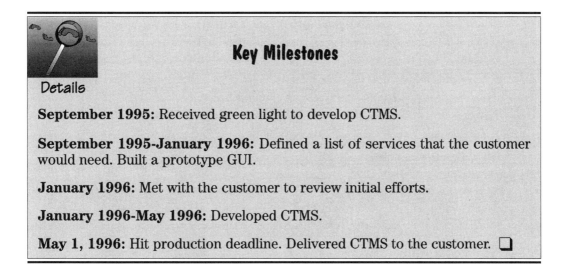

Key Milestones

Details

September 1995: Received green light to develop CTMS.

September 1995-January 1996: Defined a list of services that the customer would need. Built a prototype GUI.

January 1996: Met with the customer to review initial efforts.

January 1996-May 1996: Developed CTMS.

May 1, 1996: Hit production deadline. Delivered CTMS to the customer. ❑

Design

MCI's development team was, of course, very savvy when it came to networking—but they didn't have much experience building applications or working within a 3-tier framework. To solve this, they started learning about client/server methodologies, C++, and database technology.

At the beginning of the project, software architect Victor Koliczew showed the team a 3-tier application framework design he had developed (see the next Details box). He also proposed an application design for CTMS that included the core application modules: the CTMS server, the R2DB server, the Transformation Client, and the user interface. This "straw man" design also outlined the relationships between the components and identified the features he expected them to provide.

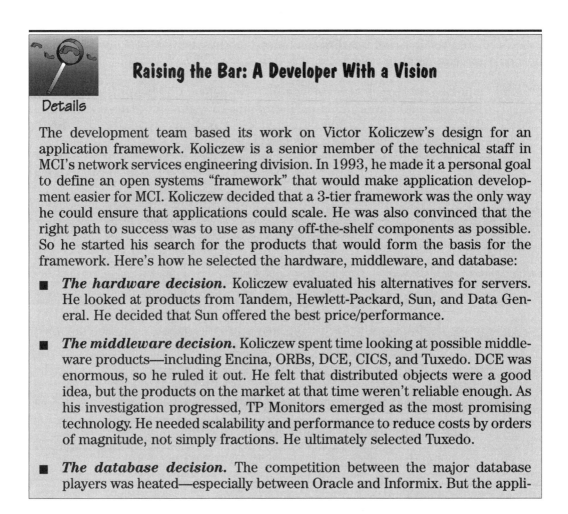

Raising the Bar: A Developer With a Vision

Details

The development team based its work on Victor Koliczew's design for an application framework. Koliczew is a senior member of the technical staff in MCI's network services engineering division. In 1993, he made it a personal goal to define an open systems "framework" that would make application development easier for MCI. Koliczew decided that a 3-tier framework was the only way he could ensure that applications could scale. He was also convinced that the right path to success was to use as many off-the-shelf components as possible. So he started his search for the products that would form the basis for the framework. Here's how he selected the hardware, middleware, and database:

- **The hardware decision.** Koliczew evaluated his alternatives for servers. He looked at products from Tandem, Hewlett-Packard, Sun, and Data General. He decided that Sun offered the best price/performance.

- **The middleware decision.** Koliczew spent time looking at possible middleware products—including Encina, ORBs, DCE, CICS, and Tuxedo. DCE was enormous, so he ruled it out. He felt that distributed objects were a good idea, but the products on the market at that time weren't reliable enough. As his investigation progressed, TP Monitors emerged as the most promising technology. He needed scalability and performance to reduce costs by orders of magnitude, not simply fractions. He ultimately selected Tuxedo.

- **The database decision.** The competition between the major database players was heated—especially between Oracle and Informix. But the applications that would use the framework didn't require leading-edge database technology—they simply needed a database that was reliable, stable, efficient, and fast. Koliczew picked Oracle.

In the spring of 1995, Koliczew was given permission to create a prototype for his framework. MCI provided the equipment—including a SPARCserver, sufficient disk for storage, and a tape backup system. At the same time, the existing 2-tier network transaction monitoring application was experiencing difficulties. As the pressure to solve its problems intensified, the mockup began to emerge as a possible platform for a new version of the application. In September, Koliczew received the green light to develop the CTMS system based on his prototype. ❏

Development

Analyze a little, design a little, code a little, test a little.

> — *Victor Koliczew*
> *(from the Booch methodology)*

The team adopted the development approach of "analyze a little, design a little, code a little, test a little." This concept came out of Grady Booch's object-oriented design methodology. Even though the CTMS middle tier wasn't object-oriented, this iterative approach allowed them to determine if they were on the right track. The team would analyze a requirement, create a design for the feature, code it using rapid prototyping techniques, and then get quick feedback. Tools such as Independence Technology's *iTRAN* code generator—later acquired by BEA and now called *BEA Builder*—assisted the team in rapidly developing system code. With iTRAN, the team created the system without ever becoming Tuxedo programming experts.

The developers reaped many benefits from working in a small team. Each developer was assigned a specific part of the project (see the next Details box). They took care of issues as they arose through constant communication, and held a more formal meeting every day. Any issues, doubts, or questions were quickly addressed in this meeting. The small size of the team simplified the job of defining the client/server interfaces. They worked together on the designs until they were in unanimous agreement.

Generally, the team adhered closely to their original architecture. If a design didn't comply with it, they carefully examined all the alternatives before modifying the framework's design. However, the developers made a few modifications to the system's initial design along the way:

- The first GUI was built for Windows 3.1, but then Windows 95 appeared on the scene. Even though the operating system was new, they decided to migrate the client to Windows 95 to extend the client's life.

- They decided to migrate from version 2.0 to version 4.0 of the Microsoft Foundation Classes—a move that was completed easily.

- When CTMS was first designed, Tuxedo didn't support multithreading. GUI windows need multiple threads to behave asynchronously. With the addition of multithreading in Tuxedo—and consequently in CTMS—the management of these windows was greatly simplified.

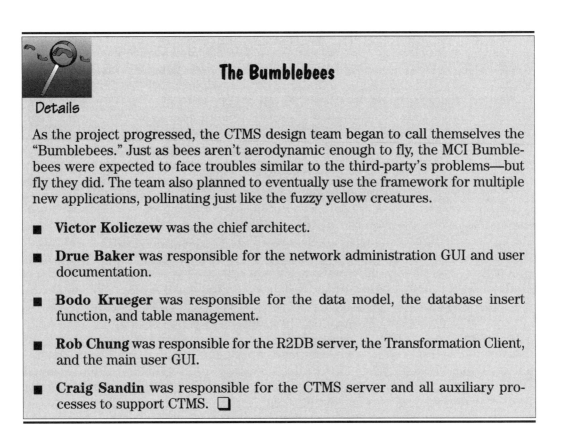

The Bumblebees

Details

As the project progressed, the CTMS design team began to call themselves the "Bumblebees." Just as bees aren't aerodynamic enough to fly, the MCI Bumblebees were expected to face troubles similar to the third-party's problems—but fly they did. The team also planned to eventually use the framework for multiple new applications, pollinating just like the fuzzy yellow creatures.

- **Victor Koliczew** was the chief architect.

- **Drue Baker** was responsible for the network administration GUI and user documentation.

- **Bodo Krueger** was responsible for the data model, the database insert function, and table management.

- **Rob Chung** was responsible for the R2DB server, the Transformation Client, and the main user GUI.

- **Craig Sandin** was responsible for the CTMS server and all auxiliary processes to support CTMS. ❑

Testing

Testing occurred throughout the project cycle. The developers used a SPARC 20 as a test system. Because they continuously integrated system components as they were built, testing ran from mid-February until the project's completion in May.

The team created a simulator to drive the system. They fed it real statistics from the MCI network servers to mimic the functionality of the Statistics Gathering client. The simulator also measured the performance of the system. CTMS didn't need to support 150 tps initially—this is close to 13 million transactions a day. However, they made it their target performance design-point to allow for future expansion. The team met this goal by fine-tuning Oracle and the operating system, and making slight adjustments to the Tuxedo services and Memory Object for greater efficiency. They now use the test system for product development and to troubleshoot bugs.

Going Into Production

In May 1996, the developers decided that the system was ready. They then released a production-level version of the product to that important MCI customer. The customer tested the system thoroughly, and CTMS completed all the tests successfully. They continued to test CTMS for a month before going live in June. MCI set up an FTP site to issue client code changes. This made it very easy for the team to quickly provide fixes to the customer when a bug was discovered. But the bugs they found were minor—the developers typically required only a few hours to fix them.

MCI also installed CTMS in its network control center in Cary, North Carolina. It turned out to be more complicated to train the network control staff than to train customers. From the network staff's point of view, some key features of the application were missing. The CTMS marketing department had focused on the requirements of MCI's customers. As a result, no requirements were gathered from the network administrators. So, it was not surprising that the control center staff immediately asked for more functionality. The developers quickly added the additional administrative features that the control center requested. Now the network control center uses CTMS to monitor and control the entire transaction transport network. CTMS provides the control center staff with greater detail about transactions running over the network. This additional view into their network lets them examine the transaction performance for a single customer or node.

In Production

The team continues to use its FTP site to deliver new versions of the client to CTMS customers and the network control center. The good news is that no bugs were found in CTMS after its first two months in production; these updates simply add new features.

THE OUTCOME

From a business standpoint, the CTMS developers solved a difficult customer relations problem for MCI. They also gave the telecommunications company a major feature to differentiate itself when selling its transaction transport services to new customers. And the staff at the network control center is very pleased with CTMS because it makes their jobs easier; it allows them to be more responsive to their customers. All of the customer feedback has been extremely positive. In fact, that important first customer told the team that they had never seen anything like CTMS and that it provides them with everything they wanted, and more!

THE FUTURE

CTMS forms the basis for a number of other projects that are being built using the same framework. The developers are now working on two new systems: 1) a billing system, and 2) a validation manager for authorizing user access to MCI's Tymnet data packet network. Both of these projects will replace existing systems. Victor Koliczew's vision has become a reality—the CTMS framework is a proven platform for quickly building new MCI applications.

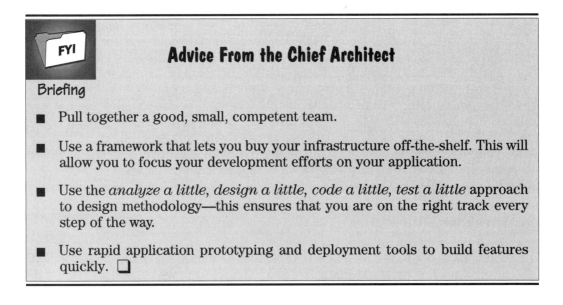

FYI

Advice From the Chief Architect

Briefing

- Pull together a good, small, competent team.

- Use a framework that lets you buy your infrastructure off-the-shelf. This will allow you to focus your development efforts on your application.

- Use the *analyze a little, design a little, code a little, test a little* approach to design methodology—this ensures that you are on the right track every step of the way.

- Use rapid application prototyping and deployment tools to build features quickly. ❏

Chapter 9

3M: Data Management for Enhanced Patient Care

As health care consolidates and hospitals come together under one umbrella organization, the goal of the 3M Healthcare Enterprise Management System was to become a repository for all of the clinical data that a healthcare enterprise could record for a patient.

— *Robert Dupont*
3M Product Development Manager

The healthcare industry has undergone sweeping changes. In the past, a patient with traditional insurance could be treated anywhere; providers of the care then received a fee for their services. With the advent of managed care, healthcare providers receive a predetermined fee for caring for a patient with a specific illness—or even receive a set monthly rate for doing whatever it takes to restore or maintain a person's health. Doing this efficiently and effectively requires the coordinated services of physicians, hospitals, clinics, laboratories, pharmacies, home care providers, and others. As a result, healthcare enterprises now face the daunting task of managing individual patient records across a diverse group of computer systems.

3M Health Information Systems is a software house that is part of the $14.2 billion 3M corporation. It provides a healthcare information system—called the *3M*

Healthcare Enterprise Management System—to address the coordination of medical services across organizations.

THE APPLICATION

The 3M Healthcare Enterprise Management System is a suite of sophisticated 3-tier client/server applications. It is used by a broad variety of organizations, ranging from 200-bed acute care facilities to large multi-facility healthcare organizations. It integrates patients' clinical data from various information systems in a healthcare enterprise. This integration provides on-line access to comprehensive patient information. The system can apply server-based expert logic against the patient data to trigger alarms and notifications about the patient's care. By relying on the 3M system, clinicians—including physicians, nurses, and lab specialists—can improve the quality, ensure consistency, and eliminate the duplication or misuse of the care being provided to patients.

An Integrated Product Suite for Comprehensive Patient Care

The 3M Healthcare Enterprise Management System consists of a group of integrated products. These products store patient records, provide access to the comprehensive patient data, apply logic against the data, and provide clinical decision support about patient treatment through alerts. The system allows healthcare enterprises to accomplish the following:

- Collect and integrate patient clinical data from multiple information systems in a consistent and useful way.

- Create lifetime medical records for each patient across all facilities.

- Provide on-line access to these records.

- Eliminate ambiguities in the information and redundancies in data storage.

- Provide the comprehensive information clinicians need.

The 3M Lifetime Data Repository

The cornerstone of the system is the *3M Lifetime Data Repository,* a database that stores patient records. The database is created by pulling in clinical data from existing information systems. Clinicians also enter data into the repository through the *3M Clinical Workstation Application.* The repository can integrate patient data records from hospital, laboratory, pharmacy, radiology, and admission/discharge/transfer (ADT) systems. Each division in an enterprise can then continue to operate and manage its separate, existing data system while also merging its records with those from other divisions in the repository.

The 3M Healthcare Data Dictionary

Patient data is encoded in the repository using the *3M Healthcare Data Dictionary*. The dictionary ensures that data definitions are consistent and valid; it also lets expert logic be applied against the data. The data dictionary automatically translates the patient data into a universal language the system understands. With 170,000 medical concepts, it's the most comprehensive healthcare data dictionary in the world.

The 3M Master Member Index

To manage the patient records, the Healthcare Enterprise Management System also includes the *3M Master Member Index*. This index associates transmitted records with a patient's permanent identification number. Then it links together all the clinical data records for a patient, including data from previous visits. This provides a comprehensive, lifetime history of the patient's health and care.

The 3M Clinical Workstation Application

Authorized clinicians can use the Windows-based *3M Clinical Workstation Application* to access and update patient data in the system. Alternatively, customers can develop a tailored user interface application.

The 3M Alert Management Software

Customers use the *Alert Management Software* to support clinical decisions by applying rules against data collected in the repository. The software can alert clinicians to adverse drug effects, contradictory treatments, or critical laboratory values (see the next Briefing box).

The Complex Problems That 3M Tackled

3M Health Information Systems began development of these products in January 1994, using a previous patient care system as its foundation. It wanted to deliver an

FYI

Paging All Doctors

Briefing

When customers use the *Alert Management Software*, the expert system's server-based clinical logic applies a series of "what if?" conditions to incoming and existing patient data. An enterprise can develop its own rules to reflect specific policies, procedures, protocols, and new medical knowledge. The expert system then generates alert messages that serve as warnings, reminders, suggestions, evaluations, and other clinical decision support notices.

When alerts are generated, they can be sent to multiple places, such as the repository's permanent record of patient data, a temporary alert review file, a beeper, a fax machine, or to other systems. An alert review file contains alerts generated from all applications.

Alert applications from 3M include *Medication Monitoring Alerts*, *Adverse Drug Event Alerts*, *Critical Laboratory Alerts*, and *Infectious Disease Alerts*. ❏

open UNIX-based system that would provide an enterprise-wide clinical data repository and a master patient index. To provide the real-time performance, high availability, and reliability that such a system requires, it was based on a 3-tier architecture (see the next Briefing box). Here are some examples of the complex problems the system enables 3M Health Information Systems to tackle:

■ *Convert data from existing systems* into the Lifetime Data Repository. This conversion is often a mammoth undertaking. A typical healthcare enterprise can consist of as many as 20 different facilities and organizations, including several hospitals, multiple clinics, and numerous other divisions such as radiology, a laboratory, and a pharmacy.

■ *Ensure that data from different systems is rendered identically* in the Lifetime Data Repository. For example, the database must accurately reflect "myocardial infarction" even when it is referred to as "heart attack" in a data record. To solve this, the 3M system codifies the data, breaking down medical values into concepts that are defined by a numerical concept identifier. This enables server-resident logic to be applied against the data. This codification is another tough job. Many concepts in medicine are very complex and can't be decomposed. Breaking apart the concept of "mad cow disease," for example, into "virus" and its effects on humans fails to represent the disease in its totality.

■ *Supply an interface subsystem* so data that is continuously collected by the existing systems can be transported to the repository in real time. This data collection provides clinicians with a real-time view of the results of patients' most recent visits as well as their lifetime histories.

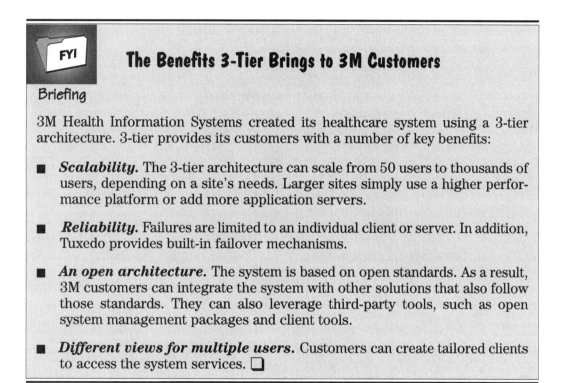

FYI

The Benefits 3-Tier Brings to 3M Customers

Briefing

3M Health Information Systems created its healthcare system using a 3-tier architecture. 3-tier provides its customers with a number of key benefits:

■ *Scalability.* The 3-tier architecture can scale from 50 users to thousands of users, depending on a site's needs. Larger sites simply use a higher performance platform or add more application servers.

■ *Reliability.* Failures are limited to an individual client or server. In addition, Tuxedo provides built-in failover mechanisms.

■ *An open architecture.* The system is based on open standards. As a result, 3M customers can integrate the system with other solutions that also follow those standards. They can also leverage third-party tools, such as open system management packages and client tools.

■ *Different views for multiple users.* Customers can create tailored clients to access the system services. ❑

THE 3-TIERED ARCHITECTURE

We don't feel that we could have built a system capable of meeting our high-end needs without going 3-tier.

— *Mark Scarton*
3M Consulting Engineer

The 3M Healthcare Enterprise Management System collects data from a variety of existing systems and integrates it in its Lifetime Data Repository (see Figure 9-1). This integrated information can then be accessed and updated from the 3M Clinical Workstation, or a custom client. In addition, the Alert Management Software monitors the data to notify clinicians of issues or inconsistencies.

The system supports both LAN and WAN environments. Users can access the system from physician offices and even from home. According to a site's needs, connection bandwidth can range from a 28.8 Kbps modem to a T1 line.

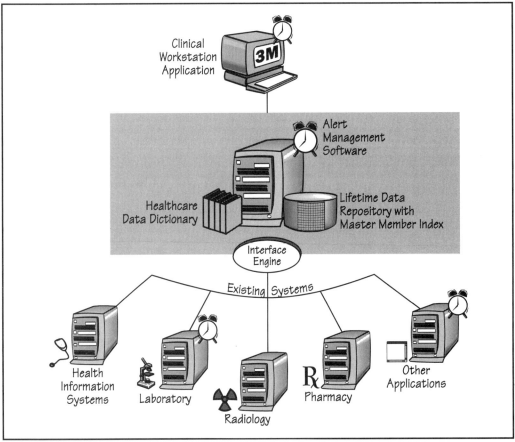

Figure 9-1. Architecture of the 3M Healthcare Enterprise Management System.

How 3M Takes Advantage of its Open Architecture

3M Health Information Systems decided to limit the number of hardware and software systems it runs its software on. This makes testing and validation of new versions of its software more manageable. So, it standardized on Oracle as its database and Tuxedo as its TP Monitor. The software runs on either HP-UX or AIX. 3M Health Information Systems is able to limit its system support while still meeting users' needs by doing the following:

- The 3M system is sold as a complete solution—including the hardware, software, storage, and, if necessary, system management. This "black-box" approach means that most customers don't care about the brand-labels inside.

- The system is grafted into a customer's environment. It interfaces to existing networks and applications—it doesn't replace them. This allows the healthcare organization's departments to function as usual, while taking advantage of the added capability that the 3M suite provides.

An Overview of the 3M Logical Tiers

The logical layers of the 3M system are shown in Figure 9-2. Here is a brief description of what is in each tier:

- *Tier 1* is a multi-layered client based on OLE objects.

- *Tier 2* consists of numerous software services that are managed by Tuxedo. For small sites, the middle tier and the database run on the same machines. In large sites they run on separate machines. At very large sites, they also distribute the middle-tier services across multiple application servers.

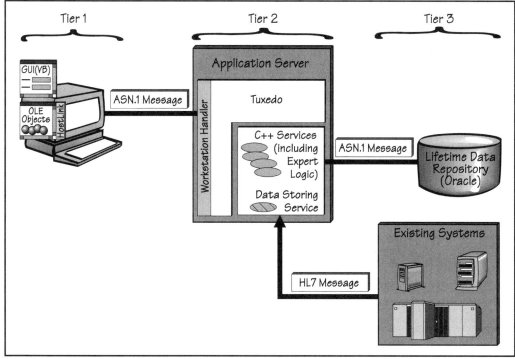

Figure 9-2. Logical Diagram of the System Architecture.

■ **Tier 3** is the Oracle-based Lifetime Data Repository, including the Master Member Index. In addition, the middle tier interfaces with a variety of existing information systems in the healthcare enterprise to create a comprehensive view of all the treatments patients receive.

Tuxedo handles the interfaces between these tiers. Tuxedo receives calls from Tuxedo /WS on the client and then invokes Tuxedo-based services on the application server. The TP Monitor manages client requests and the application's services.

Tier 1: The 3M Client

The 3M client is itself multi-tiered. It is implemented in four layers:

1. **The user interface.** The system's user interface is provided either by the 3M Clinical Workstation Application (see Figure 9-3) or by a custom interface. The Clinical Workstation is a user-friendly, Windows-based GUI. It gives clinicians

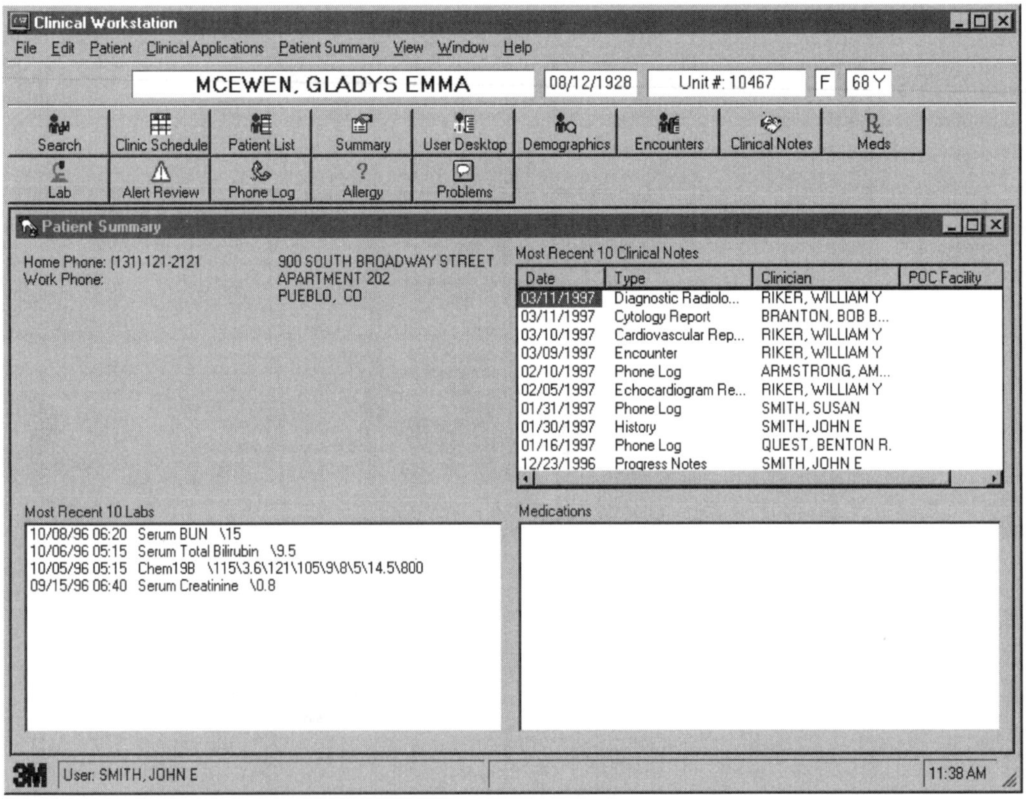

Figure 9-3. A 3M Clinical Workstation Screen.

streamlined access to detailed patient data, including physician notes, tests, medications, and results. It was developed in Visual Basic.

2. **OLE objects.** The user interface sends requests to local OLE objects. 3M created these objects so they reflect their real-world counterparts and mimic the way clinicians work in real life. For example, a lab object handles blood count data the same way a physician interprets it. The development team wrote the OLE objects using Visual C++. To let customers develop their own user interfaces, 3M publishes their APIs. Customers can then use any client platform that Tuxedo supports to develop a custom user interface; but most customers use the GUI that 3M Health Information Systems provides.

3. **The HostLink OLE object.** HostLink is a special OLE object that enables multiple clients to share a single Tuxedo /WS connection. HostLink then acts as a concentrator for passing calls to Tuxedo. HostLink also provides greater availability; if a Tuxedo connection goes down, it can automatically be restarted.

4. **Tuxedo /WS.** HostLink talks to Tuxedo /WS to access the appropriate Tuxedo service on the application server.

The 3M system uses a common message format for all communication between the client and server. It is based on the ASN.1 (Abstract Syntax Notation 1) specification—an ISO standard (see the next Details box). The client application takes the standard ASN.1 message template and fills in appropriate fields to invoke a particular service. The message is then sent via Tuxedo /WS to the application server, where services unravel the message and take the appropriate actions to provide a response.

Tier 2: The Server Side

The middle tier of the Healthcare Enterprise Management System consists of a Unix application server that runs about 120 Tuxedo services. The services access data in the Master Member Index and Lifetime Data Repository.

The 3M developers took a functional approach to defining the services. Each application task is translated into a service, which is developed in C by the services group. For example, 3M developed services such as *Add, Modify, Lookup,* and *Read* for its Master Member Index. The 3M system also uses conversational services—for example, instead of returning all the "Smiths" in the database when identifying a patient, the client and server hold a conversation to progressively refine a set of patient matches. The services frequently invoke each other, N-tier style. 3M Health Information Systems publishes the interfaces to the services so that its customers can include them in their own custom applications.

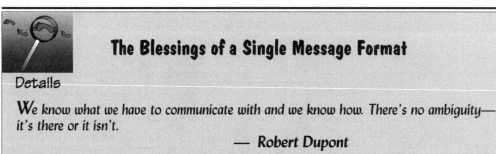

The Blessings of a Single Message Format

Details

We *know what we have to communicate with and we know how. There's no ambiguity—it's there or it isn't.*

— **Robert Dupont**

In the early stages of system development, 3M Health Information Systems decided to use a global message model. It is based on ASN.1 (Abstract Syntax Notation)—an ISO standard. ASN.1 provides a standard message template between the client and the server, and in the database. This minimizes interface issues between the client and server. The message format is self-describing. Different parts of the message are filled in depending on which request or response is being made. The average message size is slightly under a kilobyte.

The system stores the original form of each ASN.1 message as a complete, composite record. The message is also broken apart and stored as relational fields, which serve as indexes to the composite records. Consequently, the system doesn't need to reconstitute the messages through a set of joins. And because everything is stored in the ASN.1 form, it isn't necessary to revise all of the data if changes are made to the schema. ❏

The middle tier also collects data continually from existing systems that are part of a healthcare enterprise. Here's how these interactions take place:

1. Existing applications send data to the system in a Health Level 7 (HL7) message.

2. The 3M system then translates the HL7 message into its standard ASN.1 message structure.

3. A special Tuxedo service, called the *Data Storing Service*, unravels the message. This service stores many varieties of clinical data—including lab, pharmacy, and radiology data.

4. The Data Storing Service invokes another service to translate each piece of data into a relational format.

5. The Data Storing Service completes a database transaction to store the information in the repository.

All repository updates are made through this layer of server logic. Neither the clients nor the existing systems access the repository directly. In this way, 3M ensures that the data in the repository is stored and catalogued correctly.

Tier 3: The Database and Integration With Existing Systems

The third tier of the Healthcare Enterprise Management System is managed by the Oracle database. The size of the database varies at each site. The largest installation—at Intermountain Health Care—supports 70 GB of mirrored data, for a total of 140 GB.

The biggest challenge 3M Health Information Systems faces in the third tier is consolidating a customer's existing data into the repository (see the next Briefing box). Once the existing data has been loaded, 3M sets up a permanent link between the customer's other systems and the Healthcare Enterprise Management System. This connection is used to route a copy of all new data to the 3M repository. As we just explained, the 3M system expects incoming data to be in HL7 format, a healthcare industry standard for intersystem communication. The interface engine on the middle-tier application server transforms the HL7 message into the ASN.1 message format for storage in the repository (see the previous section). The 3M interface engine often doubles as a general-purpose message transformer between a site's existing systems.

Occasionally, customers want to have repository-resident data sent back to existing systems. Today, the 3M system does not provide this as a standard product feature; customers implement this capability as a site-specific project. In the future, 3M Health Information Systems may enable this capability by adding a function that transforms ASN.1 messages into an HL7 data format.

Security

The 3M security system requires a log-in and password before a user can access the applications. With a successful log-in, the system returns a coded security "ticket" to the user. This ticket is then included with each subsequent service request. The coded security ticket defines the user profile which controls the set of services available to users. When a service receives a request from a client, it makes a call to the security validation service to ensure that the user is authorized for a particular request. 3M is also planning to provide restricted access to private information.

System Management

Generally, system management is handled on a site-by-site basis. Initially, 3M expected that its Healthcare Enterprise Management System would be integrated

Integrating Existing Data: A Monumental Task

Briefing

3M Health Information Systems must create an integrated repository from existing nonintegrated data that is spread throughout the healthcare organization. To create the repository, 3M tackles two tough jobs:

- **Getting the data into the repository in ASN.1 format.** This is often the easiest part of the repository installation. Although a healthcare enterprise may have more than 20 ancillary systems—such as its hospital information, lab, microbiology, and pharmacy systems—the site has often standardized the systems on HL7. 3M then uses a tool they developed to translate HL7 messages into the ASN.1 format.

- **Checking the data.** Next, the data must be checked to ensure that it is consistent. This next step is the most complicated part of the job. The install team must sit down with the customer to double-check that their label for complete blood count, for example, translates correctly into the predefined ASN.1 code for that concept. About 85% of medical terminology is uniform, so the majority of the data is translated in a fairly straightforward manner. But an analyst must manually code the remaining 15% of the data; this is a labor-intensive process. ☐

with a customer's existing system management strategy. In practice, however, 3M often does a considerable amount of consulting with customers to define an appropriate management plan. Because its system is based on an open architecture, 3M Health Information Systems can recommend to its customers a number of third-party system management products.

An Example of a Large Installation: Intermountain Health Care

3M can leverage its modular, 3-tier architecture to maximize performance in large installations. For example, 3M has used a form of "processor specialization" to deliver strong performance results at its largest installation, at Intermountain Health Care. Intermountain's system consists of an IBM RS/6000 SP/2 with ten processors. Four of the processors are dedicated to running Oracle, another four are dedicated to running Tuxedo and the application's services, and two more processors are dedicated to I/O (see Figure 9-4). In addition, a 4-processor server runs the Tuxedo Workstation Listener. Processor specialization provides these benefits to Intermountain Health Care:

■ *Increased performance.* Nodes are dedicated to running either Tuxedo services or Oracle. Each Tuxedo node is paired with an Oracle node. The pairing boosts throughput by enabling Intermountain to individually tune the subsystems running on each processor.

■ *Higher availability.* Pairing the processors together also provides a higher level of availability by reducing the amount of time it takes to recognize and

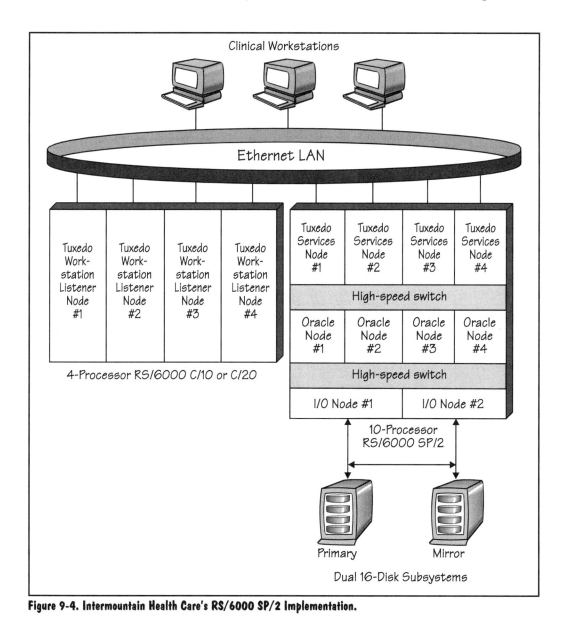

Figure 9-4. Intermountain Health Care's RS/6000 SP/2 Implementation.

recover from a failure. If one pair fails, another pair can quickly take on its workload. The I/O nodes also are paired to back each other up.

■ ***Better I/O throughput.*** Intermountain Health Care gets better throughput by finely tuning the disk I/O processes it isolates on other specialized nodes.

Intermountain's system now acts as a model for large implementations that handle thousands of clients.

THE PROJECT

Development of the Healthcare Enterprise Management System started in January 1994 (see the next Details box). At its launch, the project had the following goals:

■ Provide an enterprise-wide clinical data repository and master patient index.

■ Implement on an open UNIX platform.

■ Support the execution of expert logic on data.

■ Provide a clinical workstation client application.

Key Milestones

Details

January 1994: Project starts.

March 1994: Architecture is defined. First functionality defined as the 3M Master Member Index with support for textual data.

December 1994: Version 1.0 released.

Fall 1995: Version 2.0 released with a codification scheme to support clinical data.

April 1996: Version 4.0 released with the current codification scheme. (Version 3.0 was incorporated into this release.)

March 1997: Version 5.0 released with support for a 32-bit architecture. ❑

Design

One of the key distinguishing characteristics at 3M was the number of domain specialists and clinical people on staff. When we ran into problems of clinical interpretation, we always had someone we could go to, get it resolved, and get back to engineering.

— Mark Scarton

The initial design team consisted of people from both 3M and Intermountain Health Care, a 3M development partner. Because Intermountain was also the initial customer site for the product, 3M got direct customer input about priorities for its first release—it would include the Master Member Index, but store straight textual data.

The number of people working on the project began to grow. While the majority of the design was done by the team members, they also worked with other professionals:

- Outside consultants validated the architectural approach.
- Practicing physicians aided in the design and commented on the requirements.
- The 3M human engineering team assisted with the GUI design.

The design team quickly decided that a 3-tier architecture was the best solution; a 2-tier design could run into scalability problems. They also decided to use ASN.1 as a global messaging format to make the definition of the client/server interface consistent.

Next, the team defined the other components of their architecture. They decided to avoid inventing anything they could buy. They chose to use an Oracle database and to run on UNIX—this would ensure that the product would be part of an open environment. They chose Tuxedo as their TP Monitor. They knew it could meet the system's performance and scalability requirements. It was also well-established and supported the HP and IBM UNIX platforms that were widely used in the healthcare market.

The design team also wanted to provide standard client interfaces so that tools such as Visual Basic or Delphi could be used to build applications. This led them to a design that included building OLE proxy objects on the client for each externalized service.

Next, they created a prototype to make sure the system could compose and decompose messages. The prototype also let the developers continue to learn more about the products and the architecture as they built the system.

Development

Because the ASN.1 message is what we use to communicate with, once we have the message nailed down, people can pretty much go their own way and code.

— **Kent Stevenson, Database Team Leader**

The development organization is divided into seven groups:

- *The database server group* develops the Master Member Index and Lifetime Data Repository, including the service that maps messages to the relational database.

- *The services group* develops the application server processes and the corresponding OLE objects for the client.

- *The tools group* maintains the ASN.1 message structures and develops the infrastructure and tools for the data dictionary.

- *The data dictionary group* defines concepts and manages dictionary content.

- *The clinical alert management group* develops the Alert Management applications.

- *The systems administration, support, and performance group* assists with system configuration.

- *The user interface group* develops the Clinical Workstation Application.

When the services group completes development of an OLE object, the user interface group can start using it in development. In this way, the services group is responsible for communications between the client and server. The services group provides the user interface group with early releases of its work to get feedback. If the user interface group requests that certain properties be added or exposed, they negotiate a compromise that works for both teams.

3M Health Information Systems uses a cross-functional team to direct the project. This team is made up of software engineering, marketing, support, documentation, training, and installation staff members.

Testing

Standardizing on ASN.1 has made integration easier. 3M doesn't wait until all system pieces are complete before beginning to test them. Once new services are functionally complete, the team follows these steps:

1. They freeze development on the services and move them into a release control phase to checkpoint all of the source code.

2. The independent components are compiled and put into the controlled environment.

3. Developers run a set of unit tests on their piece of the code.

4. They run integration tests to ensure that the different components work together correctly.

Going Into Production

The install group works with the support and systems administration groups to get each customer's system up and running. Customers tend to run at least two copies of the product—one for production, and one for testing. Testing and production schedules vary by site, but typically it takes healthcare enterprises two to three months to move a major release of the product into production. In contrast, a fix for a minor bug is typically implemented very quickly.

THE OUTCOME

Healthcare organizations have responded enthusiastically to the 3M Healthcare Enterprise Management System. The system maps well to the new dynamics of the healthcare industry. It gives today's larger organizations the tools they need to manage patient data across systems. Clinicians can monitor patient status through a range of treatments. For example, a patient record can include the outcome of a visit to the doctor's office, the ensuing stay in the hospital, and the home health care that follows.

THE FUTURE

3M Health Information Systems will continue to extend its data model and upgrade its Healthcare Data Dictionary. The team also plans to integrate support for the standards that have emerged since the system was first developed. This will let 3M bring installations up more quickly and less expensively.

3M Health Information Systems is also determining how to integrate Internet access with the system and evaluating the benefits this would provide to 3M users. Although security issues would need to be addressed, extending the system via the Internet could move 3M even one step further toward providing healthcare providers with real-time patient data anywhere, anytime.

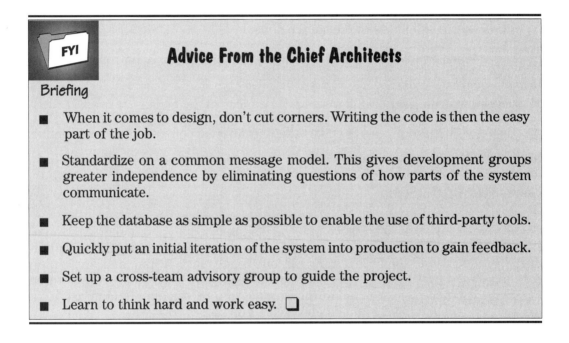

FYI — Advice From the Chief Architects

Briefing

- When it comes to design, don't cut corners. Writing the code is then the easy part of the job.

- Standardize on a common message model. This gives development groups greater independence by eliminating questions of how parts of the system communicate.

- Keep the database as simple as possible to enable the use of third-party tools.

- Quickly put an initial iteration of the system into production to gain feedback.

- Set up a cross-team advisory group to guide the project.

- Learn to think hard and work easy. ❑

Chapter 10

3-Tier Brings Car Registration Protection to Europe

EUCARIS helps to prevent the laundering of stolen cars and other vehicle fraud in European countries. Now stolen cars can be caught before they disappear into the vehicle registry of another country.

*— Hans van der Bruggen, Deputy Director
Netherlands'
Department of Road Transport (RDW)*

In Europe, an eight-hour roadtrip can take you through five different countries. This provides great access to varying cultures, but it also makes car theft and registration fraud a smooth trip for an easy rider. An enterprising cheat can buy a car in the Netherlands, register it again in Belgium and Luxembourg, and then head West through France to England—registering and insuring the car in each country. The car is then declared "stolen," and the owner collects insurance money for the same car in five countries.

But not anymore—thanks to a new vehicle re-registration system in Europe. In the early 1990s, a group of people working in the Netherlands' Department of Road Transport—RDW—envisioned a system that would let European countries share vehicle and driver registration information. That system, spearheaded by Jan

Roedoe, an RDW IT account manager, is now a reality as EUCARIS—the European Car and Driving Licence Information System. At present, six countries—the Netherlands, Belgium, Luxembourg, the United Kingdom, the Czech Republic, and Latvia—are part of the system. Many more countries are working to come on-line; the goal is to achieve Europe-wide cooperation.

THE APPLICATION

EUCARIS participants now have the capability to identify a vehicle or registration document in the country of origin. This happens on-line during the process of re-registration, letting countries maintain clean and reliable registries.

— *Erik van Nus, RDW Project Manager*

EUCARIS is a 3-tier message brokering system. Its goal is to allow any European country to retrieve car information from the vehicle registries held in any other European country. By doing so, a country can verify the identity of a vehicle being re-registered, thus ensuring the status of the vehicle's first registration. If, for example, a vehicle is stolen, EUCARIS alerts the inquirer that something is wrong. The inquirer can then further investigate the problem or immediately inform the national police.

A Multinational System

The need for an international vehicle registry network became even more critical in the early 1990s; the birth of the European Union (EU) eliminated borders between Western European countries. As a result, border checks are no longer conducted for cars traveling within the EU. This easy access between countries expanded further when the Iron Curtain came down in Middle and Eastern Europe, making even more countries readily accessible to drivers. The new political environment brought many benefits to Europeans; but it also made the illegal export and theft of cars a piece of cake. Steal a car in France and just start driving until you disappear. You can then register the car in another country. However, if countries begin to exchange registration data, the car can be tracked no matter what country it ends up in.

Surprisingly, even though EUCARIS is interconnecting multiple countries and accessing varying types of back-end data, the challenges of bringing the system on-line have been more political than technical. Because countries using EUCARIS must make their vehicle or driving-license registration data accessible to outside parties, new legislation is often required before this exchange of private information is legal. Each participating country must also make bilateral agreements with the

other EUCARIS participants to exchange vehicle information. This extremely political process can be lengthy.

The six countries that currently participate in EUCARIS are making strong efforts to add other countries to the system. They have sent information about the system to representatives of all registration and licensing authorities within the European Union—as well as other non-European countries that have shown interest. As this book goes to press, Germany and Hungary were coming on-line, and more than twenty other countries were interested in joining (see Figure 10-1).

EUCARIS as a Message Broker

The system's operation is actually quite simple:

1. A representative in Country A working on the re-registration of a car sends a request for vehicle information from its EUCARIS server to Country B's EUCARIS server, where the car is supposed to be currently registered.

2. The EUCARIS server in Country B then communicates with its back-end registry to retrieve the necessary information.

3. The vehicle information is then returned to EUCARIS server A. Alternatively, a message is returned stating that the data is not available; this signifies a possible problem. The representative can then take the appropriate action to prevent fraud.

EUCARIS' success can be attributed to its ability to link together a variety of existing, independently implemented systems. Unisys Nederland NV helps interested countries develop a way to hook up their back-end registration data—whether it's on a mainframe, on a UNIX box, or on a PC. In addition, INFONET Nederland BV provides and manages the EUCARIS X.25-based network, ensuring that data is delivered as requested. By using INFONET and Unisys, new participants can come on-line without requiring a central EUCARIS representative to manage the implementation.

EUCARIS passes small amounts of data—for example, vehicle chassis numbers and the model of the car. Consequently, the system is very responsive. Even on a relatively low-bandwidth X.25-based network, it typically returns responses within one to two seconds. This lets users check a vehicle's registration status at the time a car is being re-registered. Except for the U.K. system, all EUCARIS servers are up 24 hours a day, seven days a week. Of course, access to a specific record depends on the availability of the host country's proprietary registration database. So EUCARIS includes a central management environment that lets countries learn when other participants are inaccessible.

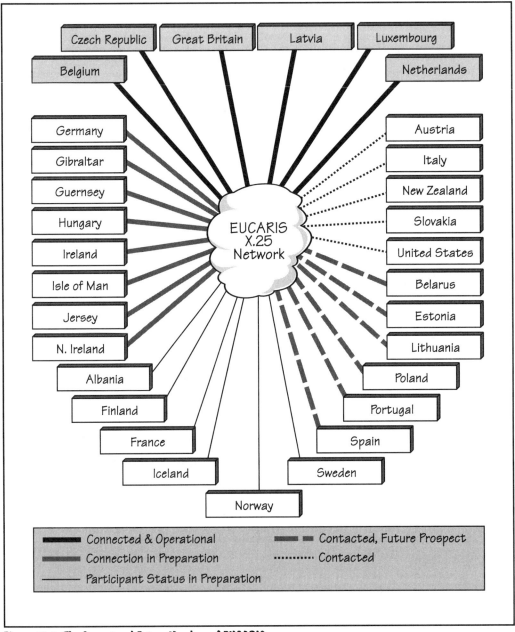

Figure 10-1. The Current and Future Members of EUCARIS.

THE 3-TIERED ARCHITECTURE

*E*ach country has a different registry with its own unique host interface. Part of the code runs in each country to hide the implementation from the application and offer a generic set of services.

> — Fred Bosch,
> Head of Professional Services Department
> Unisys Nederland NV
> Computer Systems Group

EUCARIS emerged from Roedoe's ideas, which other RDW and Unisys staff members expanded. It uses a 3-tier architecture to create a unified, distributed system environment on top of a collection of heterogeneous applications—each owned by a different country (see Figure 10-2). So in essence, the middle tier creates a virtual network of services with gateways to existing systems.

Each participating country has a EUCARIS server that acts as a front-end to their host registry database and connects to INFONET (see Figure 10-3). Here are EUCARIS' three tiers:

- *Tier 1* consists of the user terminal and the EUCARIS client software. This program runs as a native Tuxedo client on the server. The user devices in each country are either VT terminals or PCs that run a terminal-emulator program. Based on input from the user, the EUCARIS client software creates a EUROBAR message—a message format created for the application—that is sent via Tuxedo over INFONET. It is used to retrieve data from another EUCARIS server.

- *Tier 2* consists of both common and country-specific server code running under Tuxedo on each EUCARIS server. The common code transforms an incoming EUROBAR message into a C structure. The message is then processed by a Tuxedo service that acts as an application gateway. There is a gateway for each country. Finally, the requested information is returned.

- *Tier 3* is each country's back-end car registry database. The countries' existing "servers" range from an IBM mainframe to a dilapidated bookcase holding thick folders of registration papers. To return EUCARIS requests, the registries must be computerized. Unisys assists in developing an interface between the host and the EUCARIS server in each country.

Because differing host systems need to share information, EUCARIS provided a standard way for them to communicate. RDW had already created a unique message structure—called BAR—for retrieving information from its vehicle registry. RDW leveraged BAR for EUCARIS by adding electronic data interchange (EDI) data modeling to it. The result is EUROBAR—the messaging standard for EUCARIS. EUROBAR provides a standard protocol and content definition that a EUCARIS server in each of the different countries can use to retrieve vehicle information. For

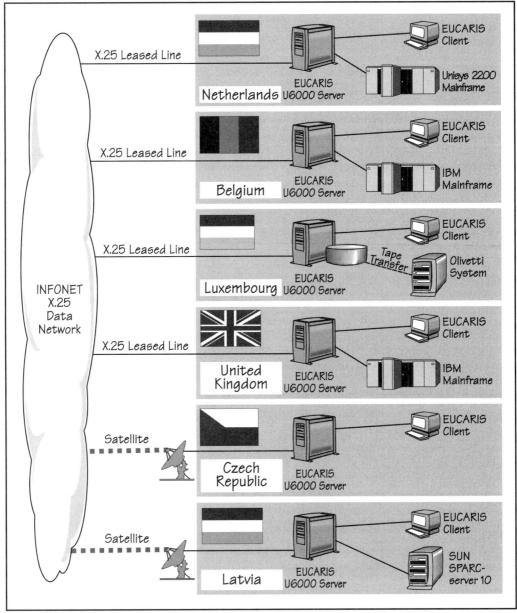

Figure 10-2. The EUCARIS Network's Physical Architecture.

example, a EUROBAR message provides a common way to describe vehicle color, even though individual country registries may track color through a numbered code or by using the color name itself.

The EUCARIS team chose a 3-tier solution for several reasons:

■ *It creates a virtual system from disparate applications.* The middle tier separates the inquiry from the software used to access information in a country's local registry. The client can interface to any country's host system via the network of middle-tier servers. Communications between the tiers occurs through a common network (INFONET) and message structure (EUROBAR). Tuxedo acts as a transport layer to manage the routing between the distributed servers.

■ *It upwardly scales.* The network must be able to grow as more countries come on-line. Tuxedo can easily manage the larger loads as connections increase.

■ *It provides maximum configuration flexibility.* Participating countries can select the client machines they like. More importantly, the interfaces to the existing registries can vary for each EUCARIS country. By not requiring a specific client or back-end interface, participating countries can maintain their independence.

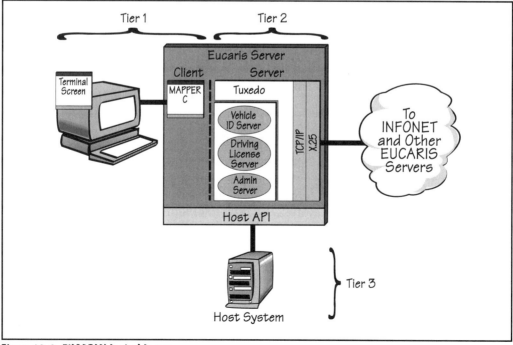

Figure 10-3. EUCARIS' Logical Layers.

A 3-tier architecture also supports the response time, reliability, and transaction management required. In any case, a 2-tier architecture just couldn't meet the system's needs. The clients couldn't be closely tied to the back-ends because they are different in each country.

Tier 1: The Client

The client portion of Tuxedo was built in MAPPER C, a Unisys 4GL. The MAPPER C terminal program runs on each EUCARIS server. This makes upgrades easy—the only programs that must be upgraded are on the servers. It's also a less expensive solution, which makes it easier to convince new countries to join. Countries can use any VT terminal—or PC that supports VT terminal emulation—to access the EUCARIS network.

MAPPER C runs on each EUCARIS server as a native Tuxedo client to route requests through the network. The MAPPER C client creates a EUROBAR message from the user input. It then uses Tuxedo calls to send the message to the destination EUCARIS server. That server then retrieves the requested data. Although MAPPER C is currently only ported to certain server platforms—including Unisys, RS/6000, and Sun systems—the team decided that its model is open enough to meet the needs of EUCARIS. To date, all of the EUCARIS servers have been Unisys boxes, so additional platform support hasn't been an issue.

The EUCARIS user interface is intentionally very simple. When a user logs on, a menu appears, giving a choice of Vehicle Identification or Driving License screens (see Figure 10-4). The primary choice is the Vehicle Identification screen. The Driving License screen is available for countries—such as the United Kingdom—that want to track driver registrations.

The Vehicle Identification screen has fields for the vehicle's country of origin and the vehicle chassis number. The user fills in these fields and submits the request. The system returns a response, with the remaining fields filled in. If a chassis number is not found, the system returns a message that states the problem. The user then recognizes that re-registration could be a problem and delays processing the new registration. If the server is not accessible, the system returns an error message indicating the server is down.

Tier 2: The Server Side

MAPPER C interfaces with the Tuxedo services, which also reside on each EUCARIS server. There are two main Tuxedo server classes in the EUCARIS system:

```
Prg/Version : EucV_Id/2.01        EUCARIS              Date : 12-04-96
Screen      : Ve-Ident/0010                            Time : 13:24:58

                              Vehicle Identification
     Country code    : NL
     Chassis select  : 63538393903
     Number select   :                        _

     Chassis number  : 63538393903
     Manufacturer    : VOLKSWAGEN
     Type            : 1300
     Commercial name : BEATLE
     Color           : PINK
     First Date      : 09 Sep 1923
     Date Expired    : 09 Sep 1977
     Number plate    : HZ-AA-01
     Fuel            : CNG
     Signals         : VEHICLE EXPORTED

  1 New     2         3         4 Menu   5         6 Print  7         8         9         10 Exit
```

Figure 10-4. The Simple EUCARIS User Interface.

■ **The Vehicle Identification server class** runs services to handle inquiries based on either a chassis number or a license plate number.

■ **The Driving License server class** runs services to handle inquiries based on a driver license number or on a driver's name and birthdate.

Each server class consists of both common services that are run on all EUCARIS servers and specific services that connect EUCARIS to each country's back-end host. The common part of the code is exactly the same for all of the countries; it was written in C. This code transforms the EUROBAR message back into a C structure. It also includes statistical services, authentication and authorization services, and logs of the input and output messages.

Even though the clients always call the same named Tuxedo service for a particular EUROBAR message, the way the content is retrieved differs depending on the country being called and how its host system handles data. The specific server code for each country's EUCARIS server is custom-built. For example, in Belgium, SNA transport software is used with SNA 3270 to access an IBM mainframe.

To date, the EUCARIS servers have all been single-processor, Intel-based Unisys U6000 boxes running Unisys' UNIX SVR 4. They connect to INFONET via X.25 lines—or, if necessary, by satellite. INFONET provides a transparent open network. Tuxedo then manages the message routing and ensures that messages are properly handled—providing real-time performance. If the load on a EUCARIS server increases, operations can run additional Tuxedo server class processes.

All of the EUCARIS servers reside in a single Tuxedo 4.21 domain. The design team expects to move away from this model to multiple domains within the next two years as more countries come on-line—this will simplify start-up, shutdown, and application management. In addition, moving to the latest version of Tuxedo will allow EUCARIS to leverage new features, such as publish-and-subscribe messaging. This could be used, for example, to provide dynamic monitoring and even more flexible statistical reporting.

The system is flexible enough to meet different country agreements and needs. For example, the government in the United Kingdom was finding that people who didn't qualify for U.K. driver licenses would forge a license and present it in another European country, such as the Netherlands. The Netherlands would provide that driver with a Dutch driver license based on the forgery. The person could then return to the U.K. with the valid Dutch license and receive in return a valid U.K. license. To meet the U.K.'s needs, the EUCARIS team added the ability to track driver licenses.

Today, the master server in the EUCARIS Tuxedo domain resides in the Netherlands' RDW. England's EUCARIS server acts as a backup. The team prefers to have all back-up administration in one location, so it is seeking the funds to put a back-up server in the Netherlands; this server will also play a dual role as a dial-in box. This will expand the EUCARIS service to mobile users, such as customs agents at borders.

Tier 3: The Database and Legacy Applications

We can talk to virtually any kind of host application. We've got the software and the skills.

— *Fred Bosch, Unisys*

EUCARIS has no single, shared database. Instead, each participating country's registry becomes a part of the system through an interface between the country's host system and the EUCARIS server. Unisys has played a primary role in creating the EUCARIS gateways to existing systems by leveraging mainframe tools or open systems tools as appropriate. Of course, countries can elect to implement their own gateways. Here are some examples of the differences among host interface implementations for the current participants:

■ *Belgium and the United Kingdom* both use IBM mainframes, so some development work was reused. These two countries run server-specific code on their EUCARIS servers to translate the C message into a 3270 data stream.

■ *The Netherlands* runs services that translate the C message into its BAR message structure to query its Unisys 2200 mainframe over an X.25 network.

■ **Luxembourg** elected to disallow direct access to its registry, which is housed in an Olivetti UNIX box. Instead, the staff copies its database to tape each morning. This data is then loaded into a database running on their EUCARIS server. As a result, the specific server code just directly calls the EUCARIS server database.

■ **The Czech Republic** has yet to make a centralized registry database available. As a result, its EUCARIS server only runs the client software on top of Tuxedo. They can query other databases, but they do not honor requests about their own.

■ **Latvia**, the most recent country to be connected to the network, keeps its registry in an Oracle database on a Sun SPARCserver 10 running Solaris. Its specific server code transforms the EUROBAR message into an ONC-RPC C structure that is transferred to the SPARCserver. An ONC-RPC server then calls Oracle in C using embedded SQL to retrieve information.

Clearly, EUCARIS demonstrates great flexibility in linking to a variety of back-end hosts. The use of a third party—Unisys—for system integration provides the pool of experienced developers that is necessary to create the back-end interfaces. It also eliminates the need for a single EUCARIS country or representative to manage technology issues as new countries come on-line.

Security

Security is a must for EUCARIS because the system is accessing data that countries consider private. INFONET provides a closed network for EUCARIS users. In addition, users have no direct access to the back-end systems aside from the services offered through the application.

To use EUCARIS, a user needs to log in to the local EUCARIS server. The user then logs in to the MAPPER C client software, adding another layer of protection. MAPPER C retains a log of user activities—and all information, including the user's name, is also logged by the EUCARIS server that front-ends the registry being accessed. This provides tracking capabilities within the system.

Not every EUCARIS server has access rights to the other servers. Each connection requires bilateral agreements between countries. If one is not in place, the servers between these countries can't communicate. Some countries don't want to share all this information. The Netherlands, for example, makes both its vehicle registration and driver license information accessible through EUCARIS, while others only allow registration information to be queried. The organization has even allowed the Czech Republic to implement a one-way system, where Czech representatives can check on cars from other countries even though other countries can't access the Czech database. Table 10-1 shows the current status of bilateral information exchange agreements between existing EUCARIS participants.

Table 10-1. Bilateral Agreements in Place for Information Exchange Between Participating EUCARIS Countries.

Country	Netherlands	Belgium	Luxembourg	United Kingdom	Czech Republic	Latvia
Netherlands	N/A	Yes	Yes	Yes	Yes	Yes
Belgium	Yes	N/A	Yes	No	No	No
Luxembourg	Yes	Yes	N/A	Yes	No	No
United Kingdom	Yes	No	Yes	N/A	No	No
Czech Republic	Yes	No	No	No	N/A	No
Latvia	Yes	No	No	No	No	N/A

System Management

A command center is set up in the Netherlands' RDW. Operations managers at this center directly monitor the status of any of the EUCARIS servers through use of Unisys' Single Point Console software, a product RDW already used. The software runs on a stand-alone UNIX box, and it provides centralized systems management for the network. This is key for a system that resides in so many different locations— and where people with technical knowledge may not be available.

Each EUCARIS server runs a daemon that sends information—including the number of users, security data, the status of legacy systems, and CPU usage—to the central command center on a regular basis. Alarms can be set for all of those values. For example, if they pass a certain threshold the command center can quickly note a problem.

THE PROJECT

EUCARIS began as a pilot project in 1990 to provide real-time exchange of vehicle identification data in the BeNeLux countries—Belgium, the Netherlands, and Luxembourg. Other countries then became involved. The current goal is to have all European Union countries join the system.

The primary design and development of EUCARIS was done by a Unisys system integration team working closely with the Netherlands' RDW staff. In January 1993,

RDW asked Unisys to develop a pilot proposal for connecting the BeNeLux countries. Unisys had the proposal ready by March, and development started in May (see the next Details box).

Key Milestones

Details

1990: EUCARIS project envisioned.

June 1991: Funding for EUCARIS denied by the European Commission.

May 1993: EUCARIS pilot agreed on by BeNeLux countries. BeNeLux pilot starts; production goal set as November 8, 1993.

October 1993: INFONET connections configured. The Netherlands connected.

November 1993: Belgium connected.

October 1994: Czech Republic comes on-line with an outbound connection.

November 1994: Luxembourg connected (delayed due to privacy issues).

December 1994: Germany agrees to join EUCARIS.

February 1995: BeNeLux pilot evaluated.

February 1996: Hungary agrees to join EUCARIS.

May 1995: Funding for EUCARIS again denied by the European Commission.

June 1995: United Kingdom connected.

March 1996: Command center becomes operational.

May 1997: Latvia connected. ❏

Design

The design team consisted of a few Unisys staff members; there was also input from BeNeLux representatives. The team quickly chose a 3-tier architecture as the best framework for the reasons we explained earlier. The goal was to create a simple, no-nonsense system that could be easily set up in new countries as they came on-line.

From the start, the designers agreed that they would use UNIX and Tuxedo to provide an open system platform. Unisys was experienced in working with Tuxedo software. In fact, Unisys has brand-named Tuxedo for its own use as *Open/OLTP*. Tuxedo provided pre-built services and administration tools. It also provided an open framework—a critical requirement when rolling out a system across multiple countries.

The design team also evaluated an RPC approach, but they decided it was too limiting—it would have required the hand-coding of all the routing. This would have increased the development time required to add new countries.

No formal design methodology was used—ideas were simply introduced and then accepted or revised. The team realized the need for a standard message definition. So they chose to leverage the message structure RDW used for its registry, transforming it into EUROBAR.

Development

EUCARIS development began in May 1993. The team assigned tasks in this way:

■ One team member developed the client code, using Unisys' MAPPER C 4GL to speed its creation.

■ Another member began looking at the networking infrastructure, such as the layering of TCP/IP on top of X.25 and the use of INFONET.

■ A third member began to develop the common server code.

■ The remaining team members started working on the specialized server code needed to interface with each country's registry.

The entire development process took only a few months—the team was able to leverage Unisys' experience with Tuxedo, UNIX, and interfacing with legacy systems. The EUROBAR message structure minimized interface issues. Later, when the United Kingdom joined the EUCARIS system, a few modifications were necessary to track vehicles by license number. The team simply defined additional EUROBAR messages, added some services, and revised the client GUI to support license-based searches. The team expects to add features to support the rollout of EUCARIS to more countries.

There was limited documentation during the pilot phase, but since that time, the team has documented EUROBAR, the EUROBAR data dictionary, the client interface, and so on. They have also written an end-user guide.

Testing and Going Into Production

When the primary pieces of EUCARIS were ready, the team began to bring countries on-line for a pilot test. The Netherlands was connected in October 1993, and Belgium followed a month later. A Unisys staff member simply went to the country, set up the connection, and voila! The system was up and running. No serious problems were encountered; countries came on-line within days (see the next Briefing box).

Initially, the system was supposed to be a pilot, but users started to query the system almost immediately. They didn't realize the environment wasn't yet production-ready. This early system use had a nice side effect, though—it made the need for additional management tools very obvious. The developers found that local representatives would bring down their system for no apparent reason. Without management tools in place, nobody was aware that the server was down until someone needed it. Because the systems are countries apart, it was also very difficult to find out what had happened. As a result, the developers decided to add the command center and tools for software distribution.

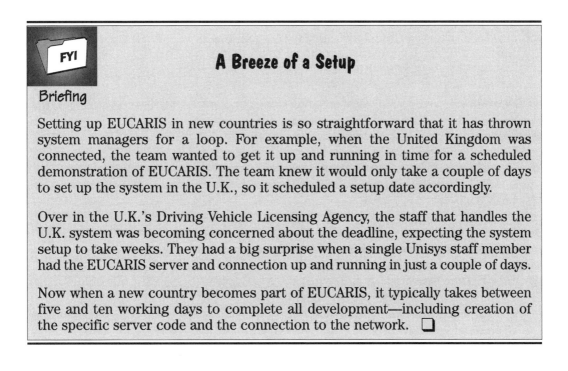

FYI

A Breeze of a Setup

Briefing

Setting up EUCARIS in new countries is so straightforward that it has thrown system managers for a loop. For example, when the United Kingdom was connected, the team wanted to get it up and running in time for a scheduled demonstration of EUCARIS. The team knew it would only take a couple of days to set up the system in the U.K., so it scheduled a setup date accordingly.

Over in the U.K.'s Driving Vehicle Licensing Agency, the staff that handles the U.K. system was becoming concerned about the deadline, expecting the system setup to take weeks. They had a big surprise when a single Unisys staff member had the EUCARIS server and connection up and running in just a couple of days.

Now when a new country becomes part of EUCARIS, it typically takes between five and ten working days to complete all development—including creation of the specific server code and the connection to the network. ❑

In Production

Because of the command center in the Netherlands, system support is a relatively easy task. Software updates can be sent out over the network to the EUCARIS servers. To date, however, there haven't been many problems with the system, so there have been few modifications. Network traffic is still not at its peak, so performance has been very good.

THE OUTCOME

Most people are surprised at the response times. They think it's done locally, not over a Europe-wide network.

— **Ruud de Ridder**
Unisys Project Designer and Developer

Participating EUCARIS countries are very pleased with the system. It meets their needs by minimizing car registration fraud and theft; it also enables them to maintain cleaner vehicle registries. And this is made possible at a low cost. EUCARIS is a success story—the system has already traced hundreds of stolen vehicles and detected thousands of other frauds. But now it faces the challenge of getting all of the other European countries to join the network.

THE FUTURE

Future development efforts being evaluated include the following:

■ ***Extending the system to mobile users.*** Currently, RDW is conducting a pilot test to let customs officials access the system—for example, at country borders or in harbors.

■ ***Using video technology.*** This would enable countries to videotape license numbers and record vehicles coming in at key border crossings.

■ ***Using the Internet or intranet technologies.*** Such efforts could further extend the system while giving users a very simple, more accessible interface. Using the Internet might also lower system costs and provide an even easier way to connect new countries. This, however, will require close investigation because security will continue to be of utmost importance.

The future of EUCARIS is really only limited by the imagination of its developers (and the budgets of the participating countries).

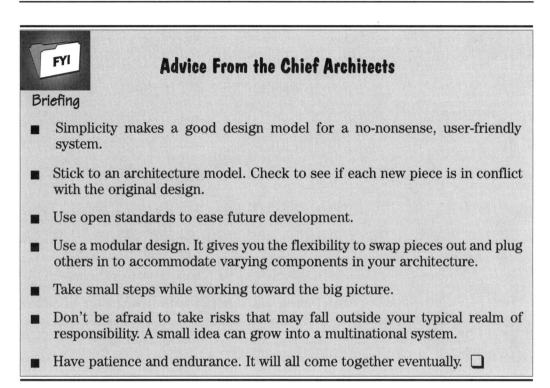

FYI

Advice From the Chief Architects

Briefing

- Simplicity makes a good design model for a no-nonsense, user-friendly system.

- Stick to an architecture model. Check to see if each new piece is in conflict with the original design.

- Use open standards to ease future development.

- Use a modular design. It gives you the flexibility to swap pieces out and plug others in to accommodate varying components in your architecture.

- Take small steps while working toward the big picture.

- Don't be afraid to take risks that may fall outside your typical realm of responsibility. A small idea can grow into a multinational system.

- Have patience and endurance. It will all come together eventually. ❏

Chapter 11

AT&T Takes On Order Turnaround

> *We had three separate platforms. We wanted to deliver a common infrastructure that gives everyone what they need, but maybe not precisely what they want. This lets us take advantage of a common platform, leading to lower unit costs.*
>
> — *Mikola Owdij, Senior Consultant*
> *AT&T's Consumer and Small Business Unit*

After AT&T was broken apart in 1984, it decided to upgrade its infrastructure to be more efficient in an increasingly competitive market. In the early 1990s, it developed an infrastructure revitalization project called *Omega*. Then AT&T began to re-engineer the applications in its *Consumer and Small Business (CSB)* business unit to run on top of the new Omega infrastructure. By doing so, AT&T can reuse applications across several CSB organizations, thus lowering costs while improving the efficiency of its services.

AT&T focused on its CSB business unit first because it is the company's largest revenue generator. It provides "Dial-1" long-distance service to residential and small-business customers. Its primary goal was to reduce CSB's order turnaround to one day so that AT&T could provide service more quickly to its customers.

THE APPLICATION

Omega is a long-range project that will have a dramatic impact on the way AT&T does business. Ultimately, it will allow AT&T to provide a single interface for its CSB representatives, called the *Universal Position*. CSB consists of three separate organizations:

- **Sales** includes both inbound sales (which handles customer calls resulting from marketing programs), and outbound sales (which is responsible for calling prospective customers).

- **Service** responds to bill inquiries, handles adjustments, and has some sales functions.

- **Call servicing** provides operator services, such as assisting someone at a pay phone to charge a call to a calling-card number.

Previously, these organizations used three separate platforms. This hindered reuse of applications. In addition, the manufacturers of products for two of the organizations had decided to discontinue their products, including some servers and some non-standard terminals that were used by service operators. Consequently, AT&T needed to replace these discontinued platforms. At the same time, the company wanted to deliver a higher level of service at a lower cost to remain a strong player in the increasingly cut-throat telephone market. To accomplish these goals, the company outlined three critical phases for Omega:

1. ***AT&T first replaced its physical infrastructure.*** By establishing a common network and equipment strategy based on open systems, any application built for one organization could easily be used in another area.

2. ***The company is now looking at the 20% of applications that are used 80% of the time and is re-engineering them to run on the new platform.*** This process starts with quick modifications to the existing primary applications to enable them to run on the new platform. Then the applications are re-engineered to be shared across organizations.

3. ***Finally, the company will look at the 80% of applications that are used 20% of the time and evaluate the need for re-engineering them.*** A number of these applications will be discarded; they are no longer useful. The remaining applications that are still considered necessary will be re-engineered.

Accomplishing these goals will eventually give AT&T a *Universal Position*, where representatives can work on any of CSB's functions. All work will be done from a single workstation using a set of applications with a common look and feel. This will lead to considerable staffing flexibility and cost savings.

Zenith: Omega's First Application

AT&T is currently in the second phase of Omega. It has re-engineered its inbound sales application—deemed most crucial to CSB's business—in a project named *Zenith*. This project was started when AT&T recognized that it sorely needed to reduce its order time for long-distance service. There was no problem getting customers to request AT&T as their carrier—1,750 inbound telemarketing representatives handled an average of 110,000 calls each day. But its batch-oriented environment meant that it could take as many as seven days to actually provide the service. A representative might take a service order at 8 a.m. one morning. That order would be batched to one system that night, then to another later in the day, and so on—possibly moving through as many as 13 systems for provisioning.

Therefore, Zenith had two primary goals: 1) to improve customer service by reducing the service order process to one day, and 2) to provide an environment that could expand to meet future needs, which is consistent with the Omega strategy. Zenith provides CSB with these major improvements:

■ ***Dramatically reduces order turnaround.*** Zenith allows inbound sales representatives to quickly process orders by interactively accessing data in AT&T's legacy systems. They have immediate access to billing, marketing, and calling-card databases. Zenith's on-line operations dramatically reduce order turnaround time.

■ ***On-line access to all customer information.*** Before Zenith, the telemarketers worked off a customer list that could have been generated three to six months in advance. As a result, many customer situations had changed considerably by the time they received a call. Zenith now provides an on-line, integrated view of customers' current status—including how much the customer is spending and what other AT&T services the customer is using. This "just-in-time" information not only improves service and sales by providing accurate data, but it also improves customers' image of AT&T by ensuring they are only contacted as appropriate.

■ ***A single ordering process for all CSB services***. This process includes new wireless, paging, and Internet services. AT&T will no longer need to maintain separate systems for each service's ordering, provisioning, and fulfillment. This will result in substantial cost savings.

■ ***Lower development costs for future projects.*** As AT&T was developing Zenith, it evaluated the needs of the other CSB organizations—it wanted to create a software project that could be leveraged in the future. The Zenith project was developed with these future applications in mind. The result is a reusable, component-based, 3-tier infrastructure. At times, this required compromises for Zenith. But—while AT&T has yet to begin the next project that proves the value of this strategy—it believes its new infrastructure will allow it to decrease future development costs and increase time to market.

The Demanding Job Ahead

To make Zenith a reality, the development team had to succeed at several tough jobs:

- *Understand the application requirements.* This was no small feat. The developers had to understand and gain consensus on the complete process for moving an order for a product or service through AT&T's multiple provisioning systems. They also had to define what each business unit required from the process. The developers then had to negotiate the right compromises between the requirements of various individual business units to make the end-to-end process work for everyone.

- *Bring batch processes on-line.* To provide faster order processing—and to deliver up-to-date information quickly to AT&T representatives—the current batch processes had to be brought on-line.

- *Become experts in objects and 3-tier technology.* The development team had little experience with either of these two technologies, and they had to master them to meet their goals.

ZENITH'S 3-TIERED ARCHITECTURE

The push for a 3-tier system was driven by the fact that if we could break functionality into smaller and more specialized areas, we had a better chance for reuse by other AT&T systems.

— Andy Schenke
Principal Technical Staff Member, CSB

Development started in March 1993. The team picked a 3-tier architecture to keep the user interface separate from the application and the application separate from the data services. 3-tier allowed them to meet these goals:

- *Support a variety of user interfaces.* For example, in certain cases, a voice-response system provides services at a lower cost than having a representative answer the call by phone. Consequently, Zenith needed to have either a touch of a pound key or a click of a mouse execute the same back-end business function.

- *Access data on legacy systems.* AT&T has a tremendous amount of data on legacy systems that could not be moved. As a result, the new applications had to be separate from the data. This separation allows AT&T to run its new applications on a common set of processors with a common infrastructure.

The developers had looked at some 2-tier solutions, but they were quickly deemed inappropriate. A 3-tier solution was obviously the right thing for Zenith.

Zenith's Multilevel Physical Architecture

Zenith is a multitiered, multilevel application that runs in a very distributed environment (see Figure 11-1). Tier-1 systems run in each of AT&T's three customer centers—in Atlanta, Georgia; Lees Summit, Missouri; and St. Louis, Missouri. CSB's representatives in these customer centers handle all inbound telemarketing; the

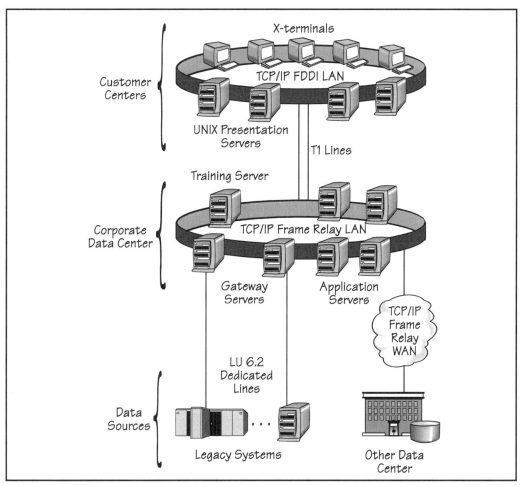

Figure 11-1. Zenith's Physical Architecture.

calls typically result from advertising campaigns and mailings. All the centers have the same capabilities, but the Atlanta center is the largest and runs around the clock. Based on business needs, AT&T can increase the staff in any of its centers to meet production requirements—for example, when running a special promotion. Each of these three centers deploys about four UNIX presentation servers to run the first-tier Zenith software. The presentation servers drive around 120 X-terminals apiece. The X-terminals connect to the presentation servers via an FDDI ring.

The presentation boxes then connect via dual dedicated T1 lines to servers in two corporate data centers—located in Alpharetta, Georgia, and Kansas City, Missouri. The dual T1 lines provide redundancy in the case of a line failure. There are about four middle-tier UNIX application servers in each center. These application servers run the main inbound telemarketing applications. Each is a 12 Pentium processor machine with about 20 GB of internal storage and a 30 GB to 40 GB RAID subsystem. In addition to these production servers, each data center has a similarly equipped training box.

The data centers also contain a number of corporate mainframes. The middle-tier servers access these corporate mainframes through specialized UNIX-to-mainframe gateway servers. The two data centers are linked by a Frame Relay-based WAN, allowing all of the machines to access each other.

Zenith standardized on NCR UNIX boxes. Standardizing on UNIX systems moved CSB toward its goal of creating an integrated infrastructure and the Universal Position. In addition to these strategic reasons for standardization, there was a number of practical advantages that led to the decision—AT&T's Business Services Division already had a lot of experience working with UNIX machines. They liked the power of smaller boxes and the lower system costs—this would allow them to purchase more computers, thus providing greater redundancy than a mainframe. And they expected to lower maintenance costs by supporting the systems in-house. Finally, they wanted to avoid the conditioning, environmental requirements, and higher staff costs that a mainframe entails.

An Overview of Zenith's Logical Tiers

Here's what goes into each of Zenith's logical tiers (see Figure 11-2):

- **Tier 1** consists of the presentation software in AT&T's inbound customer centers. Zenith's user interface is displayed on X-terminals by the UNIX presentation servers. The presentation servers run the client logic, as well as services for accessing local and remote data.

- **Tier 2** is distributed between application servers and specialized gateway servers. The application servers run Zenith's business logic, which is written as

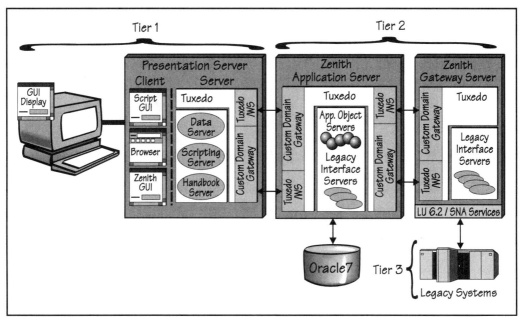

Figure 11-2. Logical Architectural Diagram of Zenith.

distributed objects. The specialized gateway servers handle UNIX-to-mainframe communications. Tuxedo is used to provide communications between the tiers, as well as for middle-tier application management.

■ **Tier 3** is AT&T's corporate data repositories. These include both mainframes and UNIX systems. They manage many key databases—including billing, marketing, and calling-card information.

Tier 1: The Client

The Zenith GUI is a native Tuxedo client. Zenith uses Tri-teal's VUE windowing manager package to display the GUI on the X-terminals (see the next Briefing box). VUE is based on Motif and X libraries. It provides users with a graphical user interface, enabling them to cut and paste, highlight, drag and drop, and so on (see Figure 11-3). VUE runs on the presentation servers now—the X-terminals simply display VUE's output. AT&T expects to move VUE to the X-terminals themselves. It believes this will reduce the processing load on the presentation boxes and enable them to run faster and support more clients.

In addition to running the GUI, the presentation servers run Tuxedo and about 24 Zenith services. One of the most important server classes running on the presentation box is the *Data Server*. The Data Server was developed in C++ and provides

```
Zenith - Customer Profile (Inbound)

 Contact  Sell  Status  Inquiry  Feedback  Forms

BTN:                              Account Status: Live
RAMP Internal ID:
Contact Name:                     LD Carrier:    AT&T
                                  LEC:      OHIO BELL TEL. CO.
                                  LEC Change Charge: $5.00
Customer Name:                    Billing Source:    LEC
                                  LEC Bill Cycle:    0
Service Address:                  ATT Bill Cycle:    0

    Billing                       Language Pref.        English
                                  Special Handling:
City:                             Toll Average - $6.00

State:          Zip:

Current Services                  Pending Services
Dial-1      Live      01/01/1995
ROS# Half Hr  Out Compl ATT


    Save      Account     Toll      Customer
   Updates   Specifics   History      Info       Reset      Help
```

Figure 11-3. Zenith User Application.

clients with data location-independence—it transparently accesses local data or data on the middle-tier servers as necessary. In this way, the client doesn't need to know where the data resides.

The presentation servers also support an HTTP daemon for on-line documentation via a browser. A number of local sales applications also run on these UNIX servers, including scripting for telemarketing, an on-line handbook, and some subsidiary GUIs for legacy access.

Tier 2: The Server Side

In the old world, we would have to go through every line of code and change it to modify a function. In the object world, you change one line and it can be inherited by the entire code base.

— Andy Schenke

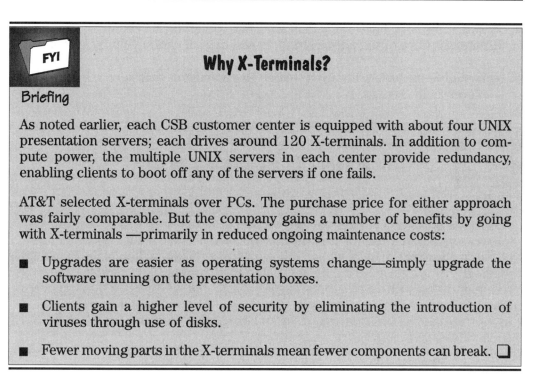

Why X-Terminals?

Briefing

As noted earlier, each CSB customer center is equipped with about four UNIX presentation servers; each drives around 120 X-terminals. In addition to compute power, the multiple UNIX servers in each center provide redundancy, enabling clients to boot off any of the servers if one fails.

AT&T selected X-terminals over PCs. The purchase price for either approach was fairly comparable. But the company gains a number of benefits by going with X-terminals —primarily in reduced ongoing maintenance costs:

■ Upgrades are easier as operating systems change—simply upgrade the software running on the presentation boxes.

■ Clients gain a higher level of security by eliminating the introduction of viruses through use of disks.

■ Fewer moving parts in the X-terminals mean fewer components can break. ❑

Zenith's middle tier is a multilevel environment that runs the application's primary business logic—it also interfaces to a variety of legacy systems that contain the information needed by CSB's sales representatives. In reality, Zenith is a distributed object-oriented system. So what ORB does it use? Tuxedo! AT&T has implemented a layer on top of the TP Monitor that, in effect, turns it into a customized ORB (see the next Briefing box).

Zenith's middle tier is distributed across two types of specialized servers: application servers and gateway servers. Tuxedo runs on all the Zenith servers. It provides inter-server communication, but in an unusual manner, through a *Custom Domain Gateway* (see the next Details box).

The Zenith Application Server

The Zenith application servers run the primary business applications—including the inbound sales application. About 1,000 C++ services make up the application. They run as objects in 70 Tuxedo server classes, and store their state in Oracle. Multiple instances of the server classes are then run to achieve better performance.

Zenith has implemented two kinds of objects:

- **Passive objects** have no persistent state other than read-only tables—for example, a table of the phone numbers residing on various billing systems.

- **Active objects** have a life cycle—such as an account that is created, updated, and eventually deleted.

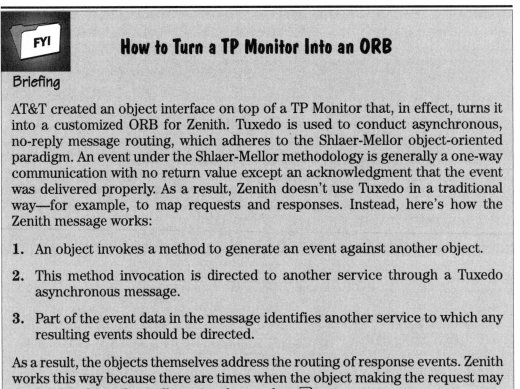

How to Turn a TP Monitor Into an ORB

Briefing

AT&T created an object interface on top of a TP Monitor that, in effect, turns it into a customized ORB for Zenith. Tuxedo is used to conduct asynchronous, no-reply message routing, which adheres to the Shlaer-Mellor object-oriented paradigm. An event under the Shlaer-Mellor methodology is generally a one-way communication with no return value except an acknowledgment that the event was delivered properly. As a result, Zenith doesn't use Tuxedo in a traditional way—for example, to map requests and responses. Instead, here's how the Zenith message works:

1. An object invokes a method to generate an event against another object.

2. This method invocation is directed to another service through a Tuxedo asynchronous message.

3. Part of the event data in the message identifies another service to which any resulting events should be directed.

As a result, the objects themselves address the routing of response events. Zenith works this way because there are times when the object making the request may not be the object that will receive the results. ❑

The Zenith Gateway Server

The application servers connect to four two-processor gateway boxes for UNIX-to-mainframe connectivity. The gateways provide real-time, on-line access to legacy data. They handle the asynchronous communications from the application servers; they also send updates and retrieve information from the legacy systems—translating Zenith messages into LU 6.2-based mainframe transactions. The boxes run about 24 C++-based Tuxedo services to provide interactive access to the legacy systems.

Zenith had a 7-by-24 availability requirement to meet. So, AT&T used multiple lines and front-end processors to provide redundancy against failures. In addition, each

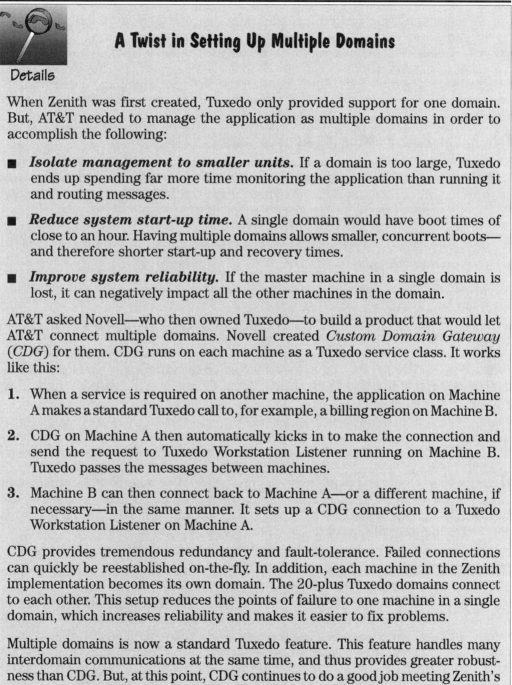

A Twist in Setting Up Multiple Domains

Details

When Zenith was first created, Tuxedo only provided support for one domain. But, AT&T needed to manage the application as multiple domains in order to accomplish the following:

- *Isolate management to smaller units.* If a domain is too large, Tuxedo ends up spending far more time monitoring the application than running it and routing messages.

- *Reduce system start-up time.* A single domain would have boot times of close to an hour. Having multiple domains allows smaller, concurrent boots—and therefore shorter start-up and recovery times.

- *Improve system reliability.* If the master machine in a single domain is lost, it can negatively impact all the other machines in the domain.

AT&T asked Novell—who then owned Tuxedo—to build a product that would let AT&T connect multiple domains. Novell created *Custom Domain Gateway* (*CDG*) for them. CDG runs on each machine as a Tuxedo service class. It works like this:

1. When a service is required on another machine, the application on Machine A makes a standard Tuxedo call to, for example, a billing region on Machine B.

2. CDG on Machine A then automatically kicks in to make the connection and send the request to Tuxedo Workstation Listener running on Machine B. Tuxedo passes the messages between machines.

3. Machine B can then connect back to Machine A—or a different machine, if necessary—in the same manner. It sets up a CDG connection to a Tuxedo Workstation Listener on Machine A.

CDG provides tremendous redundancy and fault-tolerance. Failed connections can quickly be reestablished on-the-fly. In addition, each machine in the Zenith implementation becomes its own domain. The 20-plus Tuxedo domains connect to each other. This setup reduces the points of failure to one machine in a single domain, which increases reliability and makes it easier to fix problems.

Multiple domains is now a standard Tuxedo feature. This feature handles many interdomain communications at the same time, and thus provides greater robustness than CDG. But, at this point, CDG continues to do a good job meeting Zenith's requirements for intersystem communications and multiple domains. ❏

gateway box can access the other gateway boxes and legacy systems—even in the other data center. This provides redundancy in case of a gateway failure. Intelligent routing transmits each transaction to the correct gateway, rerouting the traffic in case of a failure. And, because of Zenith's asynchronous messaging environment, the middle-tier systems can continue to take orders even if a legacy system is completely inaccessible. Once the legacy system is back on-line, the queued orders are forwarded to it.

Tier 3: The Data and Legacy Applications

Zenith's third tier consists of AT&T's corporate data repositories and their legacy applications, such as account maintenance. They are AT&T's "databases of record." The legacy systems that Zenith connects to include:

■ A billing system running on six IBM mainframes spread across the data centers

■ A marketing system

■ A calling-card system that includes incentive tracking for AT&T's customer retention program

■ Other UNIX-based data repositories, including systems for wireless and other AT&T services

Zenith's interactive access to these legacy corporate systems has enabled AT&T to implement a real-time, long-distance telemarketing system without having to migrate existing data.

Security

Security is a straightforward implementation at AT&T. Users log in at the application level. They are also assigned an ID to access the mainframe, which is tracked by the system for security audits. Every message carries this user ID. As a result, users don't have to physically log in to the mainframe at the application level.

THE PROJECT

AT&T spent a year building a business case for Zenith. Development analysts and staff from Andersen Consulting assisted this effort. The business case required Zenith to implement a common architecture for both inbound and outbound sales and for the other two CSB organizations—service and call servicing. Their original target production date was mid-year 1994. But the large scope of the project and the new technology involved in its implementation meant that a more realistic target was mid-1995. The system went into production in September 1995 (see the next Details box).

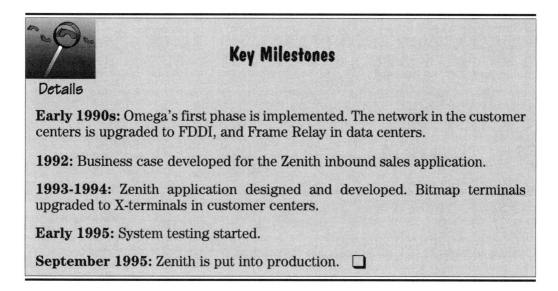

Key Milestones

Details

Early 1990s: Omega's first phase is implemented. The network in the customer centers is upgraded to FDDI, and Frame Relay in data centers.

1992: Business case developed for the Zenith inbound sales application.

1993-1994: Zenith application designed and developed. Bitmap terminals upgraded to X-terminals in customer centers.

Early 1995: System testing started.

September 1995: Zenith is put into production. ❑

Design

It's hard to build a plane if you think it has a wheel and an engine—but you don't know where it will go.

— Andy Schenke

In March 1993, AT&T assembled a Zenith team consisting of a dozen-member development group and a six-member user requirements group. The development group's analysts and subject matter experts reviewed the technical requirements. The group needed to understand all the nuances of the system and to agree on the business process and workflow. In the meantime, the user development group assembled the requirements from each business unit. Next, the development group integrated these lists of requirements. They relied on a *use case* methodology to describe the system requirements. This let them focus on the needs of their customers and business units while creating an end-to-end view of the system.

The Zenith developers used the Shlaer-Mellor object-oriented design methodology—supported by Cadre Technologies' TeamWork CASE tool—to produce models of the business environment, define the objects, and develop the core application.[1] TeamWork let the developers work with information and state models to define the objects and document their life cycles. They also used the tool to create event interaction models to show how the objects would communicate.

---

[1] Cadre has since merged with Bachman Information Systems, forming Cayenne Software.

Development

The next part of the Zenith development process focused on object definition and abstraction. This was a long process; it took about a year and a half to complete. Once the initial requirements were gathered, the Zenith project team quickly decided that they would not use objects on all three tiers. They didn't want to make the project too complicated by having to simultaneously define reusable objects for the user GUI, the middle tier, and for legacy system access. As a result, the developers decided to only use objects in the middle tier.

As development progressed, the Zenith team was divided into three groups that grew as the project evolved:

- **The Interface Group** handled communications between the objects and the legacy systems, as well as between the objects and the user interface. This group had about 22 people.

- **The GUI Group** explored and defined the framework for supporting the user. They used Visual Edge Software's UIM/X as a GUI builder for screen layouts. There were about 20 people in this group.

- **The Object Group** worked on the object-oriented framework for Zenith. This group had about 17 people (see the next Briefing box).

Getting Objects Right

Briefing

The object group probably incurred the majority of the project's challenges. They had to break down the system's concepts and processes into specific objects. For example, they looked at what an "order" was. Within that concept were multiple objects, such as name and address. Each time something was examined, it seemed to open the door to even more questions that needed to be resolved. Here are the steps they followed to develop the object-based architecture:

1. One group performed an object-oriented analysis of the business requirements. This resulted in business models.

2. A second group defined and modeled the architecture. Next they built a collection of architectural classes from their architectural model.

3. The team then applied the business models to the architectural classes.

4. Finally, the team generated the objects. To do this, they used a library to read and interpret their model data store, apply the architectural classes that they had defined to it, and automatically generate C++ code. ❏

The developers constructed a prototype to see if the different pieces of the system played well together. Some interface problems occurred between the client and server. At first, the client was too fat—it had too much business logic and was too tightly tied to the application. The developers redefined what was to be done in the GUI and what was better done by a business process. The resulting lighter-weight GUI solely displays information; it was key to meeting one of the system's primary goals—the ability to support a variety of user interfaces. By separating the business logic from the GUI, alternative user interfaces are possible.

Testing and Documentation

A separate 20-member system test group received the various parts of Zenith from the different development groups. These were then put together and tested as a whole. Each development group had written simulators and stubs to test their code, but the pieces had mainly been tested independently. Consequently, when integration began, the first real system test failed (see the next Warning box). As a result, the developers quickly set up new development and testing processes:

■ They increased the internal documentation.

■ They established an integration test area. They also implemented a policy that required the developers to perform an integration test before giving their code to the system test team.

■ Additional processes were put into place to document bugs and manage fixes.

These new processes led to improved system testing and a solid, integrated product.

After system testing was completed, another AT&T organization conducted performance and stress testing. That group configured the system and tuned the hardware and software to meet the performance goals. They advised the development team about code changes that would improve performance.

Continuous Integration Testing Is a Must

Warning

The Zenith development organization found that it is critical to test the system in a real-world, continuously running environment. The system may run very well in black-box testing—each day the system is started, tested, and shut down. But this doesn't detect problems that occur when data is accumulated over multiple days. The longer any part of the system runs—the application, the file system, the database, or the TP Monitor—the more chances it has to break because of this accumulation process. So continuous testing is necessary. ❏

Going Into Production

In 1995—about six months before Zenith was rolled out to users—AT&T put a production support group into place. The developers managed a controlled introduction of the system to test it in a real-world environment. For the introduction, they selected AT&T's customer satisfaction center in New Jersey, which takes a limited number of calls. Although the test found plenty of bugs to fix, most involved small changes to the user interfaces.

The team then began to get the customer centers ready. They upgraded the bitmap terminals to X-terminals and set up the Zenith hardware. Once the hardware was in place, they brought up Zenith and scheduled training classes for groups of users. When a group completed training, they could then use the Zenith client, although they still had access to the old order system desktop. After a year spent training about 2,000 representatives, AT&T discontinued its previous inbound sales application—all the representatives had converted to Zenith.

THE OUTCOME

Zenith is up and running, and the users are very pleased with it. They can view timely information that they haven't had access to before. They also like the on-line documentation and the look and feel of Zenith's GUI.

Most importantly, Zenith has met its business goals. Order turnaround has been greatly reduced. There are far fewer errors now because the representatives have access to current customer information. These benefits have resulted in happier customers and increased revenue for AT&T.

Of course, there have been growing pains. But Zenith is now meeting AT&T's 7-by-24 reliability requirements. In fact, Zenith's 3-tier architecture has actually improved the environment's reliability.

THE FUTURE

We accomplished what we wanted with Zenith, but now we have an even longer list of what we want to do.

— *Mikola Owdij*

We planned to show upper management that object-oriented design has a very long lead time and then a short turnaround for modifications. We know we met the long ramp-up time, but will we meet the short turnaround?

— *Andy Schenke*

AT&T is now working to complete the entire Omega project, which includes re-engineering other key applications and re-evaluating the remaining programs. This has gotten more complicated as market pressure continues to build and new services such as wireless and the Internet—and even local phone service—become AT&T offerings.

Zenith is undergoing extensive analysis to see if it met its business case goals. They expect the evaluation to be positive. If it is, the developers will begin to re-engineer the outbound sales and call-servicing applications. To make sure Zenith's objects can be reused easily, the developers are re-engineering some of the object infra-structure that they have found to be too application specific or not abstracted at the right level.

AT&T is working to provide customers with a way to order limited services from its Web page. It is also looking to leverage the Internet by putting certain customer data on-line so customers can view account information and check if the services ordered are really the best ones for them. For example, a customer could experiment with other calling plans on-line to see if another plan would generate greater savings. Other non-traditional customer interfaces are being reviewed, such as voice-response technology for ordering products over the phone without speaking with a representative and kiosks in public areas for ordering AT&T services.

These development efforts will be able to leverage Omega and Zenith. AT&T is now able to face the future head-on with a solid architecture in place.

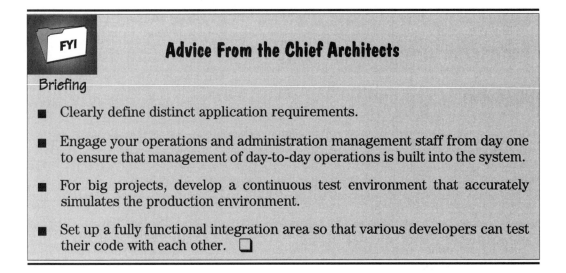

FYI

Advice From the Chief Architects

Briefing

- Clearly define distinct application requirements.

- Engage your operations and administration management staff from day one to ensure that management of day-to-day operations is built into the system.

- For big projects, develop a continuous test environment that accurately simulates the production environment.

- Set up a fully functional integration area so that various developers can test their code with each other. ❏

Part 3
The Zen
of 3-Tier

An Introduction to Part 3

The only place where success comes before work is in the dictionary.

— Vidal Sassoon

We've now come to the end of our tour—but we don't want to say good-bye until we take a look at what we've learned. The eight companies we visited deployed very different 3-tier applications. The implementations range from a software vendor providing an enterprise-wide solution to a telecommunications company that is re-engineering a business unit's entire operations.

Because of these varying needs, each company's 3-tier design is different. Nonetheless, a number of common themes for implementing successful 3-tier systems have emerged from these varied experiences. Part 3 looks at these lessons and shares with you the secrets for 3-tier client/server success:

■ We create three distinct categories of 3-tier applications. This lets us summarize how the architects in our case studies applied 3-tier to different business problems.

■ You'll learn the pitfalls to avoid and strategies to follow to make sure you're covering all your bases.

■ We'll give you tips for making the right decisions throughout the development cycle—from the initial design to the final rollout.

■ And we'll remind you to address testing, system management planning, and end-user support from the beginning.

These client/server rules of thumb come directly from seasoned experts—the architects of the systems we've just toured. Not every lesson is appropriate for every company, but these tips provide important guidelines for any client/server undertaking. Enough talk—let's go learn from the experts.

Chapter 12

The Road to 3-Tier Nirvana

Learning without thought is labor lost; thought without learning is perilous.

— *Confucius*

The companies and organizations we visited in this book used 3-tier client/server to implement a wide variety of systems. We trust that you learned many things from each of the case studies—we certainly did. This chapter is about the lessons we were able to extract from these very dissimilar applications. Confucius would be proud of us.

HOW 3-TIER IS USED

We can group our case studies into three distinct categories—or patterns—that describe how 3-tier is being used. We call these categories *Greenfield, Turbo-charger,* and *Integrator.* We're sure you can come up with more of these categories, but these are the ones we found. What follows is a description of these 3-tier usage patterns.

Greenfield Systems

Greenfields are the kind of applications we usually associate with 3-tier client/server. They are brand new systems without any legacy "drag" (see Figure 12-1). Before you turn green with envy, you must remember that Greenfield developers face that infamous blank sheet of paper—they have to invent the whole application from scratch. Greenfield architects chose 3-tier because it offered them scale, performance, flexibility, and reuse. Greenfield applications sometimes connect to existing systems, but this is not their primary purpose. The Greenfield applications in this book include U.K. Employment Service, MCI, and PeopleSoft.

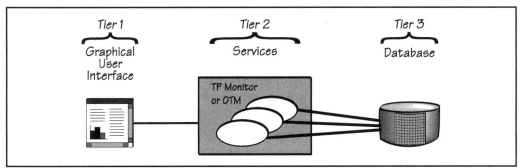

Figure 12-1. The Architecture of a Greenfield Application.

Turbocharger Systems

Turbochargers use 3-tier to front-end an existing system. They let enterprises reuse an old application in new ways (see Figure 12-2). Like a circling wagon train in the Wild West, a Turbocharger surrounds an existing system. It adds a scalable, high-performance 3-tier application environment on which to build a new application. The Turbocharger does this by offloading tasks from the existing system and multiplexing communications to it—the existing system is its third tier.

The Turbocharger often has its own middle-tier database; it manages the data it needs to improve performance and serve the client, but it isn't the database of record. Because the client and middle tier are implemented on open platforms, they are easier to program and more flexible. Consequently, the development cycle is shortened. In this book, AppleOrder Global is an example of a Turbocharger.

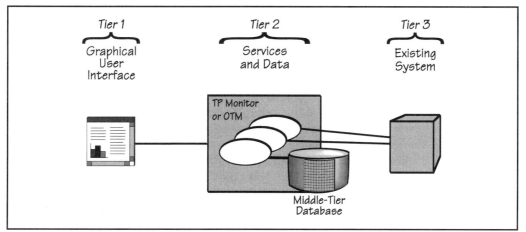

Tier 1 — Graphical User Interface

Tier 2 — Services and Data

Tier 3 — Existing System

TP Monitor or OTM

Middle-Tier Database

Figure 12-2. The Architecture of a Turbocharger Application.

Integrator Systems

Integrators—like Turbochargers—create new applications in front of existing systems (see Figure 12-3). However, Integrators have a different goal: they provide the glue that integrates previously separate systems. Integrators use 3-tier to create unified views of key business "objects"—for example, a customer, client, or patient. So companies use these systems to re-engineer their business processes to be more competitive. Once the Integrator creates an on-line version of these all-important business objects, reusability reigns supreme—the infrastructure spawns new applications that leverage a growing pool of middle-tier components.

Integrators provide a fast payoff by extending the shelf-life of existing applications. It's a lot better than rewriting them from scratch. There are often solid business reasons for recycling existing applications via Integrators—including: 1) the existing systems may support other processes that can't be changed, 2) the existing application is working perfectly well, so there's no reason to upgrade it, or 3) the last developer who knew the system retired six months ago, and no one else knows what it really does.

Because of the Integrators, older systems sprout new clients, acquire new functionality, and finally work with their neighboring systems. Integrators are the fastest growing segment of the 3-tier client/server market. The Integrators in this book include AT&T, Wells Fargo, EUCARIS, and 3M.

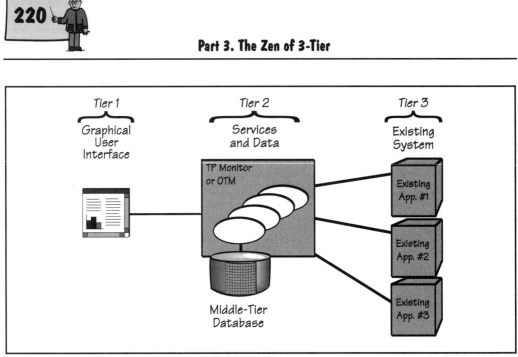

Figure 12-3. The Architecture of an Integrator Application.

3-Tier Doesn't Get Older, It Only Gets Better

3-tier's component orientation invites reuse. Most of the development teams we visited are putting this attribute to good use: they are leveraging their new middle-tier components into a suite of applications. Once the base infrastructure is in place, new applications can be added quickly. The system doesn't get older, it gets better as more middle-tier services are added. For this reason, the development groups often form a team that specializes in creating and maintaining their inventory of middle-tier components. When they get requests for new functions, they check their arsenal to see if something they already have does the job. If not, they carefully add the component (see the Wells Fargo case study). In a world of competing products and on-line services, these middle-tier components become strategic weapons for enterprises (see the next Soapbox).

Another common theme in our case studies is the Internet. It seems to be everyone's next step. After they satisfy their internal users, enterprises almost universally begin looking outward. They want to start offering their customers and suppliers direct access to at least a subset of the new middle-tier functionality. For example, AT&T is looking at ways to allow its customers to dial-in to see their account status and do rate analysis. U.K. Employment is thinking about supporting job searches through Web-enabled Java clients. 3M Health Information Systems is investigating Internet access for doctors. PeopleSoft has added Java client support to PeopleSoft 7.

The Middle-Tier Treasure Chest

Soapbox

The quickest way to new production applications isn't to write them faster, but to not write them at all. This is the promise of components. It is why the architects we visited spend time on the care and feeding of their middle-tier components. They are building a treasure chest of reusable middle-tier code. And it's pure gold. Components are additive and contagious. When you reuse components you get faster time to market, lower development costs, and—even more important—a bevy of new applications; it will differentiate your enterprise from those that opt for disposable, use-once 2-tier applications. ☐

ADVICE FROM THE EXPERTS

Enough of our own analysis—let's look at what the architects we visited said. In this section, we've assembled the most frequent tips we received for client/server success (see the next Briefing box). This list provides you with ten commandments that you must follow to design and develop a successful 3-tier application (or for that matter, any N-tier application). You'll certainly add new commandments to this list as you implement your own projects—but if you heed the advice offered here, many aspects of your project will progress much more smoothly. A drumroll, please!

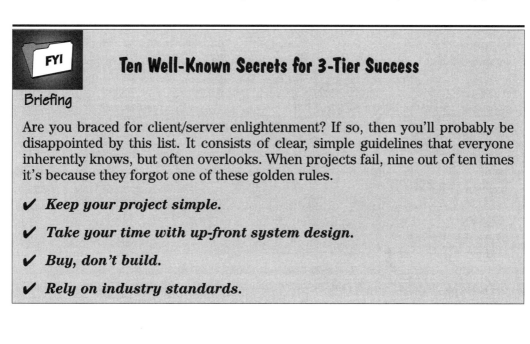

Ten Well-Known Secrets for 3-Tier Success

Briefing

Are you braced for client/server enlightenment? If so, then you'll probably be disappointed by this list. It consists of clear, simple guidelines that everyone inherently knows, but often overlooks. When projects fail, nine out of ten times it's because they forgot one of these golden rules.

✔ *Keep your project simple.*

✔ *Take your time with up-front system design.*

✔ *Buy, don't build.*

✔ *Rely on industry standards.*

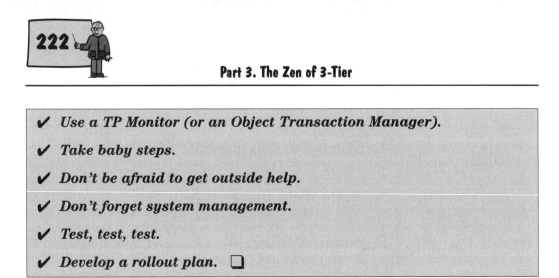

✔ *Use a TP Monitor (or an Object Transaction Manager).*

✔ *Take baby steps.*

✔ *Don't be afraid to get outside help.*

✔ *Don't forget system management.*

✔ *Test, test, test.*

✔ *Develop a rollout plan.* ❏

Keep Your Project Simple

We believe that the *real secret* to client/server success today is to rigorously apply the KISS principle: Keep it simple, stupid. Make your project scope manageable, and get the initial system up and running early. A Standish Group survey recently discovered the "sweet spot" for successful applications—it is four developers for four months. If your project is big, divide it into subprojects composed of small teams with clearly defined short-term deliverables. 3-tier's modular architecture supports this approach to applications—take advantage of it.

Take Your Time With Design

A common refrain heard among successful architects is "take your time when designing an application." It is important to get the application design right *before* you begin development—once development starts, it's almost impossible to go back. You can always fix individual modules, but it is very hard to retrofit an entire design. You never have time—and your project is usually too far gone by the time you discover the problem. Here's the good news: if you have a good design, coding the system will be the easy part. Here are a few things to keep in mind:

■ *Make sure you really understand the requirements.* Getting the requirements right isn't easy; they are often complicated—and a moving target. Sometimes your own users don't even know what they need. These are the things we simply deal with as application designers. But our most frequent mistake is overlooking the requirements of entire categories of users—for example, managers and operators.

■ *Create a prototype to test shaky parts of your design.* Take the parts of your design that you are unsure of and try them out before committing to a direction. Prototypes can tell you if the design will meet production-level requirements. Your team can also use the prototype to learn more about the system as they develop the application.

- ■ ***When you add features or components later, make sure they are compatible with your architecture.*** New components should fit smoothly into your architectural model—if they don't, seriously consider whether they are necessary before modifying your design.

Buy, Don't Build

These days there are hundreds of client/server products on the market ready for you to buy, modify slightly if necessary, and then use. They include both applications and infrastructure components. This means you can buy your infrastructure—including your database and TP Monitor or ORB—right off the shelf. You can also take advantage of third-party development environments, prototyping tools, system management packages, and so on. If someone else has already developed a good, solid product, why invest the time and money to develop your own? The job is probably much more difficult than you imagine. Unless your needs are very specific and your research shows that no prebuilt product can accommodate them, take advantage of third-party products. Don't let a "not invented here" attitude bog you down.

Rely on Industry Standards

If you build an application using open industry standards, you will gain a number of key benefits:

- ■ You'll be able to leverage third-party, standards-based add-ons and tools—such as prototyping tools and system management packages.

- ■ You'll be able to integrate the application more easily with existing applications that are based on the same standards.

- ■ You'll save money by using less-expensive hardware and software.

- ■ You'll be able to port the application to another platform or change a component if one of the products you rely on is discontinued or no longer meets your needs.

Use a TP Monitor or an Object Transaction Manager

Software infrastructure that reliably manages distributed components is an essential piece of a 3-tier architecture. It lets you break complex applications into services that it then manages. As a result, pieces of code that know nothing about each other can act in complete unison. You can then spread your application across multiple servers to serve thousands of clients, which is key to supporting the latest intergalactic distributed applications based on Internet technology.

Take Baby Steps

If you cannon-ball into a pool, you'll get soaked. This is great summer fun—but make sure you don't cannon-ball into a major project. Instead of immediately going after the whole project at once, many architects suggest that you break a project into small, iterative steps. Once you successfully complete Step 1, you've created the foundation for Step 2. By taking baby steps you can:

■ Get users' feedback along the way.
■ Make sure that all the parts of your project mesh together all the time.
■ Surface problems earlier so you have time to fix them.
■ Make frequent incremental releases so you can prove you're making progress.

Keep MCI's mantra in mind: "Analyze a little, design a little, code a little, test a little."

Don't Be Afraid to Get Help

Partners and outside consultants can make all the difference in rolling out a successful project. They can fill in wherever you have gaps in resources. They can also act as an extended arm of your staff. For example, hardware and software partners can take care of system installation. You can even rely on outside resources to conduct user training. If you are working with a technology that is new to your team, you should also bring in a few highly experienced consultants. They can provide the team with valuable guidance and advice in designing the system, and they can provide development assistance on the more complicated parts of the application.

Don't Forget System Management

All too often, system management is forgotten during application development. As a result, when a company rolls out an application, tools are not in place to ensure that the system stays up and running. Users can then become very frustrated with the new application, even if it otherwise meets their needs. If you take the time to address system management as you develop the application, it shouldn't increase your development time. If, however, you make system management an after thought, you'll spend a lot more person-hours solving the resulting problems.

Your operations staff are users of your application, too—you need to get *their* requirements. Then make sure the features they request are built into the system. Some features will be part of your off-the-shelf software infrastructure. You can add a system management package. Then you can instrument other parts of your system so they can be managed.

Test, Test, Test

If "location, location, location" is the key to riches in real estate, "test, test, test" is the key to building successful 3-tier applications. Testing ensures that the application meets user needs, that the components are working together correctly, and that the system is running at a production level of performance and stability. We suggest conducting extensive testing, as done by the U.K. Employment Service. Their testing included:

- User assurance testing
- Benchmarking
- System testing
- Performance testing
- System integration testing
- Service delivery testing
- Stress testing
- Piloting

Whenever possible, set up a *continuous* system integration testing environment that simulates a real-world environment. It will let you test the system over a longer period of time and find many hidden problems that appear only as data accumulates. As new parts of your application are completed, add them to your testing complex, add their tests to your test library, and keep testing.

Develop a Rollout Plan

A successful implementation also entails a smooth system rollout—so make sure you develop a complete rollout plan. This can be a major project. Treat it as such. Three key components to smooth rollouts are:

- Good user training and support
- Efficient hardware and software installation
- Smooth migration of existing data and systems

Plan the timing of your rollout, and select the people who will be responsible for the various steps. Be sure to enlist an experienced rollout project manager. You might want to bring in outside partners or consultants to assist with a large rollout if you feel the project will stretch your resources too thin. And don't forget to beef up your Help Desk to handle the inevitable ramp-up in user support calls. You can also conduct additional user training after the rollout to encourage users to take advantage of the more advanced features of the application.

SAYING GOOD-BYE

This brings us to the end of our behind-the-scenes tour of real-life, hard-working 3-tier implementations. We trust that you found the journey rewarding. We hope that you may occasionally find yourself thinking, "this reminds me of what case study X did in a similar situation."

3-tier applications are a reality—they are successfully meeting the diverse and sophisticated needs of many enterprises. Thousands of these applications are in production today. 3-tier—or, really, N-tier—will experience even more growth. Companies will increasingly tap into the Internet to deploy mission-critical applications of intergalactic proportions. Internet-based distributed objects will result in an explosion of N-tier applications over the next few years. The case studies in this book should prepare you for this forthcoming tsunami.

Where to Go for More Information

We compiled the following list of resources to help you find more information on the topics we covered in this book.

Client/Server

Client/Server is a huge topic. In this book, we provided enough background in the technology to understand the case studies. If you want a more thorough treatment of the entire field—including all the technology options—we recommend:

- Robert Orfali, Dan Harkey and Jeri Edwards, **The Essential Client/Server Survival Guide, Second Edition** (Wiley, 1996). This gentle introduction by your author covers all of client/server from the NOS to TP Monitors, ORBs, and the Internet.

- David Vaskevitch, **Client/Server Strategies, Second Edition** (IDG, 1995). Vaskevitch is Microsoft's VP of Enterprise Computing. This book provides an insider's view of Viper and Microsoft's client/server directions. Most of the meat is in the last part. The rest of the book is mostly about the business aspects of client/server technology. It's worth a read.

- David Linthicum, **Client/Server and Intranet Development** (Wiley, 1997). This book covers all aspects of client/server tools. It also has a good section on 3-tier and TP Monitors.

Transaction Processing

After years of hiding in computer rooms, the Internet has made transactions cool. Consequently, more books show up in bookstores. Here are some of the best:

- Jim Gray and Andreas Reuter, **Transaction Processing Concepts and Techniques** (Morgan Kaufmann, 1993). This is the Bible of transaction processing.

- Juan Andrade, Mark Carges, Terence Dwyer, and Stephen Felts, **The Tuxedo System** (Addison Wesley, 1996). This well-written guide is meaty enough for programmers—there's even real coding examples—but clear enough to serve as an in-depth tutorial if you are merely computer literate.[1]

---

[1] For more information on Tuxedo, Iceberg, ObjectBroker, or MessageQ, see the white papers at http://www.beasys.com.

■ Philip Bernstein and Eric Newcomer, **The Principles of Transaction Processing** (Morgan Kaufmann, 1997). This book provides a good overview of TP Monitors and their underlying technology.

Distributed Objects

There are tons of books on object-oriented methodologies and languages. However, very few of these books deal with distributed objects. But these good books do:

■ David Taylor, **Object-Oriented Information Systems** (Wiley, 1992). This book is a very approachable introduction to objects.

■ Grady Booch, **Object-Oriented Analysis and Design (Second Edition)** (Benjamin-Cummings, 1994). This second edition of Booch's book is superb reading. It's also an introduction but with more emphasis on language constructs, methodology, and notation.

■ Robert Orfali, Dan Harkey and Jeri Edwards, **The Essential Distributed Objects Survival Guide** (Wiley, 1996). This book is a gentle introduction to distributed objects and components. It covers CORBA 2.0, OpenDoc, OLE, OpenStep, Newi, and a variety of other topics.

CORBA

■ Robert Orfali, Dan Harkey and Jeri Edwards, **Instant CORBA** (Wiley, 1997). This book by your author is a quick guide to understanding this revolutionary new technology. It will introduce you to distributed objects and the CORBA standard, including the ORB and its services.

■ Jon Siegel, et al., **CORBA Fundamentals and Programming** (Wiley, 1996). This book covers multivendor C++ and Smalltalk CORBA ORBs.

■ Thomas Mowbray and Raphael Malveau, **CORBA Design Patterns** (Wiley, 1997). This useful book uses design patterns to explain CORBA programming techniques. It is the first design patterns book to cover distributed systems.

■ Robert Orfali and Dan Harkey, **Client/Server Programming with Java and CORBA** (Wiley, 1997). This book shows you how to program 3-tier client/server solutions using CORBA, Java, and JDBC. It can also serve as a gentle introduction to CORBA programming in Java.

Index

Index

Your Instant Guide to CORBA!

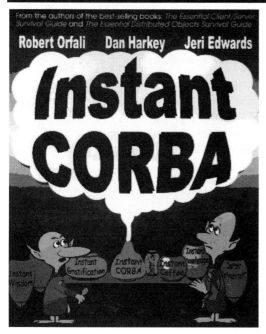

Contents at a Glance

Distributed CORBA Objects have found their killer app. It's the Object Web—or the marriage of distributed objects and the Internet. The major computing companies—including Sun, JavaSoft, IBM, Netscape, Apple, Oracle, BEA, and HP—have chosen CORBA IIOP as the common way to connect distributed objects across the Internet and intranets. Consequently, CORBA is about to become as ubiquitous as TCP/IP. Instant CORBA is your guide to understanding this revolutionary new technology. If you're in a real hurry, the book even provides a condensed tour that will make you CORBA literate in four hours or less. Written in a gentle, witty style, this comprehensive book covers:

- The Object Web—or how CORBA/IIOP, Java, and the Internet are coming together.
- Everything you need to know about a CORBA 2.0 ORB.
- The fifteen CORBA Object Services—including Transactions, Trader, Security, Naming, Events, Time, and Collections.
- CORBA's dynamic object facilities such as callbacks, dynamic invocations, object introspection, and the interface repository.
- Next-generation ORB technology—including CORBA 3.0's messaging, pass-by-value, and server-side frameworks.
- The marriage of CORBA with MOM and TP Monitors.
- Forthcoming CORBA attractions such as mobile agents, shippable places, and the business object framework.
- Products such as Iona's OrbixWeb, Netscape/Visigenic's VisiBroker, and Sun's NEO/Joe.

Available at Bookstores Everywhere

For more information visit **http://www.wiley.com/compbooks**

ISBN: 0471-18333-4, 314 pages, 1997, $19.99 US / $28.50 CAN

Your Survival Guide to Client/Server!

Robert Orfali • Dan Harkey • Jeri Edwards

The Essential Client/Server Survival Guide

Second Edition

Contents at a Glance

I highly recommend it!

It's as savvy, informative, and entertaining as anything you are likely to read on the subject. Client/server isn't one technology but many—remote SQL, TP, message-oriented groupware, distributed objects, and so on. Like the proverbial blind men feeling the elephant, most of us have a hard time seeing the whole picture. The authors succeed brilliantly in mapping the elephant.

> — *Jon Udell, BYTE Magazine*

The scope and depth of topics covered in the Guide, with its straightforward and often humorous delivery, make this book required reading for anyone who deals with computers in today's corporate environment.

> — *Bob Gallagher, PC Week*

Absolutely the finest book on client/server on the market today.

> — *Richard Finkelstein*
> *President of Performance Computing*

Charmingly accessible.

> — *Dr. Jim Gray*
> *Author of* Transaction Processing

WILEY

Available at Bookstores Everywhere

For more information visit **http://www.wiley.com/compbooks**

ISBN: 0471-15325-7, 676 pages, 1996, $32.95 US / $46.50 CAN